BASH THE RICH

TRUE-LIFE CONFESSIONS OF AN ANARCHIST IN THE UK

By Ian Bone

For Maria Spiridonova and Lucy Parsons

'It's coming yet for a' that' – Robert Burns

D1312945

1

Published 2006 by Tangent Books
3 Monmouth Place,
Bath BA1 2AT

www.tangentbooks.co.uk
01225 463983

Production: Richard Jones, Anne Smith, Steve Faragher, Joe Burt
Design: Trevor Wyatt **Cover Design:** Trevor Wyatt **&** Stanley Donwood

Thanks to: Phil Gard, Ray Jones
and everyone who made a noise. Thanks to Danny Gralton for
permission to use his pictures.
Special thanks to: Jane Nicholl, feisty, fiery and fifty fucking five

Also by Ian Bone: *Class War: Decade Of Disorder, Anarchist!*

Contact: localnews4us@yahoo.co.uk

Disclaimer
The details of all the events in this book are a true and accurate record to the best of
the the author's recollection. However, in order to protect the guilty, some names
have been changed. Also, we have substituted names to protect the identity of
individuals where they could be charged with acts of riot, conspiracy and public
order offences resulting from their attempt to overthrow the state or from having
a good old ruck with the law. In particular, when Class War caused damage to
property through riot we have substituted the names of those responsible for the
majority of the trashing and violence.

CONTENTS

Introduction

'BASH THE RICH'

In 1984, *The Sunday People* branded Ian Bone 'The most dangerous man in Britain'. They weren't far wrong. From the inner-city riots of 1981 to the miners' strike and beyond, the butler's son and founder of *Class War* was indeed a greater thorn in Margaret Thatcher's side than the useless blatherings of the official opposition. *Class War* WERE the REAL opposition! It was Ian Bone who linked the inner-city rioters of Brixton and Handsworth with the striking miners. It was Bone who *The People* spotted rioting with miners in Mansfield and attacking laboratories with the Animal Liberation Front. He was accused by *The Guardian* of being the man behind the 1985 Brixton Riot. But that was only the half of it… from 1965 to 1985, from Swansea to Cardiff and London, the mayhem spread countrywide.

In *Bash The Rich*, Ian Bone tells it like it was. From The Angry Brigade to the Free Wales Army, from the 1967 Summer of Love to 1977 anarcho-punk, from Grosvenor Square to the Battle of the Beanfield from the Stop the City riots to Bashing the Rich at the Henley Regatta, Ian Bone breaks his silence.

In the 1980s, Ian Bone was THE anarchist in the UK with a half brick in one hand and an incendiary pen in the other. How did the child who lived in a fabulous English mansion and saluted the AA man from a Rolls Royce come to be the man who famously promised to Bash the Rich and leave Hampstead a smouldering ruin?

Where do David Niven, Keith Allen, Rik Wakeman, Douglas Fairbanks Junior, Cynthia Payne, George Melly, Flanagan and Allan, Yoko Ono, Pope John Paul and Lofty from *EastEnders* fit into the story. And why did Gregory Peck send Ian Bone a get well card?

This is no dry tome destined to gather dust in leftie bookshops. Against a background of all the major outbreaks of disorder of the time, this is a startlingly honest, funny, warts 'n' all scream of rage from a gutter-level anarchist prepared to fight 'by any means necessary'. That 'the most dangerous man in Britain' is at liberty to write books rather than serving a life sentence for sedition or being hung for treason will be the first question on every MP's lips as this smouldering anarchist bomb hits the bookshelves.

BONE AND GINSBERG PLOT THE REVOLOUTION

v

SECTION ONE

THE PRE-REVOLUTIONARY EPOCH

Chapter 1

COWPAT MAN FOR THE BOLSHEVIKS!

Splat! The shit hit the smug face of the local Tory MP right in the face. Seconds earlier, my dad had scooped the fly-blown dry-crusted cowpat expertly on to his newspaper, raced across the road and squelched it deep into Sir Tufton Bufton's Knight of the Shire patrician grin. My mum followed up with a second cow shit exocet on his balding pate – gotcha! Double gotcha!

Little Ian began to shove his *Beano* under cowpat three, but was hoiked away by his mum and dad and gigglingly arm-swung off home. Plenty of time for that in later life. During that somnolent general election of 1955, every Tory poster on that road in Goudhurst, Kent was either ripped down or covered in excrement, as my mum and dad bowled home mid-afternoon from the Eight Bells to their servant's quarters at the 'Big House'. It was only a poster that received the cowpat, but as my dad served dinner to Sir George and Lady Jessel that night, he may have had other targets in mind.

My dad was a butler. But not the fawning deferential kind. He was a dead ringer for Hudson but his heart was somewhere else. He was a socialist butler. He got into it by accident. He was born in the mining village of Glenbuck, now Ayrshire's version of a deserted crumbling St Kilda, with only the plaque for Bill Shankly to stay the occasional Liverpool supporter. My dad went to school in Glenbuck with Bill Shankly and his brother Bob and it was my Granddad Edward 'Ned' Bone who would have given Shankly his first football start with the Glenbuck Cherrypickers – the mining village side that spawned more Scottish and English league players than any other. But Shankly was either too young or 'not good enough' to get into the team. For the Cherrypickers had an illustrious history of top players.

In 1901, the original gold English FA Cup had been on display in a Glenbuck shop after two ex-Cherrypickers scored the goals in Tottenham Hotspur's Cup Final victory that year. Most games in Glenbuck were not as sedate as the English Cup Final. The referee and opposing players often ended up thrown in the stream that ran alongside Burnside Park or fleeing Glenbuck under a hail of stones. The Cherrypickers was a family affair with the Taits, Wallaces, Knoxes and Bones always prominent. My granddad was the Cherrypickers' goalie, winning 13 trophies before being offered terms with Carlisle, then managed by Bill Shankly's uncle, another Cherrypicker. He walked all the way there, drank the signing-on fee and never went back.

If you take a cross between Bill Shankly and Alex Ferguson, you will get a rough picture of where my dad was coming from – that south-of-Glasgow socialist Covenanter cussedness and pride in your working-class background that you get peculiarly strongly along the Ayrshire/Lanarkshire border. A socialist and trade union consciousness was accompanied in dad's brothers by support for the Orange Order and by throaty renditions of *The Sash My Father Wore* and *Follow, Follow We Will Follow Rangers*. They grew orange lilies in council house back gardens. My Uncle George – in reality dad's uncle – had been a full-on Red Clydesider, pal of Jimmy Maxton and an Independent Labour Party stalwart. He worked as a 'professional mourner' for the big steel and ship companies along the Clyde. When an employee of the company died, Uncle George was paid to go along to the funeral to represent the grief-stricken company bosses. In between mourning, he festooned Glasgow with socialist propaganda from the back of his company-supplied black 'mourning' car.

After the war, my granddad had gone back to being a faceworker in one of the Glenbuck pits where he was in 1926 when the General Strike was called and the miners held out for nine months after the TUC caved

Bash The Rich!

Grandad playing cards when he should have been filling the pit in - the cheeky one looking at the camera

in. So my grandmother Lilly Voaden (they'd married in 1915 in Bristol when Ned was leaving to fight with the Cameronian Highlanders in Turkey) was supporting a husband and four boys on no wages for a year bringing into play her expert cadging abilities.

Any attempt to describe the hardship these days runs the risk of a Monty Pythonesque quality, but the memories ran deep. None of the rows of miners cottages had gas, electricity or water connected anyway, but dad remembered the oil for the tilley lamps running out and the village being completely black at night. They lived off stolen vegetables and hares. A washing boiler, shared between the houses in Monkey Row, was used as a permanent soup pan and gigantic steam puddings 'cloutie dumplings' were cooked in a pillow case, dried out in front of the fire by Lilly once a week and shared out in slices to all the Monkey Row kids. The toilets were just middens and dung heaps shared between two houses and there was the horror when the strips of newspaper on a string to wipe yer arses ran out! Bill Shankly said in his memoirs, 'I never saw a bathroom till I left Glenbuck.' Rugs were rags which Lilly used to chalk round every day to give the room a neat look. Her sister Alice would send food parcels up by train from Bristol including live chickens and once flannel trousers and stout boots for the boys wrapped in hundreds of mothballs which smelled for weeks. The four boys used to go climbing up Cairn Table and over to Muirkirk along the burns and all of them described their childhood in the happiest of terms.

Ned Bone, meantime, was the socialist lawyer in the Glenbuck pub, sorting out everyone's problems, running Labour Party and union business and becoming known as 'Snibs' ('his knibs') for his efforts. After the collapse of the General Strike, dad's eldest brother Eddie was picking stones out of the coal at the pithead at 14 and Len followed him down Carmecoup pit at nearby Muirkirk at the same age. It was hard and dangerous work for boys of this age as this press report showed:

'Yesterday morning, Matthew Holden, aged 14, a pony driver in Kames Pit Muirkirk was accidentally killed. Holden had left his own work to give the bottomers a hand, and by some means, he was caught by the cage and taken up the shaft. While on its way up the shaft, the cage chain broke and the cage fell back to the bottom killing Holden in its fall.'

Another press report of the time reads:

'At Davy Pit, Glenbuck, yesterday afternoon, a fatal accident befell William Wilson, 21. He was drawing the road when a large fall from the roof took place, killing him instantly. The body was removed home. His brother was killed in the same mine 18 months ago.'

And yet another death was reported thus:

'Yesterday afternoon, a fatal accident occurred by which Robert

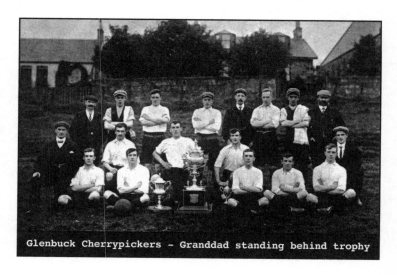

Glenbuck Cherrypickers - Granddad standing behind trophy

Bash The Rich!

Head, 17, and Robert Brown, 16, lost their lives. They were caught by a runaway rake on the dook road and owing to want of room, they were unable to clear themselves. Thomas Watson also received serious injuries, his arm being broken and one of his eyes knocked out. The lads bodies were conveyed home to Muirkirk.'

My dad, John Bone, would have followed his dad and brothers down the Glenbuck pits had they not both closed in 1933. Most of the population upped and moved to work at Kames Colliery in Muirkirk but Granddad got a contract to fill the two worked-out Glenbuck pits. In reality he was not, as Lilly had found out, over-enthused by the protestant work ethic and never worked again after 1933. A very fine photo shows him and the others contracted to fill in the pits sitting playing cards on a grass-topped slag heap – and looking a million miles from the depressed Jarrow marchers.

At the age of 14, my dad found himself in rather different surroundings. Thanks to a cousin, he was offered a position as third footman at Brechin Castle. Well, actually, he was originally employed as a hall boy, but the 14th Earl of Dalhousie knew talent when he saw it and John was fast-tracked to third footman, carrying out such vital duties as sounding the dinner gong, which turned out not to be as easy as he thought. One evening – resplendent in blue tail coat with silver buttons – he sounded the gong dead on 6.30pm. An enraged lady of the house raced down the stairs screaming that he had sounded the gong too early. John pointed to the hall clock. Her ladyship stretched up and moved the hands of the clock back to 6.25pm and ordered, 'Now sound it at the proper time Bone'. Don't think for yourself, you serf!

The other staff comprised butler, first and second footman, hall boy, cellar man, valet, four housemaids, four laundry maids, cook and three kitchen staff, two lady's maids, and two chauffeurs. Brechin Castle was an overnight stop for guests on their way to Balmoral where footmen opened your car doors and a piper would precede the arrival of dinner to the table. It was a far cry from the two-roomed miners' 'butt and ben' that John had shared with his three brothers at Glenbuck, but my dad's incongruous career in service had begun.

Every year on the Glorious Twelfth, the entire household would decamp to Rannoch Moor for the grouse shooting and dad would be out with the

Butler Bone

gamekeepers, gillies and beaters shooing the grouse into the guns of various kilted lords.

Vital though such work was, third footman was unaccountably not considered an 'exempt' occupation and, at the outbreak of war, John was called up in 1939 to fight in Monty's Eighth Army in North Africa and Italy. On the way to war, he was stationed at Hindon in Wiltshire where he met my mum-to-be Jessie Stubbs. It was an exact parallel of World War One when my Granddad had joined up in Glenbuck and met his wife-to-be in Bristol before going off to Turkey and marrying at the end of the war. As it turned out Jock (as he was always mysteriously known in England) and Jessie did a lot of their courting at The Mauritania pub in Bristol. We might have all been in the same boat during the war, but The Mauretania was arranged deckwise like the ocean liner – first class for the officers down to stowage for other ranks. They tried the same trick in a nearby restaurant where Jock had taken Jessie for a meal. Two officer types came in later and were being served first. Jock had had enough of that nonsense in civvy street and pointed out that his money was as good as theirs and got served first – as Jessie swooned at such boldness.

Bone and Stubbs were such solid yeoman-of-England kind of names that it promised to be a marriage made in the Jerusalem of England's green and pleasant land and so it turned out. But not for six years!

Faded sepia images of a whirlwind summer courtship against the darkening war clouds. Hindon populated by cheery headscarved

Bash The Rich!

'Bulge' baby and mum

landgirls and Scots battalionsmen on their way to war in Africa farewell kissing among the whitened cabbage stalks and clucking bantams of long gardens. Mum's dad Reg Stubbs was a full time Navy man and her three brothers served in the Navy throughout the war. One was called 'Uncle Tough', conjuring up Bluto-like images of dockside brawls in faraway places but in reality the back alley of their Hindon council houses was a warm and communal meeting place, populated by women called Auntie Queenie and men called Uncle Bert, who'd sit with their feet in washing up bowls of water and showing off their sweet peas like the lords of the manor they weren't.

After the war, on the egalitarian tide which swept in the 1945 Labour Government, Jock and Jessie finally got married in 1946 but the socialist victory meant third footmen weren't quite in such demand. Jessie had worked at Chilmark, Wiltshire, munitions factory throughout the war, making bombs and bullets, as well as being a right back for the Chilmark Dynamos – the women's football team named in honour of Uncle Joe Stalin's Moscow Dynamos. Dad worked briefly as a fireman at Chilmark, but early 1947 saw Jessie pregnant and the newly-married couple without a job or house or Jock with any employable skills since footmen were still out of fashion. However, a letter to his pre-war employers saw the couple's fortunes transformed, and Jock and Jessie were, out of the blue, employed as butler and housemaid at Hermongers Mansion in Rudgwick, Sussex, home of Frankie More O'Ferrall. This was one hell of a lucky break. Frankie More O'Ferrall was a true blue, Eton-educated, Irish aristocrat, but was also head of the Anglo-Irish Bloodstock Agency and horseracing was the name of his game. Ascot and Goodwood were the events on his social calendar rather than Glyndebourne or Cowes and long weekend house parties became the order of the day.

The close connections between horseracing and showbusiness meant Hermongers quickly became the place to be seen at with Princess Margaret, Douglas Fairbanks, Gregory Peck, the Aga Khan, the Maharajah of Jaipur, David Niven, Walter Pidgeon, Hugh Fraser and Lady Docker amongst the house guest A-listers, plus the exotic racing tipster Prince Monolulu. For my mum and dad coming out of wartime austerity, this was unbelievable good luck. My mum amused the rest of the servants' quarters by posing about in Princess Margaret's fur stole. My dad brought home the left over booze, the tips from the weekend house party were usually more than a week's wages. He also brought home all

Chilmark Dynamos - mum second left at back

Bash The Rich!

Reg, Queenie and kids. Mum front right next to Uncle 'Tough'

their old Christmas cards. One from Clark Gable – pictured driving a pony and trap and personally signed – had an especially swoony effect on my mum! I was often propped up for outings on the front seat of Frankie More O'Ferrall's Roller and allowed to salute the AA man (oh yes, I was born a 'Bulge Baby' in August 1947 in gran's house at Hindon). I also got to splash about in the big house paddling pool with Frankie's baby daughter Susie More O'Ferrall. She went on to marry Max Aitken, head of the Beaverbrook newspaper publishing empire. I could just see how *Heat* or *OK* might report it now: 'I frolicked in pool with Lady Beaverbrook' says mad anarchist!

When I was seriously ill with peritonitis and in hospital for months, I got sent a get well card from Gregory Peck! Yes, Gregory Peck! That one! The real one! And we had a Christmas card from Clark fucking Gable! Frankie and Jackie, the grooms, would take me out for a canter on the racehorses early morning while mum did her housemaids' work. The servants' quarters parties were legendary in Rudgwick.

Dad arranged a servants' outing to see *The Crazy Gang* at a London theatre. There was a railway carriage scene with the whole gang up to their comic capers spread right across the stage. Anxious that my mum might be missing a funny bit in the train toilet, dad shouted across to her. 'Jessie, Jessie – look at the shithouse'. The rest of the Hermongers staff gasped in horror and shock at this coming from the head of the servants quarters!

The Crazy Gang – in particular the songs of Bud Flanagan and Chesney Allen – encapsulated the after-the-war attitude of 'We're as good as they are'. Mum and dad took them at their word, the housemaid looking glamorous in her frock and dad flashy with his spivvy kipper tie and his favourite sports jacket as they bused it down to racy Brighton for the weekend.

We lived in the Lodge at the entrance to the driveway to the 'big house'. Wherever we were it was always the 'big house'. One day, my mum was walking me down to work when I spotted a ten bob note in the hedge. We found a further £20 and raced to the butler's pantry to show my dad. He was straight back out hacking at the hedgerows with a polo stick. We found over 120 bloody quid! They had been coming back from Goodwood the night before counting the winnings and some had blown out of the car window. They never looked for it. We never offered it. Finders keepers. I got a nifty red tricycle out of it. Ripping off the rich at the age of three. Tops!

Frankie More O'Ferrall moved on. Good times came to an end. The furniture van turned up. We sat in the back on the settee as the back lanes and the byways of Sussex and Hampshire flew by.

Dad was next employed as butler to Captain Alexander RN (ret) at Corsley House in Wiltshire. Here, mean spiritedness rather than generosity was the order of the day. Dad spotted that his employer's wife was stealing the servants' tips left by house guests. He marked a ten bob note one day before Captain Alexander's wife could nick it. Sure enough, it turned up in his pay packet. The furniture van arrived again – having your butler accusing your wife of being a thief never goes down well with the landed gentry. This time the van took us to Goudhurst in Kent, home of Sir George and Lady Jessel. By now, the brief escape from the drabness of post-war austerity, utility furniture and ration books that Hermonger's had provided had well and truly vanished.

The return of the Tories in 1951 seemed to eclipse hope of a better life and constraints of a life 'in service' became increasingly irksome to my dad. Being a butler isn't like any other job – you can't just clock off at the end of the day and say 'sod the boss'. If you see them out and about in the village, you're never off duty – you have to take on the expected

Brighton rocks… off duty!

deference. Throughout his career in service, my dad was always referred to by his surname, even by the children of those he worked for. In return, he would have to address even the youngest child as Master John or Master David. In all the 'big houses' my dad worked, my mum also worked as a housemaid. Both their livelihoods were completely dependent on them satisfying the demands of their employers. If they were sacked, they were both jobless and homeless at the same time. The tied cottage system was like a throwback to the slave trade. More often than not, their employer was chair of the local magistrates and on the local council, so any appeal to the courts for stay of eviction or to the local authority for council housing would be blocked. Wages were at an appallingly low level. From 1947 to 1951, dad earned £5.50 a week with no rise in four years and even by 1958, he was only on the basic agricultural worker's wage of £12 per week.

There was a brief return to the glitzy high-life world of 1950s show business when dad appeared on *What's My Line* on BBC television and beat the panel of David Nixon, grumpy old Gilbert Harding, Barbara Kelly and thieving toff Lady Isabel Barnet who was convicted of shoplifting and committed suicide in the bath. Dad returned with a full autograph book including a message to me in Gaelic from Eamonn Andrews! Butler Bone had beaten the panel but then it was back to the workaday life of opening letters with silver knives, ironing the newspapers and helping aged toffs put their longjohns on!

Cowpat Man For The Bolsheviks!

Goudhurst was the tipping point, but it had started at Rudgwick in 1951. At a Labour party meeting in Horsham, an agricultural labourer, an exiled Polish airman, had vividly complained about being ordered out of his tied cottage with this family after being sacked from the estate of Lord Winterton, the Tory MP. On the walk home from Horsham, Jock and Jessie ripped down all the Tory posters en route, including those from their employer's front gates. The cowpats would take another four years. Goudhurst was a beautiful, traditional country village set in the Weald of Kent, the garden of England. The centre of the village was the pond with its swans and a village bobby who held up the traffic to let the ducks cross the road. The church, the school and the football team were the village's pride and a trip to Tunbridge Wells by bus once a month was a highlight.

The village was largely composed of agricultural labourers whose attitude to their employers remained that of forelock tugging and grateful thanks that they were given a job. Rural deference was the order of the day and voting Tory was the established pattern. Labour voters were so few and far between as to be considered weird rather than a threat to the social fabric.

In the summer, the calm of the village was rudely shattered by the noisy arrival of the hop pickers. Down by the lorry load from the East End of London, they would stay in the 'hopper huts' for the two or three week duration of the season. These huts were just corrugated tin shacks or large cowsheds with no floor covering. The arrival of the hoppers would totally transform the village. Up would go the 'No Hoppers' signs in the pubs and shops. Barbed wire would be erected round the counters and regular village customers would be served at the back door. At weekends, the hoppers would bring their own jellied eel and whelk stalls to the centre of the village and have a carnival atmosphere whether the locals liked it or not.

While the local labourers tut-tutted with their masters about the feckless and thieving nature of the no-good Londoners, the hoppers themselves were openly contemptuous of the forelock-tugging attitude of the locals and unmercifully sarcastic in their treatment of the local squires and gentry – many of whom used to flee for the length of the picking season. Mum and dad met other workers who were confirmed Labour voters and whose cheeky attitude towards his own employers came as a welcome change.

Two incidents involving Sir George deepened dad's feelings of disgust for his employers. Tom Poyle was a 76-year-old widower who had worked on the Jessel Estate all his life. He lived with his elder daughter Ruby in a tied cottage with no bathroom and collected rainwater in an outside barrel to wash in. The day he collapsed and died, he was up early in the morning, working as usual.

On the day of his funeral, Jock was astonished to find that Sir George had absolutely no intention of attending it. When he finally decided to attend after being reproached by his Butler, it was only to inform Tom's daughter, Ruby, who had lived in the house for 52 years, that she 'would have to be out within three months'.

Then I intervened by getting dad the sack. I was beeping the horn on my bicycle to amuse the groom's baby, when a thundery red-faced Sir George stormed towards me shouting 'turn that bloody thing off' – a fearsome sight! I told mum who told dad who stormed in to give Sir George a right rollicking. He might be a wage slave but Ian was not on the payroll so leave him sodding well alone! How dare he tell his son off! The furniture van arrived. We landed in 1958 at Jenkyn Place, Bentley, Hampshire, as Butler and Housemaid to Sir Gerald Coke.

But I for one was sorry to leave Goudhurst. On my way home from school there was a grave in the churchyard of one of the notorious Hawkhurst gang of smugglers who battled the local gentry in the 1830s. I used to scrape the lichen off to read the inscription: It revealed a large skull and crossbones. I always felt drawn to that sign of blood curdling rebellion and revolt. The Hawkhurst gang had attacked Goudhurst then caroused all day long in the Eight Bells, the pub my mum and dad drank in. 'Beer first, business later' as the *Class War* (the anarchist paper I was later to edit) slogan was to say a quarter of a century later. Their leader was Goudhurst-born Thomas Kingsmill but other desperados of the gang were monikered 'Bloodthirsty', 'Cold Toast' and 'Slipjibbet'. Wouldn't it be a fine thing to belong to a gang like that I thought. I'd doubtless have been called 'Bones'.

Jenkyn Place, Bentley, was the home of Sir Gerald Coke Esq, grandson of the Earl of Leicester and millionaire chairman of RTZ. Soon after arriving at Bentley, dad joined the local Labour Party for the first time, actively working during the two General Elections of 1964 and 1966 and quickly ending up as chairman of the Petersfield Constituency Labour Party. Amid wide publicity, a resolution he proposed on the tied cottage issue was adopted for discussion at the Labour Party's national conference. Labour party motorcades had a habit of ending up in Jenkyn Place driveway. Labour Party election posters were prominently displayed on our doors and windows which were just inside the entrance to Jenkyn Place itself. Following his boss's retirement from the Parish Council, dad himself stood for the vacant seat and was subsequently elected as the first ever Labour member, despite a 'Ban the Bone' campaign led by local farmers

Dad's Labour election leaflet for Bentley Parish Council from May 6th 1964 was a masterpiece of class war speak heavy with understated nudges and winks in its appeal to latterday Captain Swingers :

Dear Elector
Are you satisfied with your present council?

For years now your council has been made up mainly from a VERY SMALL SECTION of the community. We think this should be altered.

We candidates think we represent A BETTER CROSS SECTION OF VILLAGERS, and know more about their problems. If you come along and

Bash The Rich!

vote for us, you can be sure THE MAJORITY of the village is represented on the Parish Council.

Signed: John Bone (butler), Reg Parfitt (woodworker), Hillier Furze (maintenance engineer), Margaret White (secretary).

If they'd put their opponents occupations down they would have read: 'Landowner, Squire, Farmer, Vicar'.

It was the first contested Parish council election in Bentley for 30 years and the class lines couldn't have been drawn more clearly. And there was the Labour address at the bottom of the leaflet: 'Published by J Bone, Little Jenkyn, Bentley'. Little Jenkyn was the name of our house within the gates of Mr Coke's mansion Jenkyn Place. This Bolshevist clarion call had been issued from within the belly of the beast itself!

From that day Mr Coke and the rest of the Bentley squirarchy knew the cap doffers were a dwindling minority. On election day, many voters told dad they'd accepted lifts to the polls off the local farmers but voted Labour in secret!

Imagine the humiliation of your butler taking over your seat on the Parish Council! All this political activity from one's butler in direct opposition to one's own views was made even harder to stomach for Sir Gerald by the election to two successive Labour governments.

At Bentley we got our first car – a Ford Popular – we were so proud of it. I can still remember the number plate now. Where are you 135BKK? On our first big drive up to Scotland to visit dad's brothers for our annual summer holiday, we overtook a Jaguar on a dual carriageway. It seemed to take an age to draw alongside and pass. We whooped and we hooped and we cheered. We hadn't just passed a Jaguar, dad's Stirling Moss heroics had shown that we were every bit as bloody good as they were!

Guests at Jenkyn Place were hardly the post-war glamour pusses of Hermongers but dad was entrusted regularly with the spare glass eye of John Christie, the founder of Glyndebourne, on his visits and with

16

Yehudi Menhuin's violins. More interesting to dad was Field Marshall Montgomery of Alamein who lived at Isington Mill just outside Bentley. Monty only came to dinner at Jenkyn Place twice but dad was anxious to share his Eighth Army credentials with him. He must have informed him – on

That Ford Popular – proud as punch!

the quiet, like – of their joint campaign in North Africa and Italy when he greeted him at the front entrance. On the second occasion, Monty found some excuse to come into the butler's pantry after dinner. Dad was amazed to hear Monty divulge that, after problems with Alton Council not giving planning permission for his mill conversion, he had contacted Aneurin Bevan and the Prime Minister Clem Attlee to see if they could help him out! Otherwise he threatened to live in his old war caravan in the garden! At that prospect, Attlee got it sorted – according to Monty anyway. Dad chanced his arm and ended the conversation by asking if Monty would join the Bentley and Froyle Labour Party! I often wondered if Monty had picked up from the Cokes some mention of his left-wing politics for otherwise, why would he be discussing Nye Bevan with his neighbour's butler?

Both mum and dad had left school at 14 and, like a lot of their generation, valued education for their children beyond anything else. They really slogged their guts out to make sure I would have that opportunity and I did, thanks to them.

I got my three A-levels and, when I left home to go to university, Dad felt a new sense of freedom to break the ties that had so long shackled him. He was increasingly irritated by the dinner table discussions on the Labour government, and education in particular, which he was forced to listen to every night. Though obviously unable to join in, his politics were so well known by the guests that he often felt the conversation was more for his benefit than the other guests. Mr Coke's three sons had all gone to Eton, but inexplicably the old school tie had failed to get John Coke into Oxford. Forced to go to Durham University instead, he bitterly complained at dinner one evening that the place was 'full of grammar school yobs and miners' sons'.

Taking this as a direct attack on himself and me, dad tackled an embarrassed John about it the day after. It was the beginning of the end. Soon after, Mr Coke informed him that 'because of your government, I can no longer afford to employ a butler' and that his wife was increasingly annoyed by his 'brusque Scottish manner and embarrassed by his Labour Party posters when her friends called for lunch'. He would, of course, have to give his house up as well.

But without a job, mum and dad had nowhere else to move to and refused to move out. My lurking long-haired presence had been noted

Dad with union banner at Tolpuddle commemoration – free at last!

by the Cokes and dad told Sir Gerald I would bring rent-a-mob down from the London School of Economics if he was forcibly evicted!

Sir Gerald agreed to rent mum and dad a house he owned in nearby Alton. The furniture van appeared again amongst the puddle-wonderful and mud-luscious springtime Hampshire lanes and brought to an overdue end their life in service. Dad got a job making artificial limbs at the Vessa factory in Alton where he was able to join a trade union for the first time in his life.

The following summer was one of his proudest ever days. He carried the FTAT (Furniture Trades and Allied Technicians) trade union banner on the annual Tolpuddle Martyrs Commemoration in Dorset. Commemorating his own release from rural servitude as well.

Chapter 2

PUNCH CRAZY

I'd discovered anarchism by chance in an article in *Punch* in a dentist's waiting room in Alton, Hampshire when I was 15.

'Jesus!' I thought 'This is it. This is what I am – an anarchist.' Well, you couldn't really blame me, could you, with that background in class hatred. My dad's democratic socialism seemed to offer scant hope of revenge on any of the bastards who employed him and mum. Anarchism offered not only this, but the exciting prospect of doing away with the wealthy and privileged altogether.

I noted the address of Freedom Press – 'the anarchist HQ' – in *Punch* and composed a letter to Freedom that night, but added the cautious footnote requesting that no-one visits my house. For weeks, I had nightmares of a bearded anarchist turning up to our door, or, even worse, the door of the big house. I needn't have worried that the anarchist movement was that efficient! Three months later, a copy of *Freedom* dropped through my letterbox. I never looked back. For the next two years, I made the frequent solitary trip to London visiting Freedom Press, Indica and Better Books, bringing back to Hampshire Lenny Bruce, Alan Ginsberg, The Beats and incomprehensible copies of *Anarchy* magazine.

In *Freedom*, a meeting of the 'Anarcho-United-Mystics' at Finch's in Portobello Road was advertised. I wanted to go but didn't have a clue what a 'United Mystic' was. The only one who I thought might fit the bill was Aleister Crowley who I'd read about in one of my London book imports to Bentley. Then I got lucky – it turned out Crowley Ales, where Aleister inherited a lot of his money from – had been based in the Hampshire brewing town of... Alton! I thought if a 'united mystic' asked me a question I'd say I was a relative of Crowley's from Alton. I went. It was full of the beautiful people: Long-haired, velvet-jacketed eye-shaded beatniks who looked a different species from the spotty, speccy adolescent sitting in the corner. My cover story claim to fame was not needed. No one spoke to me. No one noticed me, but did I care – did I fuck! I was in seventh heaven!

Back at Bentley, my dad was well involved with the Labour Party, fighting the 1964 election in deepest feudal Hampshire. He came up with some surprising people in the quiescent villages. There was Bill Eve, a veteran Communist living in Froyle; Arthur Griffiths, the Spanish Civil War veteran in Alton; and a Captain Swing house down towards The Hangers in Selborne with the faded 'an injury to one is an injury to all' inscription just above the door jamb. Shades of the Tolpuddle martyrs and history echoing down from the rick burners till the present.

But the trumpet call beckoning me to trash the threshing machines and rise up with the hop pickers was not strong enough. My hair was rapidly curling over my school collar. I may not have been a united mystic, but I sure was an anarchist. The only one in the village! But not, I hoped, in Swansea where I had been accepted for a university place.

There's a Fogg on the Line

I was leading a double life... one older than the other. Sitting in my bedroom at Bentley in the long wood pigeon-cawing late summer evenings reading Lawrence Ferlinghetti and Gregory Corso. Then every other Saturday, going off to Aldershot with my dad – and often my mum – to the Recreation Ground to support 'The Shots' complete with matching scarf and bobble hat.

Aldershot had never won anything. One of the only two teams at the time never to have been promoted. In their matchday programme under 'Honours Won' listed: 'Semi-finalists Southern Floodlight Cup 1952-53' – a useless reserve team trophy to pad out dead time for the big London clubs.

Bash The Rich

But there was hope. The first game I ever saw, we beat the mighty Gateshead 8-1! Then nothing. Then we suddenly had a half-decent team. The brilliant Chick Brodie in goal – how we were proud and happy for him when he was sold to Wolves! Flying wingers in Chris Palethorpe and local hero Alan Burton, the midfield schemer Alan Woan (the Johnnie Haynes of the Rec) the mighty colossus of Dick Renwick at full-back and, for one season only, big-boned bustling elbow-flexing Ron Fogg at centre-forward. We had other notable centre-forwards, such as Jack Howarth, but it was Ron Fogg that pressed my g-spot. Nowadays, he'd be called Ronaldinho Foggio or somesuch but Ron Fogg was the perfect name for those Fourth Division dismal days as he battled gamely on, chasing every ball. I think he was sold on to Weymouth or Hereford but we'd had our 15 minutes worth by then.

Somehow, we'd got through to the third round of the FA Cup and we had been drawn to play away to Aston Villa. Me and me dad got the special supporters' train which took about three weeks to get to Birmingham. It was pissing down with rain at Villa Park and the tie was nearly postponed. After 89 minutes of Alamo defending in the quagmire, Villa were awarded a penalty! Horror! Black despair! I was sick to the pit of my stomach.

What an unequal contest the penalty was to be. Step forward sleek black-haired Tony Hately for the Villa. Step forward for us – Davey Jones – known as The Ancient Mariner – 'he stoppeth one of three'. Jones was like something out of a comic book with big roll-neck green jersey, flat cap, and leather boots concreted into the mire. Hately lashed a ferocious drive arrowing into the top right corner. Jones – who never did anything remotely similar before or after – took off from the mud (I swear he left his boots behind) and flung himself skywards and palmed the ball over the crossbar. Ferlinghetti, Fuck Off You Waster!

We won the replay 1-0. You couldn't see the goal at the other end because it was a dead foggy night. We'd scored direct from a corner but we couldn't tell until we saw the Aldershot payers running back towards the half-way line. There was a minute's delay between the goal being scored and the roar going up! YEEES! Where are you now Billy Wright... Jack Kelsey... Tom Finney... Alan Ginsberg... Jack Kerouac... Walt Whitman... Hart Crane... eecummings...

There' only one Ron Fogg! But could there be another?

We lost to Swindon in the next round but so fucking what! I'd decided to model my own willing-chaser, never-say-die football style on Fogg. I WOULD force my way into the school team as a 'gangly striker from the Ron Fogg school of hard knocks', scoring goals-a-plenty with knee ricochets and belly-ins.

But there was a problem. Tony Goodchild – admittedly a much more skilful player –had kept me out of the team all season. To make things worse, he insisted that I couldn't play inside-right or inside-left because these were 'specialist positions'.

'Bone is no Johnnie Haynes,' he would opine. I didn't want to be Johnnie bloody Haynes anyway – though I secretly thought I could make a decent stab at Tosh Chamberlain.

However, come the last game of the season, I was picked to partner Goodchild up front. A nondescript goalless game followed, in which my influence was far from Haynes-like. Goodchild spent the game shrieking at me to give him the ball and raising his arms to the heavens like a supplicant every time I ignored him.

Then we won a corner, which was taken quicker than I expected. Seeing some cronies sloping off home early, I had turned to give them a mock bow in salute of my performance. At that moment, Goodchild hit a thundering volley which cannoned off my preferred backside and

Bash The Rich!

into the roof of the net! Yeeeesss! Fogg scores! Hysterical with glee, my cronies forsook the delights of an early trip to Alton's only Expressso Bar and hoisted me shoulder high to the halfway line. 'Credit the goal to Fogg' I demanded of our maths teacher refereeing the match. 'No, Goodchild's goal' he snapped back.

Whaaaat?' I entreated, I begged, I implored, I swore. I showed him the mark of the ball on my otherwise spotless arse. To no avail.

Come back Ferlinghetti. Come back Lenny Bruce. Come back Jack and your greyhound buses – all is forgiven. I realised that I couldn't hope to be Ron Fogg and Aleister Crowley. Football was the loser – from now on, it was politics all the way. Swansea Town FC would be the loser – but what the hell – they'd just got to the FA Cup Semi-finals without me!

SECTION TWO

SWANSEA

Chapter 3

JACKTOWN

The first time I set eyes on Swansea, I thought I was landing on Mars as the clanking train pulled in through the cratered moonscapes of the lower Swansea Valley. I tried hard to recall what the university prospectus had invitingly said about golden beaches and Walter Savage Landor's hyperbolic description of Swansea Bay. In the event, I didn't give a toss because I only set foot twice from the university campus in my first year and that was to watch Swansea Town get relegated to Division Three – seeing Ivor Allchurch but just missing out on the glories of Derek 'Didi' Draper. The 'Ugly Lovely Town' as Dylan Thomas described it, was to be my home for the next 17 years.

The hall of residence was a bit of a shock, though, in the Indian summer of 1965, the site in Singleton Park was a rare thing of beauty. Gowns were still worn to dinner where there was a high table as which arselicking sporty types would grovel before the warden. Swansea was trying to be a poor man's fucking Oxbridge. There was a particularly vile visiting tutor called Henderson who invited some of us out to his house on the Gower one night. Turned out he was a full-on white Rhodesian Ian Smith fan. I started calling him 'Bwana Henderson' after a few drinks and got thrown out into the pouring rain and had to walk all the way back to Singleton Park from Bishopston... with a bit of a smirk among the raindrops, it has to be admitted. It felt like I'd done my bit to oppose the Rhodesian UDI.

The students were even worse. There were three black students in the hall. The two Africans were quiet and, therefore, seen as OK but the West Indian was known as 'cocky wog' because he'd once turned the television channel over in the Common Room. I got pissed one night and one of the rugby boys cut all my hair off while I was asleep on the floor. I grew a Manfred Mann beard as a symbol of defiance. It was a bit of a style minus but it was the thought that counted. I moved out of the hall at year's end by when a couple of fellow long hairs had turned up.

Swansea Anarchists came into being in October 1966 and our main activity was strolling around outside the Griffin Bar in the town centre on Saturday afternoons hoping people would stare at us – sort of United Mystic wannabees. We all had long hair and were generally only pestered by kids with the enquiry in a lilting Swansea

Revolutionary student chic 1968.

accent 'Are you a boy or a girl?' But, what the fuck, it was a start!

There were still a lot of 'Gentleman Only' bars in Swansea where our long hair would be greeted by the hilarious: 'Sorry girls, this is gents only'. We did however pile into quite a few of them – boys and girls – and the gents only bars gradually vanished.

One night, a few of us got on to the blue and yellow Llynfi Valley motorbus to go to Maesteg to see The Crazy World of Arthur Brown play. Whoever booked Arthur to play there was fucking bonkers. When we got there – all hair and army greatcoats – they let us in for free because they thought we must be with the band. Long hair had yet to reach Maesteg. About 10pm, all the suit-wearing Saturday night drunks piled in and we huddled down the front in terror.

My mate Phil Thomas – aka Vile Phial – was waving a joss stick about. 'What's that?' enquired a drunken suit. 'Joss stick,' replied Phial factually. Wham! The suit laid Phial low with a Saturday night haymaker. 'What'd ya do that for?' I asked. 'He called me a spastic,' said the suit. Arthur let us flee into the band's dressing room and we were smuggled out in Crazy World of Arthur's van.

I was wising up that being stared at in Swansea was likely to end in getting thumped – not quite eliciting the same desired response as the gilded Fauntleroys in Portobello Road! Indeed, I don't think any of the hippie crowd hanging around outside the Griffin Bar would have past muster in Finches – apart from Peter Cowley always dressed from top to toe in black. Where the beautiful people of London shopped in Granny Takes A Trip and I Was Lord Kitcheners Valet, the Griffin poseurs just cobbled together what they could from wherever. I was wearing my dad's cast offs – a long black army coat with one of dad's kipper ties tied around the elbow like a poor man's bandana. It was a matter of class – they had it and we didn't – but the Griffin crowd were working-class hippies whose experiences were far removed from the over-chronicled swinging London.

Kustard, Sweeney and Junkie Ginge were the first town hippies that I met – can you imagine one of the Portobello Road hippies being called Junkie Ginge? I'd seen them outside the Griffin but not spoken to them, then they turned up outside my door one evening! Brilliant – it meant I was part of a wider scene beyond the university.

They were all wearing cloaks – Junkie Ginge's being made simply by cutting a hole in a hairy blanket like a poncho! Kustard always wore a black cloak with incongruous cowboy hat while Sweeney had a fine metal clasp on his. 'Did I want to go 'posing' up the Uplands Hotel?' asked Ginge. I felt made up breezing into the Uplands with this top-quality stare material in tow!

Kustard's name was all over Swansea – he'd carved it, written it, painted it on every available surface but particularly carved into the seats at the Bun House (Social Security) in Castle Street. The good burghers of the town had grassed over a bank on the main road into Swansea but Kustard had immediately creosoted in huge letters 'USTARD' onto it. Working backwards (don't ask!), he'd been nicked

– brown creosote-handed – before he could flourish off the 'K'. In the magistrates court, Kustard sat silent in the dock – as always – wearing his cowboy hat and reading the *Beano*. His defence arguing that he had been on the beach and had just found the creosote pole and barrel when the cops turned up! Later, he rolled a tyre down Constitution Hill which luckily caused no fatalities. Sweeney (Gerald Castle) was a local legend for having escaped from the cop shop and gone on the run after a drug bust. Junkie Ginge said we should organise a march from the Griffin one Saturday to the cop shop round the corner – no particular reason. When we got there he put on a tin helmet with an anti-slug smoke pellet on top, walked into the police station reception lit the pellet and started dancing about wildly as the flare exuded choking orange smoke. We ran to the pavement opposite as he exited the cop shop pursued by gasping red-faced Keystone Cops. Those were the days, my friend.

In October 1967, we produced our first leaflet *Swansea Anarchists Are Revolting* and furthered our great leap forward from the university into town by getting to know some of the cannabis suppliers. Harold Wilson visited the Guildhall and we met some anarchists from Llanelli

Swansea anarchists with 'fish face' banner

holding a banner which read: 'Go home fish face', which certainly stood out from the usual platitudes.

We followed this up with another leaflet *Sex, Drugs and Vietnam* which was very exciting because we got to meet some girls from town. We started up our weekly paper which was like a duplicated version of *Oz* without the sex and pictures and graphics – so not a lot to it really!

One of our number, John Plant, had taken over the moribund student arts festival with a sizeable budget attached and brought such auto-destructive luminaries as Gustav Metzger down to bewilder everyone with dripping pipes plus a weeklong showing of the *Eating, drinking, pissing, shitting* film and an experimental music festival. It wasn't exactly a Strasbourg University appropriation of funds but when we blew the rest on taking a coach load of freeloaders up to the 24 Technicolour Dream at Alexandra Palace, it certainly felt like ten days that shook the university!

While the beautiful people from swinging London's demi-monde drifted conspicuously by in a cocooned serenity of drug haze, I could only fumble with the contents of a Benzedrex nose inhaler bought from the 24-hour Boots Chemist in Piccadilly. You had to remove the filter papers, screw them up and swallow them. They'd unfold in your throat and choke you and did nothing for me except make my breath stink, but I convinced everyone I was hallucinating just as much as they were. Yoko Ono was having bits cut off her clothes as some sort of auto-destructive happening – or similar, what the fuck did I know – and emboldened by my stinking Benzedrex, I cut a bit off her collar. No longer the anonymous geek in Finch's – I'd made my mark at last. Look at me now ma!

We headed back to Swansea with a coachload of *Oz*'s, *International Times* and a total cultural superiority complex.

We had a Swansea Anarchists float – I kid you not – in the annual Rag Week procession through town. We had someone in a cage, Junkie Ginge reprised his tin hat smoke flare act, and – god knows why – we had a giant papier-mache mushroom on board. When we got back to the university, we set fire to the mushroom on the grassed area in front of the main college building and danced round it waving our red and black flags. The proletariat – in the shape of the college porters armed with fire extinguishers – chased us off.

Then, incredibly to our eyes, news came that Pink Floyd were to play Port Talbot at the Afan Lido. We thought it

Blocking the Mumbles Road

would be another Bash a Hippie night like Maesteg but, all of a sudden, there were hundreds of people just like us there. I wasn't quite sure if this was good or bad at the time. No one asked me if I was a 'boy or a girl' and we weren't the centre of attention I'd imagined.

Actually I was a crap hedonist – the drugs didn't work, I couldn't 'hear the colours', I couldn't even see the fucking colours and the cover of *Their Satanic Majesties Request* did not move for me, I couldn't see how Arnold Lane was 'psychedelic', I seemed the only one unable to hallucinate and got loads of morning glory seeds stuck in my teeth for weeks – for nothing. I must have sat through more idiots talking bollocks that year...

I was interested in the politics of hippiedom then yippiedom, not the brain numbing banalities of dopedom. One day I discovered the quote: 'The creative personality does not seek to shock or entertain the bourgeoisie but seeks to destroy them'. That'll do for me I thought and I was gagging for the Summer of Love to end quick and usher Street Fighting Man centre stage. I'd found a fellow spirit in Julian Ross who worked in the college bookshop and we shared a flat together.

Against the continual backdrop of the Vietnam War, the mode of the music was changing and the walls of the cities were about to shake in 1968. Beatnik hippy narcissism didn't seem to be an appropriate response given the daily slaughter reporting on TV from Vietnam. The

Bash The Rich

Anarcho-United-Mystics no longer had me in their thrall. The nightly flickering images from Vietnam of Agent Orange and Napalm and blowing peasants to bits politicised hundreds of students in Swansea as across the world.

I missed out on the March 1968 riot against the Vietnam War in Grosvenor Square, but John Plant reported back to the rest of us on the joys of rucking with the cops. It seemed, at last, we were going to match the Zengakuren in Japan and the thousands of others all over Europe and the USA who were rising up.

We took our Swansea Anarchists banner on the Easter Aldermaston march where we bumped into some other Swansea marchers – including Paul Durden who went on to scriptwrite *Twin Town*. At the end of the march, we heard about the shooting of Rudi Dutscke in Berlin and the anarchist faction broke away from the CND stroll to head for the German Embassy. We ran out of steam after about 30 minutes because no-one knew where the Embassy was and the bastard cops wouldn't tell us! We recovered by heading back to the Axel Springer building in Fleet Street where my rucking with the cops virginity was finally lost!

Back in Swansea, our University Anarchist Group grew overnight to 60-70 members as news of worldwide insurrections broke out. We listened into Radio Luxembourg for nightly news of the Paris rioting. One night, the reports said: 'The black flag of anarchy is flying over the Bourse which is in flames'. It seemed like revolution was possible and we weren't going to see Swansea left out. We occupied the university Registry for four weeks, blocked Mumbles Road, abolished the Students Union Executive under the slogan: 'All power to the forums', sent telegrams of support worldwide and hoisted the red and black flag on the university flagpole. Anarchists Albert Meltzer and Dennis Gould came down to speak at meetings. Heady days…

My paper-selling career was well underway as I flogged shitloads of *Oz, IT, Black Dwarf* and *Freedom*. Our time was surely coming, and 28 October in Grosvenor Square would surely be the date.

The press build-up to the Anti Vietnam War demo in Grosvenor Square was hysterical, with scare stories about a revolution planned to take place on the day. Army units and Marines were said to be on duty. If anyone got through to the American Embassy in the Square, it was said the Marines would shoot to kill. In return, groups such as Orpington Anarchist Group – which I knew consisted of a very nice middle-class father and daughter – were said to be building tanks! There was the classic 'Anarchists have tanks' headline. If only, I thought, wising up rapidly on how easy it was to wind up the media. The list of groups in the Anarchist Federation of Britain published in *Freedom* multiplied to 60 or 70 from only about a dozen a year earlier. Foreign anarchists led by Danny Cohn-Bendit were said to be arriving mob handed. London quaked. But it was the Trots in the Vietnam Solidarity Campaign who held centre stage. Tariq Ali, Pat Jordan and all were able to portray themselves to a gullible media as leaders of the Anti-Vietnam War Movement. Then a few days before the much desired attack on the Embassy, the fucking Trots – led by Tariq Ali – decided the march should not head to the Embassy at all, but go to listen to a rally of speakers in fucking Hyde Park! Abandoning revolution for a picnic in the park. I have never forgiven fucking Ali for this disastrous abnegation of revolutionary duty. Indeed, 35 years later, the same Oxbridge educated crowd – Tariq, Pinter, the Redgraves, Ken Loach – have led the anti-Iraq war movement into the same cul-de-sac of mind-numbingly boring rallies in Hyde Park instead of direct action on the streets to bring effective opposition to the war. The new generation of anti-war activists have had themselves saddled with the very same movement leaders who so effectively bottled it in Grosvenor Square in 1968.

The decision not to go to the Square was vigorously opposed by the anarchists and a small groups of Maoists. We were so fucking annoyed in Swansea that we refused to share a coach with the Trots and organised our own two coaches – two fucking coaches mind – to London with our very own Swansea Anarchists banner flying up the A4 all the way to the revolution. We stayed at the occupied LSE the night before the 28 October – a flavour, or so it seemed, of what the Smolny must have been like on the eve of October 1917. Earnest debates and discussions everywhere. John Rety – who was the editor of *Freedom* at the time – was debating with Tariq Ali why we should go to the Embassy and not the picnic in the park. I always had a lot of time for John Rety – still do – a proper bearded anarchist with an East European accent, a mischievous twinkle in his eye, and a good selection of one-liner put downs. The room was packed out and Rety looked an especially romantic figure with his beard and red and black neckerchief. He was the only anarchist anyone had heard of and gave Ali a good sneering run for his money. The anarchists would join the Maoists and go to the Embassy – an 'ultra-leftist adventure' snarled Tariq the Toff, making sure everything stayed peaceful for the authorities.

The revolution would not be televised, but not for lack of trying on 28 October. The anarchists were, as on the Dutschke demo, completely disorganised. At first, we tail-ended the Trots. Then we picked up momentum and ran alongside them as they queued up for their picnic. 'Ho Ho Ho Chi Minh!' chanted the Trots. 'Ho Ho Rubbish Bin!' chanted the anarchists (well, you think of something better!).

The truth is, we were lost again. How did you get through to the Embassy? The cops were keeping secrets from us again. Where were our logistics units? But now, at last, the truth can be told: Ian Hunter – aka Junkie Ginge – one of the Swansea mob we'd brought with us, suddenly appeared by the Hilton Hotel pointing down a service alley where we could out-manoeuvre the cops and get to the Embassy. We suddenly found ourselves in South Audley Street with lines of cops barring our way. To the north side of the square, we could see the white helmeted Maoists. We could outrace them in our bid to get gunned down by the Marines inside. We pushed up, fought, and shoved against the cops. After 20 minutes or so a surreal scene was developing. A quite nasty ruck with the cops in the front three rows, but a few yards back people just standing around chatting. The whole thing fizzled out. On the way back to our coaches, a crowd of kids waving an American flag got in amongst us – the revolutionary Trots fled in terror. The working class had finally put in an appearance – on the wrong side!

I went back on the coach to Swansea bitterly disillusioned. If we couldn't do anything with 100,000 people at our disposal, what the fuck was the point of going up to London in the future. We needed to do work in Swansea to get kids like those we'd just seen on our side. Then we might come up again and make a difference. Tariq Ali – you're a cunt!

CHURCHILL'S DEAD

The Rt Hon Reginald Maudling was a money grabber in the pay of John Poulson and taking every backhander going from his friends in the north. He got his comeuppance — dying of cirrhosis of the liver during the winter of discontent when the strikers wouldn't let his ambulance through the picket lines into the hospital. Top work comrades! He'd spoken at a Tory election rally I'd attended at the Brangwyn Hall in Swansea in 1966. Churchill had just died and the Tories hadn't realised the depth of hatred towards him in South Wales because of the memories of Tonypandy, when, as Home Secretary, he deployed troops to force miners back to work in 1910, or 'drive the rats back down their holes' as he put it.

Towns such as Merthyr Tydfyl raised the princely sum of 2/6d, a coat button and three Green Shield stamps for the Churchill Memorial Appeal. When I'd gone on a Freshers' coach tour of Swansea the year before, the driver had pointed out 'the scab's house' just outside Ystradgynlais as we came back from the delights of Dan-yr-Ogof caves. 'When was that?' I asked the driver as we filed off the coach. '1926,' he replied. It wasn't just because of the Tonypandy Riots that Churchill was hated, it was the General Strike in 1926 and the Llanelli railway riots of 1911 — these things were not forgotten. The tinplate town of Llanelli raised even less than Merthyr for the appeal. I could add the death of Peter the Painter (but he never died said I) in the Sidney Street Siege in the East End of London in 1910 to Churhill's crimes but why bother — everyone loathed him already.

Boz Morris, a popular student at the university with a deeply rational hatred of Churchill, got on the stage at the Brangwyn, pushed Maudling off it, and arms raised shouted 'Churchill is dead!' to an audience of the party faithfuls. Morris was chucked off his teacher's training course at the university but he'd impressed me with the first bit of direct action I'd ever seen. The second bit I did myself. Roy Jenkins had brought in the Race Relations Act and the first person to be prosecuted was, needless to say, a black man. Michael de Freitas. Michael X. He was banged up in Swansea Prison. I spray painted 'Free Michael X' on the prison walls with perforated 'cut here' hyphens. I proudly walked past it for weeks making sure it was still there. If you know where to look, you can still see it.

Chapter 4

WE GOTTA GET RID OF THE TROTS!

The ramshackle and inadequate nature of the anarchist movement was becoming more obvious as the better organised Trotskyists started to clean up on the student radical market with the International Socialists (IS), International Marxist Group (IMG) and Revolutionary Socialist Students Federation (RSSF) pre-eminent. By contrast, the anarchist groups listed under the Anarchist Federation of Britain in *Freedom* came and went with bewildering rapidity. I'd thought that if the anarchists had been better organised at Grosvenor Square, we could have fought our way into the Embassy as an organised force rather than relying on Junkie Ginge to show us the way. The Anarchist Federation of Britain didn't have any practical existence so, despite the libertarian nature of the student revolts, it was the Trots who were making the running.

We'd established our own links with a lively anarchist group at Aberystwyth University, the renowned 'Aber Anarchists'. Prince Charles was due to study there to learn parrot Welsh before his investiture as a sop to the nationalists. We were staging our own mock investiture in Swansea – 'A fanfare for a prince is a fart in the face for the people' – and sent Big Tony Levene to Aber on his motorbike to invite the Prince along. By chance, the university authorities were holding a press conference to announce how secure the Prince was going to be during his stay. Tony and the Aber Anarchists hid behind curtains in the room and leapt out halfway through the press conference making a mockery of the vaunted security arrangements. From then on, we linked up a lot with the Aber Anarchists but surely we could do the same nationwide. At the start of 1970, I attended an anarchist conference in York organised by Keith

Bash The Rich

Nathan of the Organisation of Revolutionary Anarchists and others aiming to form an more coherent anarchist movement. However, there was no follow up and the impetus was frittered away – as usual.

On the CND Easter Aldermaston March in 1968, I'd bought a pamphlet entitled *The Death of CND and the Committee of 100 at Grosvenor Square*, published by the Solidarity Group. I was impressed and subscribed to the journal *Solidarity* and assorted pamphlets they published. Rumour had it that it was *Solidarity* who had produced the infamous *Spies For Peace* pamphlet detailing the locations of secret regional seats of government in the event of nuclear war, The publication broke the Official Secrets Act and caused uproar but no one was ever prosecuted. Word had it that the Solidarists had thrown their typewriter in the River Thames after its production to avoid detection. Action as well as theory! The main activists in *Solidarity* had split from Gerry Healey's Socialist Labour League in the late 1950s and gone on to develop a well thought out form of anti-Leninism, heavily influenced by the writings of Paul Cardan (Cornelius Castoriadis) of the French Socialisme ou Barbarie group.

Things came to a head for me in October 1969 when there was a huge demo against The Springboks Rugby Tour in Swansea. Hundreds of RSSF members flooded into the university the week before – I mean really sexy-looking gels and geezers – and our Swansea Anarchist membership ebbed further through horizontal recruitment. They seemed to have a perspective of how a revolution might be achieved, whereas we were 'just a local anarchist group with no analysis' as some plum-in-the-mouth wanker from Essex University told me!

We recovered somewhat by engaging the cops in a full scale riot outside the rugby ground while the RSSF narcissists just stood with their banners but the lack of any perspective beyond the local niggled away. The riot itself – outside the St Helens ground that is – was quick and vicious and thank fuck they didn't have cop cameras and after-riot witch hunts as they do today. We'd charged up the Mumbles Road arms linked when the cops lines broke and charged at us. The fighting spilled on to the beach with bits of old railway sleepers, handfuls of sand and bottles being lobbed at the coppers. We then launched a few choruses of 'Harry Roberts is our friend – he kills coppers' – unaware that demonstraters inside the ground were taking a terrible beating from the cops and rugby steward vigilantes.

Chris Pallis

The Swansea riot and subsequent police inquiry into the brutality inflicted on protestors inside the ground by collusion between cops and rugby vigilantes set the tone for the rest of the tour. Unlike the peaceful Anti-Vietnam War protests, it felt the violent protests outside the rugby grounds had a real effect on bringing an end to sporting links with apartheid and were replicated to good and brave effect in New Zealand later. But again we could have been better organised – hardly any anarchists from outside Swansea had turned up

By the time the RSSFers drifted back to the radical languor of their chaises longues at Essex University, I was for forming a national organisation with full-on fucking analysis! Solidarity must be it!

I threw myself into selling *Solidarity* pamphlets and the regular journal. Here was some coherent and innovative thinking with excellent pamphlets and a chance to think beyond Swansea. To be honest, I didn't understand the Paul Cardan/Cornelius Castoriadis stuff but the analysis of the *Kronstadt Commune, Paris May 1968, Irrational in Politics, Bolsheviks* and *Workers' Control* were revelatory. Plus, I got introduced to Victor Serge and Council Communism and Workers' Councils and

Bash The Rich

Self-Management and Wilhelm Reich. More to the point, the *Kronstadt Commune* pamphlet in particular enabled us to wipe the floor with the Trots and Leninists in argument. They were like sitting ducks as I moved round the university coffee bar demolishing them with my new-found analysis of the iniquities Bolshevism. I even had Tony Cliff, the SWP's founding father, on the backfoot – and he was a fucking good speaker – as he burbled on about white guards and other slanderous rubbish.

I liked selling mags anyway and sold shitloads of the *Paris May 1968* one. I used to really look forward to the postie delivering the rolled up bundles of mags – what a saddo! In 1971, a group of us – all current or ex-Swansea University students – decided to set up a Swansea Solidarity Group. I had by this time stopped calling myself an anarchist but opted for 'libertarian socialist' instead – all down to *Solidarity!* The main people involved were Ian Garvie, Kevin Gaynor, Jock Spence, Eve Spence, Dave Lamb, Max Milburn and myself. I can't recall how the original approach was made to London for the franchise but I think Ken Weller and Chris Pallis came down to Swansea to check us out. Joe Jacobs and Arnold Feldman from London Solidarity became regular visitors. They'd talk all night as I fed baby Josie with one hand and went off to work as a postman at 5am with Arnold asking what time I'd be home so we could continue talking! But it was well worth listening. These were men in their 50s and 60s with tales of Cable Street – not callow youths like us lot and their experience and stories and commitment and grasp of what made for real revolutionary action was dead impressive to us. People like Ken Weller had been active in wildcat strikes at Ford's Dagenham and other car and engineering plants. They were real fucking workers like we were always looking for and they were with us rather than the fucking Trots. I was in dreamland.

There was a particularly impressive group called South London Solidarity formed around Ernie Stanton who all worked in the construction industry – mainly at the Kingsnorth and Isle of Grain power stations – and produced the best examples of work-centred working-class writing I'd ever seen. Not the *Socialist Worker* kind of triumphalist agitprop clichéd nonsense, but a real sense of what it is like to be a worker resisting the order givers on a day-to-day basis. I regretfully never got to meet them.

Throughout 1971 and 1972, we produced our own *Swansea Solidarity* paper and the main political thrust of the group was encouraging workers on strike or facing redundancy to organise sit-ins and take over the running of their workplace and kick the bosses out. Following on from the Upper Clyde shipbuilders' sit-in, *Solidarity* had produced a pamphlet on the Fisher Bendix factory occupation and we sold this outside many factory gates alongside our own paper. The spread of factory sit-ins seemed to validate *Solidarity's* workers self-management approach and we were all very excited. Of course, all of this had a bit of Citizen Smith absurdity to it as none of us were working or even looked remotely like any of the workers we were flogging our paper to and it all smacked of Socialist Working Party (SWP) opportunist paper-selling. No matter – it didn't seem like that to us at the time. We found ourselves in some strange places at 6am in the morning as the night shifts clocked off at the Trostre and Velindre Tinplate Works in Llanelli, or the Rheola Aluminium plant in Resolven up the Neath Valley, at British Steel's huge steelworks at Margam in Port Talbot, at the Wagon Repairs in Swansea and the Alcoa Aluminium plant in Waunarlwydd. I tell you – we couldn't be faulted for sheer effort!

One week, we heard about a forthcoming strike by construction workers at the Milford Haven oil refineries. We rushed out a special edition of *Swansea Solidarity* and Ian Garvie dragged the lot down to Milford with him on the milk train. We were beside ourselves with frenetic anticipation all day awaiting his return and news of how many he'd sold. SEVEN. He'd only sold seven. There had been many exits and entrances, the site was miles from the station, most people came whizzing out in cars... whatever, we were disconsolate. But as the evening wore on, we decided seven wasn't too bad after all. In fact, by the end of the evening, it was bloody good! Who knows how many people might read those seven copies, they were probably being passed eagerly from hand to hand as we spoke. Probably.

There was a big blast furnaceman's strike at the Port Talbot Steelworks. Unknown to us at the time, London *Solidarity's* Chris Pallis was in fact Dr Chris Pallis, one of the country's leading neuro-surgeons. He wrote under the name Maurice Brinton to avoid press attention. He was now treating Rudi Dutscke who had come to Britain with a bullet still lodged in his brain from the assassination attempt in Berlin. One of the conditions the then Home Secretary Reginald Maudling placed on Dutscke's entry into Britain was that he didn't involve himself in politics. Chris Pallis had brought Dutscke to meet some of the striking blast furnacemen at Port Talbot, and Maudling jumped on this as an excuse to throw Dutscke out of the country – a particularly mean-spirited act which led eventually to Dutscke's lonely suicide. It contrasted strongly with Robert Carr's more generous approach to the imprisoned Angry Brigade women a few years later.

By now the formation of a national Solidarity organisation rather than a collection of autonomous groups was on the agenda. I think the leading lights in Solidarity – Chris and Ken – were dubious about turning Solidarity into some form of federal organisation, but got more or less pushed into it by the rest of Solidarity groups around the country. I was all for turning it into a full on revolutionary organisation – somewhat missing the point of what Solidarity's politics were all about.

But before the question of organisation could be addressed, something happened. One night a member of London Solidarity visited out of the blue and introduced us to a newcomer to Swansea from London – Hilary Creek of The Angry Brigade. Things were never quite the same again.

Chapter 5

ARMED LOVE

After months in gaol, two of the Stoke Newington Eight women – Hilary Creek and Anna Mendelson – were bailed to Hilary's parents' house at Pennard on the Gower. The Stoke Newington Eight were those charged with The Angry Brigade bombings. Like Rudi Dutschke, a condition of their freedom was that they weren't supposed to get involved in local politics or meet local anarchists, and like Dutschke, they could not but break these rules. We'd followed The Angry Brigade bombings and arrests from afar – now all of a sudden we seemed to be in the middle of it. I'd lie if I didn't say it was exciting. It was dead exciting and a real adrenalin buzz. After years of toiling away at local radical politics, we seemed to be part of something bigger – much more exciting than flogging papers outside aluminium smelters and wagon repair works.

I'd been in the dole office when news of the bombing of Robert Carr's house had come through – greeted with hilarity and punched fists by our *Dole Express* readers (see Chapter 7). But in reality I'd always thought bombings were a sign of failure, a sign of giving up on the working class in favour of a few (self-appointed) revolutionaries acting (in their own eyes) on behalf of the working class. In reality this was not 'on behalf of' but 'instead of'. You can't blow up a social relationship after all. The Angry Brigade slogan 'If you want peace, prepare for war' that we'd later take up in *Class War* but as Martin Wright wrote in *CW* 'for us that means getting out on the streets with a paper in one hand and a petrol bomb in the other, as part of a mob'. Or as John Barker later put it... 'petrol bombs are far more democratic than dynamite'.

But no matter, the Stoke Newington Eight were innocent and their politics were almost identical to our own. Indeed, Hilary, Anna, John Barker and Jim Greenfield had produced a pilot paper called *Strike* in Manchester which we had got a copy of and written back for more. *Up*

Bash The Rich

Anna And Hilary

Against the Law Motherfucker was another SN8 journal close to our hearts. We hit it off with Hilary and Anna straight away and, after some understandable caution, they both put their trust in us – in particular myself and Lin Harwood. For them, it was a chance to talk politics again after months of isolation, and to plan their defence.

By this time, I was living with Lin in the Uplands and our first child Josie had been born in January 1971. After a brief stint as a hospital porter, I was working as a postman in Sketty delivering the mail in Derwen Fawr. Our house at 18 Windsor Street quickly became the place away from Hilary's parents where they could meet up with friends from London, sit and laugh and drink wine amidst the piles of interminable depositions of evidence. On sunny afternoons, Hilary would drive us out to the Gower languidly flicking her wrists to get in and out of the traffic before looping across the sands to Three Cliffs or Port Eynon. We threw ourselves headlong into the SN8 defence campaign – what could be more important than defending our comrades. Nothing! We produced our own *Swansea SN8* bulletin.

The house sprawled with visitors, imparting a London radical edge to our previously Swansea-centred politics. Many were from the London Claimants Unions, Hackney and Islington Gutter Presses, West London community papers *Ned and Nell Gate, Up Against the Law Motherfucker*, the Women' Liberation and Feminist Movement. Our political outlook was transformed with a new up-to-speed metropolitan consciousness. The women who had flour-bombed the Miss World contest, the stroppiest women in London, were in and out of our house. Month on month, our Swansea self-imposed isolation was burst open. But for all that, it was a strange out-of-sync summer – almost poetic in its sense of doomed love and snatched moments of fun as the trial loomed ever nearer. I can't put it better than I wrote in *Anarchist*!:

'*Vapour trails tracing back to the summer of 1972 when Hilary and Anna had been bailed for a last glance of freedom for a decade to a blissful Gower summer. Doomed women facing a life stretch, hugging naked on Oxwich beach. Kiss flicking under broody Swansea rainstorms waiting for the turnkeys' chastity belts. An intensity of repressed desire as they lolloped, wine-drinking among the depositions on the ever darkening summer nights as the sea raced into Three Cliffs Bay. Dancing among the fireflies at Rhossili – a last summer idyll before the storm would break around their heads. Suspended time like patients in remission, pulses racing as they scrabbled home from the Parkmill Happy Shopper through reedy streams and distant headlight beams and time closing in with the tide.'*

Our second child Jenny was born at 18 Windsor Street in August 1972 and Hilary and Anna were among the first to see her, melancholically heightening the sense that their own chances of motherhood could soon be taken from them forever. At the same time, we got a sense of the pressures and political culture of London and the current gender clashes in the newly-emerged Women's Liberation Movement. Many women were making the political choice to come out as lesbians rather than one based on desire and sexual proclivity. Remaining heterosexual was almost siding with the enemy. Hilary in particular was getting heavy grief from some of the visiting sisters for remaining a 'het' as the term was dismissively denunciated. Maybe she had other things on her mind I thought, especially considering her boyfriend John Barker was still banged up – not afforded the bail privileges of The Angry Brigade women. But that was the exception. Somehow it was a blissful, joyful, life-affirming few months despite the gathering gloom. Kevin Gaynor from out Solidarity Group, was to become a Mackenzie Advisor at the trial. Darcus Howe and the *World in Action* team came down and filmed interviews on our flat roof at Windsor Street with Hilary and Anna for transmission at the end of the trial. Hilary and Anna insisted Darcus give us £50 for use of our electricity, knowing how broke we were. And then the tearful cheek-kissing farewells as they headed back to London and who-knows-what gaol sentences.

Lin and I visited them up at Ilford where they were staying in the days before the trial. But we looked and felt like a couple of provincial hicks again as the London radical milieu swarmed round them. Anna I never saw again. Lin would visit them both in nick taking the kids with her. Hilary would return to Swansea after gaol with John Barker and get involved with *Alarm* and rekindle our friendship. The sentences were passed. Ten years. We were desolate. The Swansea *Evening Post* ran a sneaky front page story 'Angry Brigade Girls Bathe Topless' with a blurry photo of Hilary and Anna in Hilary's parents' garden at Pennard. Somehow it seemed a suitable bummer of a footnote for a summer of heart-stopping highs and lows.

We'd stayed at Ken Weller's place in East Ham while visiting Hilary and Anna and I was impressed by the perpetual clanking of the duplicator as shifts of Solidarity members churned out the pamphlets all hours. But in truth Solidarity had slipped from our priorities that summer. Most of the group had been university-based and had moved on. I for one had no more heart for paper selling at 6am. My friends were in gaol and Ted Heath was in power because England always votes Tory. Wales, as always, voted Socialist. Maybe it was time to go it alone.

Chapter 6

FREE WALES

In the late 1960s, Welsh nationalism was on the swell. The saintly Gwynfor Evans had given it an electric jolt up the back passage by sensationally winning the Carmarthen by-election in 1966. Plaid Cymru subsequently pushed Labour very close in by-elections in Rhondda and Merthyr and Cymdeithas Yr Iaith Cymraeg was busy ripping down English language road signs throughout the Principality. The eager queue of anoraked Aberystwyth students and wispy-haired Methodist ministers demanding to be arrested for pulling down 17 'No Parking' signs as they deposited them outside their weary local cop shop cut no ice with me, but the wilder shores of the nationalist tide were throwing up some interesting nuggets.

The Free Wales Army had been founded by Julian Cayo Evans, a Lampeter horse breeder of wild gaucho Argentinian stock, who was (in theory at least) to wage a military war against English occupation unlike the reformist quislings of Plaid Cymru. Cayo dressed his men up in a mish-mash of green combat clothing from the Army & Navy Stores and proceeded to strut about towns such as Llanelli and Lampeter in the gap between lunchtime closing and evening opening with a few Alsation dogs in tow. Cayo was careful to commit no crimes but gave the impression of cocking a snook at the English authorities and developed a cult following among students. Then Cayo pulled his master stroke – his March on Rome, his Munich Beer Hall Putsch. He took a Flying Column (the FWA had flying columns long before Ricky Tomlinson had flying pickets) of 50 'Boys' in full FWA uniform over to the annual Easter Parade in Dublin. It has to be remembered that at this time in the early 1960s the IRA was moribund – there was no ongoing military struggle – and the sight of the 50 uniformed Welsh storm-troopers strutting past the Post Office was very impressive to the Sinn Feiners. Seizing the time,

Bash The Rich

Cayo produced a farmer's shotgun and fired it into the air achieving front page photo news in Ireland and Wales. He finished the finest hour off with a nicely judged melodramatic touch of offering to lend Sinn Fein his 'Boys' for a few months.

Flushed by this success, there had even been drunken talk of hijacking the Rosslare to Fishguard ferry and sailing to Patagonia on their triumphant return to Wales!

The Easter Parade act of big bold brassiness transformed Cayo from pantomime villain to Welsh Che Guevara. On his return, he organised a mega strut through Llanelli with over 100 uniformed FWA members attempting the semblance of a military formation. Cayo informed a credulous *Western Mail* reporter that: 'The FWA had two flying columns in Lampeter alone of 1,000 men in each.' Since the population of Lampeter in total was only 1,800 this might have seemed a little far fetched, but adopting the 'Bigger the Lie' approach never did Cayo any harm and this chilling threat to English rule duly appeared on the front page of the *Western Mail*.

The formation of this now-to-be-taken-seriously, anti-imperialist movement in Wales was slightly undermined by the antics of its Second-in-Command. Dennis Coslett had learned well from his Commander in Chief and vied with him in wild claims including an assertion that the FWA possessed an aeroplane – a Free Wales Air Force! Coslett had lost an eye in a shot-firing accident in the mine where he worked and struck an imposing figure with his black eye patch, brass Eagle of Snowdon badge, home made army uniform and a   loyal Alsation called Gelert. He was later to be immortalised as 'Dai Dayan' by David Frost because of the similarity of his eye patch to Moshe Dayan's! As Plaid Cymru engaged in a cliff-hanging attempt to win the solid Labour seat of Rhondda in a razor-edged by-election, they struggled to distance themselves from the FWA and stay respectable. At a pivotal election meeting addressed by Saint Gwynfor himself, Coslett arrived early and occupied the front three rows of the hustings with a phalanx of uniformed FWA members.

Coslett decided to enliven the meeting and strutted on stage in full military regalia before sending the aspiring MPs diving for cover by discharging a starting pistol into the air. Plaid Cymru blamed this incident for their narrow failure to take the seat and repeatedly urged the police to arrest their fellow nationalists.

In the meantime, Cayo Evans faced an unexpected dilemma: his Flying Column in Dublin had impressed the Irish Republicans more

Cayo Evans

than he realised. A consignment of Thompson sub-machine guns was delivered to his Lampeter farmhouse for FWA use, courtesy of the IRA. The Commander in Chief kept his cool and immediately dumped the lot in Tregaron Bog. And he had good reason to. Bombs were going off in Wales. And guess whose name was in the frame? A wild gaucho horse breeder not a million miles from Tregaron Bog.

At the time I was just an observer of these events. I was living in Swansea for sure, but a million miles away culturally, politically and socially from Cayo and his Welsh 'Boys'. I was a 1967 Summer of Love hippie turned 1968 Student Power Revolutionary. I wonder what would have happened if Cayo Evans had turned up to the 'Dialectics of Liberation' Conference at the Roundhouse instead of Stokeley Carmichael? Apparently Hitler and Lenin were, at one time, on one day in the same square in Vienna. Cayo Evans inhabited the same time span as the 24-Hour Technicolour Dream and the Battle of Grosvenor Square. But they were completely different worlds co-existing but never

Bash The Rich

meeting. The FWA existed on the periphery of my consciousness but I knew none of them or sympathised with their nationalism. In the early 1970s, I did meet up with some of the major players so can pick up the story from closer quarters.

Gethyn ap Iestyn (aka Keith Griffiths aka Gethyn ap Gruffydd) was gaoled for 13 months in the big FWA show trial in Swansea in 1969 along with Cayo Evans and Dennis Coslett. I subsequently got to know him when I flirted with socialist republicanism in the mid 1970s.

On release from gaol, Gethyn had set up his own organisation – the Welsh Socialist Vanguard (WSV) – based on Pencoed Estate just outside Bridgend. The WSV consisted of Gethyn, his wife, his brother and Pedr Lewis, a veteran nationalist. Pedr had been involved with the future leaders of both the Official and Provisional IRA, Cathal Goulding and Sean MacStiofain, and in a gun theft from a public school at the time of the Coronation in 1952. Pedr Lewis had a burning hatred of Plaid Cymru leader Gwynfor Evans which had led him to stage a sit-down in the driveway of Evans' house. In 1974, he had persistently heckled Evans during an election meeting in Bridgend. On his way to the hall, Pedr Lewis had noticed a tank on a low-loader being transported through the town to the army firing range at Sennybridge in Brecon. A bemused Evans was abused throughout the meeting for doing nothing 'as even now English tanks rumble through the streets of Bridgend.'

Eventually Gethyn and I joined up in a new organisation Cymru Goch which involved his entire family, plus the brothers Cris and Meic Haines from Swansea and assorted anarchist cronies of mine from Swansea and Aberystwyth, the legendary 'Enrico' and a few other nutters of Gethyn's acquaintance. The organisation never amounted to much apart from stealing an electric typewriter from Swansea University Registry building, but Gethyn proved to be a solid socialist, if firmly of the Leninist variety, giving the lie to the belief that all the FWA members had been right wing semi-fascists. In fact, Gethyn ap Iestyn was probably the only person within the FWA who had some idea how to build a political movement.

He'd started to build up an anti-investiture campaign and proved to be an honourable and committed revolutionary and still remains so.

After the demise of the FWA following the Swansea trial, various tinpot nationalist groups had emerged, from the Patriots' League to the Welsh Socialist Vanguard and the Lost Lands League. None of these having a membership into double figures. The Lost Lands League campaigned for the return to Wales of lands 'seized' by the English, such as Oswestry and Shrewsbury. I later discovered the list of seized towns was remarkably similar to the list of English teams allowed to play in the Welsh Football Cup which at the time included Kidderminster Harriers and both the Bristol clubs. It has to be understood, therefore, that the historical base for the Lost Lands League was not all it might have been.

However, I was persuaded to attend a secret meeting of the League where some dramatic direct action was to be discussed. I questioned how welcome I might be at this meeting as I was pretty obviously an English cockney hippie with hair down to my backside, but my contact saw no problem with this. And he was right. In all the time I was involved with the wilder shores of Welsh Republicanism, I was never ever given any grief because I was English nor did anyone ever raise an eyebrow about my involvement. The meeting of the League was held in a darkened room just outside Ammanford and attended by about ten men. The speaker outlined the need for direct action to seize control of the centre of one of the 'lost' towns for several hours to make a symbolic point. He had checked out the disposition of the police in the town and assured us they were weak in numbers and morale. 'How the fuck does he know that?' I thought to myself, feeling increasingly uncomfortable. Usually at similar meetings with the 'Boys', there would be a lot of hot air and booze and no action, but this time the speaker invited us all to make a firm commitment to the action which was to be followed by the taking of some sort of Oath! 'Oh Jesus,' I thought, 'not a fucking oath,' with a mixture of fear and derision. I seriously thought, 'Well, the last bus to Swansea goes at 4.30 from outside the Post Office and I must be off – Ymlaen Y Werin Gyfeillion. Hwyl Fawr'. (Forward with the workers comrades and cheerio). But I sensed I was already in too deep. I was also struck with fear. Not about the action itself but that I would have a fit of the giggles during the oath taking.

The speaker produced maps of the mystery town showing a central bridge which was to be taken and held. 'Other forces would join with us,' we were assured. 'Oh yeah?' I thought, 'I'd heard that one from nationalists before – we'd be fucking lucky if the speaker turned up'. But I was stuck with it. At the end of the meeting, the speaker would reveal the name of the town to us. Hereford! Fucking Hereford! Jesus Christ fucking Hereford! Home of the fucking SAS! We'd be fucking slaughtered! Our idiot leader had checked the 'dispositions' of the local police and indicated regular army units were stationed over 40 miles away, but he'd made the slight minor oversight of overlooking the fucking SAS. I beckoned my contact towards me before the oath taking and mingling of blood with this tactical colossus could begin. I felt I was too much of a newcomer – and too English – to raise this delicate matter. He took our leader aside. A series of oaths followed, but not the ones we had been promised: 'Fuck, shit, fuck, fuck, fuck'. Within half an hour, we were in the pub and the Lost Lands League's finest hour was lost to history. Thank fuck!

Away from the FWA as Joke stories Gethyn ap Iestyn was a committed revolutionary. At the Swansea trial, he had been the one who, as the trial teetered on farce, had refused to disavow his actions or claim, as others did, that the FWA was not a serious organisation. But why had he been on trial in the first place? For that we must return to Tregaron Bog.

At the same time that Cayo was dumping the IRA weapons, Army Sergeant John Barnard Jenkins was launching a one-man bombing operation for real in Wales. His Mudiad Amddiffyn Cymru (MAC) blew up water pipelines, the Temple of Peace in Cardiff, the Welsh Office, the RAF base at Pembrey where an officer had his arm blown off, and a series of other attacks which the police seemed incapable of solving. As the investiture of the Prince of Wales at Caernarfon in 1969 drew closer, the bombings intensified with an attempt to blow up the Royal Train at Abergele resulting in the bombers George Taylor and Alwyn Rees losing their lives. The Abergele martyrs are celebrated still. Later John Jenkins was arrested and gaoled for ten years.

On his release, I met up with him a few times to interview him for yet another magazine I was producing – *Penderyn*. He proved to be another solid socialist who had been politicised by his time fighting the Greek National Organisation of Cypriot Fighters (EOKA) with the British Army in Cyprus. In 1983, he was gaoled again for his involvement with the Workers Army of the Welsh Republic (WAWR) bombing campaign which led to the smashing of the increasingly influential Welsh Socialist Republican Movement. However, our interest here is in what happened to the Free Wales Army while John Jenkins conducted his bombing campaign. In a strange way, both John Jenkins and Cayo Evans had got lucky with each other.

As the Welsh Secret Police – the detested Heddlu Cudd – hunted for the bombers, Cayo realised Dame Fortune had smiled kindly on him again. After every bombing, Cayo would appear on television claiming responsibility for the bombing on behalf of the FWA and promising further ever more daring acts. The public and media were infuriated by this, demanding their incompetent coppers arrest the FWA leader and commandants as the evidence stared them in the face. But, of course, there was no evidence because no one in the FWA had any connection with the bombings or even knew who was doing them. Cayo and his band of merry men continued to strut about West Wales with impunity as the bombing campaign intensified giving credence to his claims as a skilled urban guerrilla leader.

I think the only time any of this appeared on anyone's consciousness beyond Wales was a drunken appearance by the FWA Commandants and their leader on *The David Frost Show*. This did not rate up to the

Bash The Rich

yippie takeover of *The David Frost Show*, but the FWA were considerably more drunk than the yippies were stoned and considerably more incoherent. In their pantomime army combat gear and pissed out of their skulls on BBC hospitality freebies, the show effectively knocked Cayo's claims to credibility cold. Cayo clawed back, by claiming they had been 'drugged by the Brits'. But the repeat show could be seen in Lampeter, Tregaron, Llanelli, Bridgend most Saturday afternoons when the FWA Commandants met up to sing re-fashioned IRA songs: *Tramp, Tramp, Tramp the Boys Are Marching* being the FWA anthem sung as the Eagle of Snowdon banner was held aloft in a back bar under the slogan Fe Godwn Ni Eto – We shall rise again.

And it was the 'Boys' who marched. There were no women in the FWA. At the Swansea trial, the 'FWA Wives' finally put in an incongruous appearance with their beehive hair-dos, mini-dresses and stilettos just at the time their English sisters were slipping into dungarees and boiler suits. It was a matter of class. Unlike the middle-class leftist organisations of the time, the FWA, apart from its gentleman farmer leader, was overwhelmingly proletarian – similar in class composition to the paramilitary organisations of Belfast – coming from the windswept council dreg estates of the Valleys, Swansea and Llanelli. My impression was that the FWA was made up of divorced men in their 30s searching for a club that women couldn't join.

Gethyn filled me in on some of the more farcical elements of the FWA. Their main activity had been regular survivalist type manoeuvres in mid Wales which could only be accessed by those who knew the password. The trouble was, most of Wales knew the password.

On being challenged at a 'checkpoint' on the way to the training camp, the FWA member would be confronted by the question 'Is this the road to Abbey Cwm Hir?' To which the correct reply of 'Llewelyn rest in peace' had to be given. One journalist seeking access to these manoeuvres forgot this simple password but was waived through the checkpoint after simply asserting he was 'one of Gethyn's boys'. But apart from training and strutting about, the FWA never took any actions to forward their cause, living simply on their notoriety obtained by self-association with John Jenkins' bombing campaign. Of course, this suited John Jenkins' purpose also by diverting endless police hours to following FWA suspects all over West and South Wales while he got on, unsuspected, with his single-minded campaign.

Alarmed by the nationalist tide, the Labour Government had cynically decided to invest Prince Charles as Prince of Wales in a grand ceremony at Caernarfon in 1969. There were real and valid fears for his safety as the unsuccessful attempt to blow up the royal train en route was to show, plus there was widespread opposition at such a waste of money. This should have been a golden opportunity for the FWA. Instead of making any real attempt to mobilise opposition on the streets and in the communities to the investiture, Cayo Evans resorted to ever more desperate claims to make the headlines. Reservoirs were to be poisoned and packs of wild dogs were to have gelignite strapped to their backs and be herded into the centre of Caernarfon on the day. Actually this was quite a neat idea. Gethyn told me that Cayo had far more complaints from dog owners than anyone worried about the safety of the Prince.

One night, Cayo and his men drank long drafts of Welsh Mead before the flickering embers of the fire and Cayo was cajoled with the honeyed words: 'You are a man of destiny Cayo – let's get the guns out the bog and do the fucker.' Cayo consented. But the following morning, he was back in his fantasyland of poisoning the water supplies. The authorities finally tired of their antics and devised an ingenious way to prosecute their leaders who had, of course, not committed any illegal acts. They resurrected the public order laws designed to deal with Oswald Moseley's Blackshirts in the 1930s against the wearing of paramilitary uniforms. Eleven FWA members were prosecuted under this law, not used since 1936, and three – Cayo, Coslett and Gethyn – were gaoled. The trial, on the eve of the investiture, could have been an opportunity to make political capital but, as ever, descended into farce as some of those charged tried to wriggle out of the charges by denying their involvement and ridiculing their own organisation.

The main evidence against them came from the journalists who'd believed their wild claims. Coslett's gun in his uniform holster was revealed to be a toy. The case of one of the defendants, Dafydd y Dug – who was, bizarrely enough, another to be prosecuted again in the WAWR trial in 1982 – piled farce on farce. When asked what anti-English acts he had committed, he replied that he had chopped down his neighbour's apple tree because he was English. Next to the Eagle of Snowdonia insignia on his combat jacket was a Robertson's metal golliwog. The judge pompously enquiring as to whether this denoted any significance in military rank within the FWA, had to sit through a long explanation from Dafydd y Dug on how you had to save up so many jam tokens and send them off to Robertsons to get the badge!

And yet... and yet. Gethyn was convinced it needn't have been like this. He cited the one occasion on which the FWA had tried to link with a local struggle as an example of what might have been. The Aberfan disaster in 1966 had moved everyone in Wales, yet the Labour Government had tried to use money from the Disaster Fund to level the remaining tip rather than give the money to the families involved. The FWA had visited the families' committee and threatened to blow up the National Coal Board offices if the money was used to level the tip. The Government capitulated and, in September 1967, they gave the money to the Families Fund. The FWA action was thought by many in Aberfan to be the best support they got and, to be fair, it was Dennis Coslett who'd initiated the action. If Gethyn and Coslett had been able to build on such community campaigning, things might have been different, instead, a month later Cayo and Coslett were arsing about on the *Frost Show*.

However much I might be inclined to portray Welsh Republicanism in a heroic light, farce is never far away. I attended an Owain Glyndwr commemoration on a hilltop at Corwen in North Wales where Glyndwr was said to have first raised his standard. About 20 of us were listening to speeches on a windy day when a ruddy faced Manchester rambler chanced upon us .'What's going on?' he enquired seeing the berets and flags. 'Commemoration to Owain Glyndwr,' he was told. Getting out his Ordnance Survey map he helpfully observed that it was the 'wrong mountain. It's that one over there where Glyndwr raised his flag... cheerio,' and wandered happily off. 'Bloody English' came the muttered oaths as we headed off to the correct spot.

DIG FOR VICTORY!

There were some half-decent people in the Swansea International Socialists (IS) in the early days. I used to spend half my time in the university coffee bar arguing with Tony Tate and Reg Jones about Kromstadt or the CNT anarchists in the Spanish Civil War. The anarchists and the IS would tug of war each other for recruiting new members. The IS had the advantage of having a very articulate and charismatic philosophy lecturer, Colwyn Williamson, as a member but we made up for that with our far longer hair. At the time the IS still had a libertarian socialist wing at national level with people like Peter Sedgwick and David Widgery who where a far cry from the later SWP party builders, and non-sectarian in their approach.

Seeing my evident discontent with the chaotic state of the anarchist movement, Pete and Jill Branston — affable leading lights in the Swansea IS — invited me over for dinner one night. They profusely praised comrade Victor Serge, claiming him as one of their own, testing my weak spot. Fucking hell! They where trying to recruit me, I thought. I knew that practically everyone wanted a piece of Serge, so remained unmoved. They did a better class of dinner, however, than your average anarchist but there was no sight of the rumoured horizontal recruitment!

Affable though they were, the Branstons blotted the Swansea IS reputation one night during the Port Talbot blastfurnaceman's strike. Arriving late for the vital evening strike meeting at Aberavon, the IS contingent spotted workers entering a working man's club. Not being familiar with the world of Club & Institute Union (CIU) clubs and the British Legion, they were told they couldn't enter without membership, which they didn't have. They waited patiently for three hours outside, struggling to flog *Socialist Worker* to the stragglers. Finally, they had to return to Swansea before the meeting concluded so they asked the doorman to pass a message to the meeting. The doorman agreed and the message was duly passed to the chair and read out: 'Comrades, we, the Swansea Branch of the IS, salute your heroic struggle… Recall the TUC… Betrayal… Not since the general strike… From Addis Ababa to Aberavon…'. Later, they excitedly phoned the club asking how their message had been received by the meeting. 'No one could understand it' came the reply. 'Why not?' they asked, 'it was simply written'. After a slight pause, the reply was given: 'Well, we're not used to messages of solidarity at the AGM of the Port Talbot and District Allotment Society.'

Chapter 7

THE BUN HOUSE BUGLE

We wanted to turn to the working class but we didn't know anyone who was working! So we organised where we did know people – down Swansea's Employment Exchange in Northampton Lane and the Social Security (SS) offices in Castle Street. We'd had some contact with the National Claimants' Union Movement, so decided to set up the Swansea Claimants' Union. We met every week in the Red Cow in the High Street. We decided to produce a paper called *Dole Express* to hand out to people signing on every week. In Swansea, the SS was known as 'The Bun House' – so the paper had the title *Dole Express* on one side and *Bun*

Swansea Claimants' Union outside The Housing Office

Bash The Rich

House Bugle on the other. We handed it out in Castle Street. We offered help to people to get the right money and get 'special needs' grants. We also helped people at appeals tribunals if they had their dole money stopped for not taking a job. At the time, the hated 'four week rule' was being implemented which meant they could stop your money if you didn't take a job they offered within four weeks. Quickly our popular slogan became 'They give you a job – we'll fight your case!' Ho! Ho!

Dole Express was two duplicated sides of A4 – all about the cases we has won, the iniquities of the Social Security and lots of jokey stuff abut the length of the queues to sign on. We had one member who could throw his voice and he'd amuse everyone by shouting 'supervisor box 4 please' and everyone had a good laugh as a perplexed Supervisor came out the back to the bemused counter clerk on box 4. *Dole Express* went down a bomb – handed out free, we'd get more than enough donations each week to pay for each issue. It was my first experience of producing a paper that ordinary people wanted to read.

A big group of big women – proper council estate proletarians from Bonymaen – quickly became the hardcore of the group led by the redoubtable Rose Barnes. They'd represent people at appeals tribunals. Well, they wouldn't so much represent people, as sit alongside them and 'argue' their case with the tribunal. They had an astonishing success rate with 'special needs' applications. They won a grant for a washing machine for a mum with four kids, then fridges, tumble dryers, more washing machines, holidays, clothing, bedding, beds, furniture, toys, carpet, lino.

At the time, in the Castle Street SS office, a little shutter would go up, your name called, and you'd actually be handed cash – not a boring time-delayed giro. This made for a dramatic feeling of solidarity on Friday afternoons when people were desperate for money for the weekends. When you got your cash loud cheering and applause would ring out, and a couple of quid was chucked in the Claimants' Union bucket. Then people would wait for their mates' claims to be sorted out before leaving. Often the last claim would be paid out at 4.30, but there would be the whole afternoon's punters staying behind to cheer the last cash handout.

Rose, Gaynor and Sandra from Bonymaen, formed the cutting-edge hit squad of the Claimants' Union. Sit-ins at the Department of Health and Social Security (DHSS) became common place until grants were paid up or benefits restored. Once Rose sat on top of the manager in his office until he agreed a cash payment with his possibly his last breath. All done with spirit, energy, laughter and organising with people at the bottom of the shit pile – not the aristocracy of Labour or horny-handed miners but working-class people from the disabled to the old or weak. The one big Claimants' Union gave power to 'em all. We even had our own song *Edward Wilson, Harold Heath them on top, us underneath.*

In June 1972, the nascent National Federation of Claimants' Unions held its first conference in Swansea at the university. We had a lot of contact with Hackney Claimants' Union and the Hackney Gutter Press. They were mostly single mums and we'd assured them adequate crèche facilities would be available. In the event, our house at 18 Windsor Street in the Uplands was to be the crèche and I was selected to run it. It proved impossible to squirm out of this, what with the sudden advent of the Women's Liberation Movement and men being forced to atone for their oppressive crimes. I waited anxiously for the maybe five or six kids from London to arrive with their parents. Horror of horrors! A coach turned into Windsor Street – a full on coach with about 40 kids on board, two women and a driver on the verge of suicide. The Hackney crew had rounded up every kid they knew with the promise of a free weekend at 'the seaside'. Most of the mums had not even come to the conference but had simply had a kiddy-free weekend in London – on me! The kids ranged from six months – I kid you not – to 15 or 16. No names, no food, no nappies, no bottles, no nothing! The Claimants' Union women legged it as soon as they were off the bus after handing me a lucky dip of medicines. I spent the next 48 hours in a Hieronymous Bosch painting.

Bash The Rich

I sent a message to the conference on Saturday afternoon pleading for help – dismissed as typical sexist male behaviour as I recall – and slept for two nights on mattresses on the floor in the mock-up of a Dickensian slum surrounded by hungry screaming shitty infants. Miraculously, there were no losses or deaths.

On Sunday lunchtime, I marched this raggle taggle urchin army down to the university to hand them back. To get to the venue of the conference, we had to pass by the university refectory which just happened to be hosting a Swansea Rotary Club lunch addressed by Harry Secombe. The tables were all nicely laid out with serviettes and bread rolls as Secombe was introduced. Then – unleash hell! At the sight of the food, the urchin army charged into the refectory, bombarded Secombe with bread rolls, scoffed and pinched everything in sight and raised and pillaged 'til there was only scorched earth left. Truly the expropriators had been expropriated!

SKOOL'S OUT!

School kids were walking out on strike all over the country. Spilling over from unrest at the university, we leafleted Swansea secondary schools in the name of the Swansea School Anarchist Alliance (SSAA). There were spontaneous walkouts over petty school discipline and uniform wearing at Llwyn-y-bryn, Mynyddbach, Penlan, Dynevor and Olchfa schools. At Olchfa, the head teacher reacted with fury, disciplining one of our SSAA members, Wilbur O'Kelly. We leafleted outside the school and the head teacher himself — nicknamed 'King Kong' by the kids and our leaflet — came storming out. He tried to rip the leaflets out of Tommy Trumpet's hand, and the Olchfa school kids raced out to see him engaged in a furious brawl. Tommy had him in a headlock and wasn't letting go and the bullying head got more than he bargained for. The police arrived and moved us on, but news that the Olchfa school bully had been stood up to spread like wild fire.

There were other forces than the anarchists at work now. The International Socialists were making their usual opportunistic effort to take over and at Penlan School, there were two particularly aware and politicised kids in Andy Bevan and Rob Sewell, who went on to become leading lights in Militant. They set up a more broad-based Union of Progressive Students and, like the IS, tried to foist on that movement a whole list of ludicrous Trotskyist transitional demands including nationalisation of the fertilizer industry. Wot! This wasn't quite what the kids had been chanting as they poured out of Bishop Gore and Glanmor Schools, but the Trots contrived to bore this spontaneous and dynamic movement to death.

In the meantime, our house in Windsor Street had become a centre for kids 'mitching' off school and a hotbed of ideas and actions, general rebelliousness and fun. At one time, five of the Swansea schools had their own anarchist groups, and nationalisation of the 100 monopolies wasn't on their agenda. I once asked Rob Sewell to name the 100 monopolies Militant wanted to nationalise and he fucking did — off pat! Fertilizer was Number 98! Chwarae Teg!

Chapter 8

THE SWANSEA MAFIA

Swansea was as corrupt as fuck in the 1970s. Council houses, teaching jobs, building contracts, planning permission – all available from your local Labour councillor. Your local one-party-rule, tin-pot, twin-town. Freebies, backhanders, extensions to your semi, jobs for the boyos. Being a Labour councillor made you up for life. There were councillors whose occupation was given as 'school caretaker' who were living in mansions in Derwen Fawr and holidaying abroad five or six times a year.

The money changed hands in nightclubs. Everyone knew about it – it wasn't a secret. It was talked about openly. Most of the fucking town had benefited in some way anyway, so who wanted to blow the whistle? The local paper knew. The cops knew. Meanwhile, the property development boys carved up the ugly, lovely town. The Swansea Mafia had the town by the bollocks and had Gerald Murphy, the council leader, in their pocket. Every development that went through the council came back to these five 'businessmen'. They were the smart ones – make millions from planning permissions in return for a free side of salmon or artexing some councillor's bathroom extension.

What do you do when everyone knew about it and no one gives a toss? What do you do when most of the heavyweight villains, scrap merchants, bouncers and freelance psychos are already on the Mafioso payroll? You could pay some bouncer to kill their own granny in Swansea and till get change of a tenner... WHAT YOU DO IS THIS: You research like fuck in council minutes and Companies House. You write a 20-page anonymous pamphlet called *The Swansea Mafia,* detailing payments for contracts and every corrupt act you can discover. You sneak off to

Birmingham and get 5,000 printed in a leftie printshop. You bring them back on a scheduled bus service to Swansea sweating like you'd going to rip off some Colombian cocaine cartel. You distribute them at dead of night – all in one night – through 5,000 letter boxes on every big council estate in Swansea. You're exhilarated, but scared shitless. You move house. You barricade your door. You have weapons by the bed. You've lit the blue touchpaper, but will anything happen?

For a week, fuck all! Then bingo! Front page of the *Evening Post*, *Western Mail*, and on TV. Council denials. Every fucker in every pub reading it. I see pink copies, green copies, upside down duplicated copies. Photocopies of photocopies, overnight photocopier millionaires, copies written in longhand and copies in bus queues. I see dogs distributing copies out of knapsacks. The fuckers have had their day. Murphy and five others go to gaol. We don't get carved up. The Swansea Mafia pamphlet has revealed the power of the mass-distributed political tract and I have taken good heed of it! Of course, nothing really changed. A few corrupt councillors who didn't play by the rules and got found out were gaoled – but the ones who did play by the rules were just as bad. The five businessmen Mafioso escaped unscathed but we weren't campaigning for honest councillors or honest businessmen – we were anarchists for fucksake! We didn't want any councillors or any businessmen. Good or evil: they were all fucking bastards to us.

It was good to see our arch-enemy, the council leader, carted off to gaol – Leyhill open nick, naturally – but the next one would be just as fucking bad. No political movement had been created. The publicity had forced the authorities to clean up the more blatant acts of corruption but the Swansea punters remained inactive. Could we have taken things further without an automatic return to the status quo? Could you galvanise the punters with this kind of anti-corruption stuff or would they remain spectators? We found an answer and it was called *Alarm*. I can say without any doubt that *Alarm* was to become the most effective political paper I have every seen.

Chapter 9

THE ALARM

What we discovered with the *Swansea Mafia* pamphlet was that it was possible to engage the political attention of the punters by concentrating on local issues but not by presenting it in an overtly political way. People told us that the pamphlet wasn't political because it was 'the truth.'

People who would never read any of the leftie papers and who considered themselves non-political were fighting to get their hands on the *Swansea Mafia* pamphlet. So all was not lost with the working class – there was a way to get political ideas across after all! What was needed now was something that wouldn't just gain their interest in a passive way but would encourage them to organise and to act for themselves.

The other surprising thing was that, though most of the information in the pamphlet was common knowledge, the fact that someone had had the bottle to write it down, print it and distribute it emboldened loads of other people to speak out about what had been going on for years. So how could we take this further? We decided that we had to produce something that came out regularly, that we couldn't continue to be anonymous but would have to sell it on the streets and pubs. We also decided that it should concentrate on exclusively local issues, and that it should be funny and not 'political' in a party-building way. We would not label ourselves socialist or anarchist. We thought it should contain swearing – we wanted to write as people spoke.

One of the best compliments I had in my *Alarm*-writing days was that I wrote just like I talked. Since every other word I use is 'fucking', to write without swearing would have been impossible. The swearing issue caused a lot of arguments – some people thought we'd be restricting our audience to youngsters or politicos or punks (this was 1977 by the way!) or men. I stuck firmly to the 'let's have lots of fucking swearing' line. If you called the council leader a 'wanker' in print that was fine, but if you called the council leader a 'fucking wanker' that was even better. If you called the council leader a 'FUCKING WANKER' and stuck it on the front page, that was better still. Circulation would shoot up, you'd see people pouring out of the city centre boozers on Saturday afternoons trying to find more

On the march against the
Swansea Mafia

copies. Of course, there were contradictions. People felt compelled to moan about the swearing but went on buying more copies. One of our regular bulk buyers had a long chat with me about 'the swearing' one rainy Saturday afternoon. He said we were: 'spoiling our case, we had the information, we didn't need to use language like that... we weren't going to be taken seriously... I can't show it to the wife.' Then he went on to increase his weekly order from 50 to 100 copies. People aren't swayed by rational arguments. They complained continually about the swearing but really they liked it because it was part of the ferocity of the paper's response to a town stinking in corporate greed. But let's go back a bit before the (close to my heart) swearing issue takes over.

It was Autumn 1977, and one of those happy coincidences when some very sparky, imaginative people all happened to have come together in Swansea, the 'Gateway to Glorious Gower'. Among them were The Angry Brigaders – first Hilary Creek and then John Barker – fresh out of prison to Swansea and getting stuck back in to radical politics straight away. *Alarm* no.1 appeared in October 1977. As ever, it consisted of two duplicated A4 sheets stapled together. Its first print run was 50 copies, price 2p. The first few issues were distributed within our social scene and printed on a duplicator repossessed from the bourgeois academics of Swansea University. It was to come out every week – duplicated Friday afternoons, distributed Friday nights and Saturdays. Its contents were at this stage corruption news, Swansea scandal and gossip, gratuitous abuse of the Swansea crachach, gig reviews, good café guide, bad pub guide etc . By Christmas we were selling 500 a week just through social contacts. January saw our great leap forward out to the streets and pubs. We would sell for two hours Saturday mornings in the town centre, go to The Duke in Wind Street for two hours – change the 2ps up into notes and get sloshed – then return to Oxford Street for another three hours of drunken rumbustuous paper-selling.

We advanced to a scanned illustrated cover page but often the duplicator was so bad you could hardly read the contents. When people talk about how important presentation, layout and graphics are in newspaper production, I think back to those Oxford Street days when punters would be holding the paper up to the sunlight to try to decipher the names hidden in the folds of the creased-up stencil duplicated pages. Fuck the presentation – get the fucking contents right first. And *Alarm*'s contents were more than fucking right. Despite the gaoling of Murphy, the Swansea Labour council had still been enmeshed up to its cesspit ears in shit. As a result of the *Swansea Mafia* pamphlet and *Alarm*, the Labour Party was swept away in the May 1978 election and the Ratepayers returned with a sensational majority. This was a seismic change in a town totally dominated by Labour for 50 years.

The Ratepayers continued as Labour left off – totally fucking corrupt and playing ball with the Swansea Mafioso who didn't mind who the fuck was in power as long as they were partial to a free lunch. Music to our ears. We were like pigs in clover – we couldn't fail to hit the target. Octogenarian Ratepayer leader Sidney Jenkins quickly became a laughing stock as *Alarm* christened him Sid 'Vicious' and the Ratepayers became the 'Ratpack'. Information on dodgy deals flooded in – pressed into our pockets on scraps of paper on Saturday afternoons, anecdotes, stories (some of them 40 years old), anonymous tip-offs, meetings in quiet pubs. We started doing our pub runs on Friday and Saturday nights. Five car loads of *Alarm* sellers would divide the Swansea pubs up between us and hit them with paper sales between 8pm and 11pm. The nearer to 11pm it was, the riskier it was, but the more papers you sold. These weren't sales in friendly, anarcho-leftie-alternative culture pubs; these were the most vicious, blitzed, no-go area pubs no sane leftie would ever set foot in. The Cadle Mill in Blaen-y-Maes, the Rum Puncheon in Townhill, The Bonymaen Inn, the Gatehouse, the Gors Inn – where no paper-seller had trod before or since!

We would sell 50 or 60 in every boozer – the punters wondering why we were late, buying us pints, showering us with written and verbal information, more scraps of paper and articles by proletarian wordsmiths who'd never put pen to paper before, arguments breaking out, drunken assaults on us by Mafioso payroll merchants compensated for by the local heavies kicking the shit for us back. Unofficial minders looked out for us, the scrap metal boys from the Haford riding gunshot for us buckshee. Grinning Blaen-y-Maes villains telling us stories of how they'd been paid to do us over by you-know-who, but if anyone touched us just mention our names to them – the Lenny McLeans of Swansea tilting the balance of terror in our favour; John Barker hanging out in the Gatehouse pub, with his Jacques Mesrine persona, knowing more about the Abertawe armed blags than the cops. The criminal underbelly of Swansea with its lunchtime boozing in shitty pebble-dashed council estate pubs was a second home for John.

The pub sales functioned as political meetings. People who would never contemplate going to a meeting in their life would talk politics with us in the boozers for hours. Rowdy ramshackle arguments involving 20 or 30 people. Shouting, cheering, laughing, jostling. It was as hairy as fuck – you didn't know if the big fucker coming at you was going to press a fiver into your palm or a knife into your stomach. We were bombarded with money. Commonplace to get £1 for a 2p paper, but often fivers, tenners or £20 notes handed over with conspicuous effect.

The circulation went up to 2,000 to 3,000 to 4,000 to 5,000 a fucking week in a town the size of Swansea. We ended up selling in every boozer in Swansea every week. No shithouse landlord dared ban our paper-sellers. The *Evening Post* paper seller in town used to sell *Alarm* as well, hidden under the *Posts*.

Our town paper sales on Saturdays used to turn into sprawling political debates. Pop into any town centre boozer on Saturday afternoon or evenings and every fucker was reading *Alarm*. The political ideas flowed thick and fast – abolish the council, scrap the mayor, we don't need no fucking council, occupy the Guildhall and the Mansion House.

Reports from factories and workplaces flooded in – shit and scandal on the factory bosses: Ford, Baglan Bay, Mettoys, Port Talbot steelworks – the paper-selling on the shopfloor slagging off jobsworth foremen and anyone who took the boss's side. News from schoolkids, from nurses and porters in the hospitals slagging off the consultants and the rip-offs, a football column allegedly written by the Swans manager Harry Griffiths and later by Tommy Smith – 'Tommo Talking' – sales on the North Bank at home games. School sales, hospital sales, sweatshop sales. At 5,000 a week, practically everyone in Swansea read the paper.

The paper was ferocious – I used to describe it as 'an organ of organised class hatred' – with a vulgar humour which often had you laughing for days afterwards. The Mafioso were on the run. The Ratepayers collapsed. When Sid 'Vicious' Jenkins was arrested on corruption charges as he came out of the Guildhall, he shouted to a TV reporter waving a copy of *Alarm* at him: 'I haven't read it but it's all untrue. It's all the work of anarchists!' How we laughed our little cotton socks off that night.

For two years, we had created an authentic weekly people's paper in Swansea. Like the *Mafia* pamphlet people said *Alarm* wasn't 'political' because it told 'the truth' as opposed to the 'political' lies of the council. We had made our version of what was going on in Swansea, the common-sense version. We'd inverted the usual process where we are the loonies and the authorities have the common sense.

Could this be translated to a newspaper at a national level where you couldn't concentrate simply on local issues, I wondered. How could it be done? While the Left cried into their beer over Thatcher's election victory, I was pondering this question as I finally thought about shifting gear out of Swansea up to the Big Smoke.

SID 'VICIOUS' IS A WANKER

We stood four *Alarm* candidates in the Swansea local council elections in 1978: Jan Green (Port Tennant Alarm seller), Louise Graham (girlfriend of convicted Angry Brigade bomber John Barker), Michael Aldron (standing in Mayhill against his own auntie Lorna Aldron) and me, Ian Bone (later described as 'the most dangerous man in Britain' by the *Sunday People*). Campaign manager was Phil 'The Div' Williams – the hardest man in town who had just been gaoled for hospitalising a leading member of the Swansea Mafia in his own nightclub.

Phil ran an 'unorthodox' campaign. He had the idea we should hire a hot air balloon and get 'Sid Vicious is a wanker' on it in huge letters and hover over the city on the day of the elections. It was a neat idea but too weather dependant and not really a runner. But Phil had plan B. Dominating Swansea was the blackened mass of Kilvey Hill. We could put a huge Vote Alarm on the side of the hill. 'How would we do that?' I asked? 'With quick lime,' said Phil. I passed. On the night before the election, Phil rounded up 12 mates to drag the lime up Kilvey Hill. It poured down. Half of them landed up in hospital with lime burns as the bags split in the downpour. Phil persisted. The following day you could just make out the top part of letter A if you knew where to look. Undeterred, Phil came to pick me up on election morning in his smart brand-new Citroen car. 'Have a look at this,' he grinned. He'd sprayed 'Vote Alarm' all over the sides of his car. Brilliant! We motored up and down Kingsway all day with our megaphones. He got fed up with our candidate for St Thomas, Jan Green, and threw her out. Leaving me alone with the hardest man in Swansea. 'Only six more hours,' he said.

ALARM 2p

No. 51

STOP PRESS EXCLUSIVE

MURPHY IN PRISON BREAK ATTEMPT

Late Friday night Gerald Murphy walked from his penthouse
suite at Leyhill Open Prison and climbed on to the top of
the prison.He is reported to be starring as 'Fiddler on the
Roof'.

**SWANSEA MAFIA PAMPHLET○○○○○○○○
EXCLUSIVE INTERVIEW**

Its almost three years now since the people of Swansea woke up to find
the SWANSEA MAFIA pamphlet pushed through their letter boxes.The pamphlet
caused more shit to fly in Swansea than anything else ever produced,
alleging as it did of the corrupt links between the five Swansea Mafia
businessmen -Trevor and Derek Vignall,Brian Cornelius,Kbxx Terry Francis,
and Malcolm Struel - and Gerald Murphy leader of the City council.The
effect of the pamphlet was widespread,resulting in the eventual downfall
of both the Labour council and Gerald Murphy and other businessmen.
Many people however remain wondering who produced the pamphlet and why,
and above all whether there will ever be another Swansea Mafia pamphlet.
Now some of the answers to these questions can at last be revealed as
ALARM has managed to track down those who produced the pamphlet and
interview them.The second part of the interview will appear next week.

ALARM: Why did you produce the Mafia pamphlet?
MAFIA PEOPLE: It was widely felt that there was a lot of corruption
going on in Swansea.People knew about bits of it here and there,but often
their stories were confused or they had different versions of the same
story.The whole lot of information needed to be put together so that some
sense could be made out of it.This meant pulling a lot of research into the
various companies involved at Companies House (where all the Company
records are kept) in London on who was involved with which companies etc
Gradually a pattern emerged where Mafia owned companies were time after
time being awarded contracts by the city council and were selling off
property they otherwise could not sell to the council for vast sums of
money.This was beginning to effect the daily lives of ordinary people
living in Swansea.....for example the Vetch Field development scheme
meant knocking down hundreds o' good houses in the Sandfields,the Rees
and Kirby built houses at West Cross were almost falling apart they were
so badly built,and the Glanmor Park flats remained empty when they'd
been built despite the hundreds of homeless people in Swansea.Yet all
those involved Mafia deals with the city council,at the front of all these
goings on we had a Labour council,in power continuously for 40 years and
seemingly irremovable,which made out to be interested in the welfare of
the people of Swansea but which was in fact bleeding them white right,
left and centre.And of course the Tory and Ratepayer opposition parties
though they knew what was going on did nothing about it as the only thing
that annoyed them was that they werent getting a share of the loot.The
Evening Post also knew what was going on but was too scared and dependent
on Mafia and council advertising to do anything about it.So the people
of Swansea were being kicked in the teeth and no one dared do anything
about it.

ALARM! 2p

Staff walk out on Swansea's Mayor

GUILDHALL LICE SCARE PROBE! FULL REPORT

ALARM! No. 72

A DAY IN THE LIFE OF A COUNCILLOR 2p

72

ALARM! No. 74

RATEPAYER SPLIT 2p

RATS SEEN LEAVING SINKING SHIP

Chapter 10

PAUL RINGER IS INNOCENT!

For three years in Swansea, I made my living making badges at markets and summer carnivals and shows. These were often at god forsaken places up the Swansea Valley where I'd park my stall next to the beer tent and happily knock out 'All coppers are bastards' badges to the local drunks – usually incorporating the name of the local copper! By far my best-selling badge at the time was 'I slept with Lady Diana' – a right little earner that summer but more often you'd be standing in a ploughed field at 6am and be lucky to make the stall money. However, once I had a lucky break.

The Wales vs England rugby international of 1981 was something different. Socialist Wales v Tory England. Red in the claw pit prop forwards vs Maggie Thatcher. Thatcher's programme of cuts in the steel industry, headed up by her hatchet guru Sir Keith Joseph, was the start of the Tories decimating industry in South Wales and was causing widespread anger. The build-up to the rugby clash was toxic, like England vs Argentina would have been during the Falklands War. 'I just want them to go up there – Twickenham – and give it to the swine,' said Owen Reynolds, a Port Talbot steel worker speaking for many in Wales.

The game started in bruising fashion. After ten minutes attempting a charge down, Paul Ringer had clattered (accidentally!) an English forward and been sent off. The steel works closure was compounded by a second injustice! I seized my chance. I'd already had some success selling badges outside the Arms Park such as 'Billy Beaumont walks on water... which proves that shit can float' My trusty badge-making machine toiled through the night before the next home international. 'Paul Ringer is

Innocent!' proclaimed the badge on my board as I took my place along side the ticket touts outside the Arms Park. They flew out. I'd sold the lot – six hundred – within the hour and was on the train back to Swansea before the game kicked off. I was quids in! The badge was featured on welsh telly and the newspapers and by the time of the next international

The Scorcher reports that Ringer story

there was wall to wall 'Ringer is Innocent' merchandise on sale. Before that, I sold them outside Llanelli's Stradey Park ground. Ringer came out to have a look – friendly like – asking about his royalties!

I always had a fascination for the red-bricked tinplate town of Llanelli. Dunno why. One day I'd just finished flogging badges outside a Scarlets vs All Blacks match. Roger Forsythe, the judder-man singer with Llanelli's and my favourite band, Andy Pandemonium, came ticketlessly forlorn round the corner. We mooched back into town for a drink. The sun shone down on the Turk Tinnopolis, glimpsing dapples among the silted docks and mud-flatted Loughor estuary. The marooned groynes tracing a finger to Stebonheath amid the scrubby warehouses, derelict tinplate sheds, coal dust lumber. 'Baby, baby, baby you're out of time,' we sang. 'I am just a dummy for your love.' Something would happen here one day. Something big.

Another time, I'd spent a desultory afternoon drinking with some striking Duport steel workers. We mooched around the back of the works drinking cans of Felinfoel, sitting on old railway sleepers amidst the thrusting nettles. 'Fuck Duport,' they laughed, throwing the cans at a shed. We found the works loco and ripped up the rails so it couldn't be moved. 'Fuck Duport - fuck work.' We laughed in the sunshine at the warmth of our day-long friendship which would never be renewed.

There was a sort of 'out-of-time-sync' strangeness up the Swansea, Neath, Amman, Afan and Lynfi Valleys. Dame Adelina Patti's opera house at Craig-y-nos, the moving mountain at Godre'r Craig, Emma Goldman's husband Jim Colton in Ammanford, colonies of Maoists in Glyncorrwg and Cymmer, Palestinian printing presses at Ystradgynlais, Spanish civil war veterans in Gwaun-Cae–Gurwen, strange artists communes at Tafarn-y-Garreg, miners' week at Trecco Bay and Paul Robeson's voice crackling over the phonelines to Alfie Bass at the Porthcawl Miners Eisteddfod in 1956. Try walking along to the waterfall at Melincourt in the gloaming when there's no one else about, the old Thomas Ward shipbreakers yard at Briton Ferry where huge ocean liners loom Marnie-style at you out of the mud-flats, the ferocious hand-to-hand piratical fighting with billhooks and axes along the River Neath wharves during the dockers strike of 1972, Rocky Marciano mooching in his socks and sandals round Swansea Market looking for the big one that floored the Aussie at the Adelphi in Wind Street, Dick Richardson and Brian London's mobs belting each other with chairs in the outside the ring fight of the century at Porthcawl, and most, mysterious of all, why is Maesteg full of Rush fans? You learn a lot about cultural difference selling badges and all people in Maesteg ever wanted were badges featuring Canadian band Rush. 'What not Arthur Brown,' I chanced!

My badge-selling career had another rugby uplift in London when Erica Roe ran out topless at Twickers. The following game me and Piers Buckingham were outside Twickenham flogging 'Fuck the rugby! Where's Erica?' badges. They flew out, but the class composition of the buyers was different from the Arms Park. Cavalry twilled sheepskin-coated rugger toffs. Never again – I flogged the badge machine and diversified into Deely Boppers. Nicer class of punter.

BOMBING THE GUILDHALL

'It's like Beirut in there!' someone told the
Evening Post headline writer. Well not quite, but
The Angry Brigade had struck again! We flour bombed
the City Council meeting. Me, Phil the Div, John
Barker, Lindsay the Punk, Jay Jay, Louise Graham,
and the rest of *Alarm*'s disparate rent-a-mob. Early
morning, I was in a belly-buster cafe in Landore
as Phil Williams and me filled up paper bags full
of flour, gleefully aided by a desperate crew of

Bash The Rich

Landore villains and scrap merchant boys. We doled them out by the Guildhall and sneaked them into the public gallery. There was a minute's silence for the death of Lord Heycock — the unlamented money-grabber from Port Talbot. 'Good riddance!' we shouted. Gratification could be deferred no longer. The first flour bomb arced through the air and exploded on Tory councillor Paul Valerio's head. The next scored a direct hit on Councillor Brian Ludlam. But Phil the Div was furious. We were supposed to have waited until he gave the signal. Too late now! The rest of the flour bombs exploded on the Tories and Labour indiscriminately. The whole chamber was enveloped in a thick floury fug. A Labour councillor attacked pink-haired Lindsay Morton but got more than he bargained for as Lindsay pulled him over the balustrade into the gallery and kicked him on the floor. Lindsay was the most 'fuck you' punk in town and had to be levered off. Police sirens wailed, we legged it, and The Angry Brigader did the communiqué to the *Evening Post*.

Me and Lindsay were later arrested on fairly serious public order charges. They had to move the case out of Swansea because most of the magistrates were witnesses — the chairman of the bench, the Lord Lieutenant of Glamorgan, the High Sherriff, various other mace-carriers, Black Rod wannabees, party leaders and endless hawk-eyed councillors determined to get revenge on *Alarm* at last. My solicitor, John Morse, laughed his head off when he saw the list of the great and the good. 'We'd better get a decent barrister for this one,' he told me. He did. My barrister was masterful. He led each councillor on, eager to exaggerate the flouriness of the attack. 'Yes it was terrible… hundreds of flour bombs: everything covered in thick flour: you could hardly see in front of you!'

'Well, you could hardly see my client then, sitting 40 yards away, could you?' It was a clear political settling of old scores rather than reliable identification evidence. Case dismissed! Thrown out before it even got to the jury!

John Morse had previous with me… and afters! Tory councillor Richard Lewis alleged I'd smashed up his car one night. 'What's the evidence?' asked Morse. 'He says he saw me do it,' I replied, fearing this might be telling. 'Ha!' scoffed Morse. 'What kind of rubbish evidence is that? He saw you do it! No forensics, no fingerprints?' he inquired.

'No,' I said, relieved to learn that someone seeing you smash up a car was regarded as useless evidence. I saw him a couple of weeks later crawling around outside Lewis' front garden with a measuring tape. In court, he had Lewis claiming to have seen me smashing up his car on the darkest night in recorded history — 'no moon, your worships' — from his 'heavily curtained' bedroom window through a '14-foot tree' and a 'high garden wall'. By his diagrams and elevations, he proved it was impossible for Lewis to have even seen his car. Case dismissed. No need even to call the defence evidence. 'You do bring me a bit of light relief,' said Morse.

Chapter 11

PAGE 3

It was variously named Dirty Doras... Pandoras... Circles... The Pit... Marina Nitespot and was a fantabulous fleapit which had hosted The Sex Pistols, Slits, Buzzcocks and Sham 69 as well as spawning every legover in the town. It was all managed with massive indifference by Howard. It was also the only venue in which Swansea's home-grown punkers – The Next Step, The Autonomes, Venom, The Urge and The End, plus Llanelli's greatest ever export, the utterly brilliant Andy Pandemonium – could get to play outside the usual Top Ranksville wankdom.

I'd put Crass and Poison Girls on there. When Howard turned up, there was a queue of tiny 10 year olds trying to get in with their 'Fight war' T-shirts. 'They can't come in, she only looks about eight,' said Howard to the door staff. Steve Ignorant hid the offending eight-year-old in the back of a speaker and carried her past the door gorillas. I was talking to Howard later when the eight-year-old walked between us swigging a pint like a veteran alkie. Howard shrugged and hid in his office.

But tonight was Page 3's debut gig... mucho fucking hyped. Howard told me the Dutch band Focus – no, me neither mate – had pulled a record crowd of 900, but we were pushing it fucking close. We had strippers 'fucking good-looking ones,' enthused Ray Jones, our singer. He was right. They were supposed to strip seductively when Ray burst into his Troggs cover version of *Can't Control Myself*. Instead they just raced on stage naked and danced about before rolling around on top of each other laughing hysterically. The surge from the back towards the stage was almost of Hadj-like proportions.

Page 3 had started in the Coach and Horses a month or so earlier. Beer talk –

<< Jock Mcveigh

start a band. 'Porno Rock,' that's what we'd be – songs all about sex – but political, funny, subversive like. Our strippers would subvert the idea of stripping, wouldn't they? Well, yes... that doubtlessly accounted for the Doras surge.

I wrote about ten songs all over one weekend, hummed the tunes to Ray and Stuart who worked out the music. 'Every one a fucking winner Ian,' enthused Ray moonlighting from his other band Dyfatty Flats. We recruited everyone else from the pub regardless of musical ability – punk as fuck or wot? Jock McVeigh (exotic dancer), Glen, Hugh, Trevor, Jonathan, Carolynne, Gaggsy, me, Ray Jones, Rhian, Stuart, Sheralee, Sarah Bewara, Amanda Bewara. Three rehearsals up at Cockett Studios and we're off. Our set included such classics as *Sexist Twat*, *Bitches on Heat*, *Premature Ejaculations*, *Swallow it Down*, *Can't Get It Up*, *One of the Boys*, *Clap Clap I Wanna get the Clap*, *Prostitutes' World*, *John Bindon*, plus the evergreen singalong *God Bless You Queen Mum* and a couple of Reg Presley covers. Ray was a bit dubious about singing the impotence song *Can't Get It Up* but accompanied solo by Sarah on oboe, he did it proud.

The gig was a storming success – musically as well as sexually. I'm not sure that our cogent analysis of the commodification of sex and the reification of emotion in the society of the spectacle was appreciated, or understood, by all, but Howard seemed to buy into it because he immediately rebooked us in a back office overflowing with cash.

I decided to help our notoriety along a bit further. I phoned the *Evening Post* and told them that Jock 'Negative' McVeigh had been tragically killed in a car accident in the south of France. The *Post's* front page ran 'Page 3 Exotic Dancer Killed In French Crash' – which sounded both glam and tragic! Oh how we laughed. Jock had never been further than Briton Ferry in his life and to see this lovable, tattooed, gay proletarian Swansea ne'r do well described as an 'exotic dancer' in print was mirth inducing. When up before the Swansea bench in the future, Jock would always give his occupation as 'exotic dancer' then argue he was 'dead' so couldn't be charged, producing the crumpled *Post* front page as conclusive evidence. I followed up with a further call to the *Post* complaining the story was untrue – cue another front page 'Band Victim Of Cruel Hoax' and giving full details of our next Circles' gig naturally. Jock now describes himself as 'a living legend' in the town – a name the band was later to take on. After one gig, we were indeed living legends in the pretty shitty city.

We'd chosen the name Page 3 by sticking a pin in a book and agreeing to be called whatever it stuck in. But now with the strippers, it became obvious there was a connection in some crazed Swansea minds between us and *The Sun*'s Page 3 girls. So I decided to exploit this as well:

> *Dear Editor,*
> *I recently went along to see a concert at Circles nightclub in Swansea. Advertised as Page 3, I naturally thought it would be sponsored by* The Sun *and feature your delightful Page 3 glamour girls. Imagine my horror to see the crudest pornography, vile lyrics, live sex and a song wishing the Queen Mother would die of cancer etc etc.'*

The hope behind the letter was that *The Sun* would run a sensational article on the band denying any connection and spreading our notoriety nationally, but it didn't quite work out like that!

Our second gig was at the Highwayman Nite Spot in Ystalyfera – a ponderosa-style scampi-in-a-basket club but temporarily managed by Gwyn 'Bomber' Dawe, one of my Welsh Republican acquaintances anxious to spread the porno-rock message up the Lower Swansea Valley. The gig was a total fucking shambles on all counts. Our stripper, had been chatted up by a camera-toting 'merchant seaman' by the bar and was posing for photos. Later, she breathlessly told us that the 'merchant seaman' was in fact a *Sun* journalist. The poor unfortunate, hoping that the journo line was more likely to get her into bed than the merchant seaman ploy, had blurted out the truth.

Our two roadies – famed Townhill hardmen, Ianto and Ado Craven – took his camera off him and threw it in the river. Ado then performed a perfectly executed head-butt on him which stretched him prone on the ponderosa floor as we headed home. Further gigs were put on hold as Jock Negative was in Swansea gaol for a month on shoplifting and assault charges. Still nothing in *The Sun*. The day Jock was due for release, we booked a gig at another chicken-in-a-basket joint – the Rainbow Club in Gorseinon. That morning, we met Jock coming out the Oystermouth Road nick – or Cox's Farm as it was still known in Swansea. He was very excited – as you would be after four weeks inside. But no, it was more than that. The night before, he'd had a writ served on him in the gaol by a solicitor acting for *The Sun*. The whole band was summoned to appear before the High Court on The Strand on infringement of copyright charges – *The Sun* claiming to have copyrighted 'Page 3'.

Page Three in action. Ray Jones in front, me behind in comedy shades!

Bash The Rich

Page 3 only ever played six gigs. The last one in Swansea being at the university. There was a huge crowd as usual and we had our full complement of Swansea footie hooligan 'roadies'. On this occasion, it was Mac, Conkers, and the legendary Hank, who threw anyone off stage who tried to get near our strippers (theoretically), but, in fact, threw anyone about they didn't like the look of. Our new strippers for the night were the electrifying combination of Siobhan and Alison. Alison was one of the hardest girls in Swansea and part of a group of hardnut women who always seemed to be biting each other's ears and noses off in Circles, then heading down to St Lawrence Hospital, Chepstow, to get them sewn back on again. Whatever – she had this stunning eagles' wings tattoo across both breasts which was eagerly looked forward to. Alison limbered up by throwing excitable students off stage with practised ease. Everyone was hyped-up as fuck and completely gaga pissed. But Siobhan stole the show. She sashayed onto the stage wearing high heels, stockings, suspenders – no knickers naturally. Little was left to the fervent imagination of the students as to the destination of a handful of Jelly Babies she produced. When members of the audience at the front were invited to retrieve them there was a massive surge to the front and pandemonium around the stage as our roadies fought with the Jelly Baby tongues. Paul Durden (*Twin Town*) smashed the fire alarm and the fire brigade stormed in to a scene of utter mayhem – Sodom and Gomorrah meets Fight Club. That was our last Swansea gig.

There was still the matter of the High Court appearance. Fourteen of us trouped into the No. 8 court on The Strand, dressed for the occasion. Jock Negative looked especially fetching in his thigh-length leather boots, informing the judge he was an exotic dancer before the proceedings started – 'just to break the ice like'. Ranged against us were a battery of be-wigged barristers representing *The Sun*. Ranged with us was Keith Allen, a friend of Ray Jones through his Swansea background who had a gig that night at Raymond's Revue Bar (and was to become briefly the Living Legends' drummer). *The Sun*'s barristers listed a litany of our vile behaviour and how 'Page 3' was copyrighted by *The Sun*. They asked for judgement in their favour and 'exemplary damages'. Our case was weak and feebly-presented by myself and Jock Negative. But then, horror. I'd made the mistake of bringing a copy of my original 'complaining' letter to *The Sun* and was writing notes on it. The judge asked to see it! He looked long and hard over the top of his glasses at it – he must have seen the handwriting was the same. But he simply looked at me and handed it back with a 'thank you, Mr Bone'. Did I imagine a wink. He found for *The Sun*, and told us we had to stop using the name, and refused to give damages. The Sun's barrister asked for costs – £80,000. 'Both sides can meet their own costs in the matter,' he ruled. Was there another wink or was I dreaming?

'Why don't you play Raymond's Revue Bar with me tonight?' asked Keith. Why not. Keith rustled up a few instruments. We sang acapella, pissed and chuffed as fuck. We played London but Page 3 was no more. 'We're Living Legends!' shouted Jock from the stage, as he lay on his back gurgling free booze. Not quite yet mate, but we will be!

A Swansea class hero...

I'd transferred my fickle loyalties from Aldershot Town FC to Swansea Town FC. Firstly, I thrilled to the magical inside forward line of Keith Todd, Jimmy Mclaughlin and Ivor Allchurch who'd come within a disputed penalty of making the FA Cup Final the year before I'd landed in town. But later it was Alan Curtis, Jeremy Charles and Robbie James who set our North Bank pulses racing.

One day, I breezed into town from Mayhill for a lunchtime drink with Ray Jones at the Coach and Horses where Ray was to play me his unreleased hooligan classic *Trouble on the North Bank*. The delirious promenade of shoplifters with empty carrier bags was making its daily excursion to the big shops. Soon they'd be touting joints of beef, big chunks of cheddar and super-sized coffee jars round the lunchtime drinkers. I moped around Oxford Street until opening time. XXXX a newspaper seller, *Alarm* enthusiast and a top source of gossip, beckoned me over animatedly. The poster on the front of the metal newspaper stand said 'Welsh Cup stolen from Vetch Field'. Within the metal stand was a large black bin bag. 'Here 'ave a look in 'ere Ian,' XXXX laughed, eyes flashing. And there stood the very fine and the very same Welsh Cup. Far more impressive than the English FA Cup incidentally.

'How the fuck did you get that?' I asked.

'Two kiddies nicked it from the Vetch, tried to sell it to the Buy and Sell shop in St Helens Road, then I brought it off them for a tenner!'

Newspaper buyers were reading the front page story little knowing the stolen Welsh Cup was within arms' reach.

'What are you going to do with it?' 'You can 'ave it for twenty quid,' XXXX replied... seriously! 'Or I'll flog it to Cardiff City – they'll want it.' 'For fuck's sake, Cardiff City will want the Cup, but they need to win it. They can't just parade it through the streets after it mysteriously vanished from the Vetch, no questions asked like.' XXXX looked crestfallen. 'But I know Ritchie Morgan (Cardiff City Manager),' XXXX countered hopefully. I raced home to get the £20. The Welsh Cup would look very fine on the mantlepiece of my council house I mused. I got back too late. The Cup was gone. 'What happened?' 'Struel (Swansea City chairman) offered a £500 reward so we've taken it back.' Brilliant. Fucking brilliant. Top work.

Apart from the Swans, my other Swansea sporting hero was Jimmy Wilde. There were two boxing Jimmy Wildes – both from South Wales. One was the legendary Jimmy Wilde 'The Mighty Atom' or 'The Tylorstown Terror' fighting out of the Rhondda and the smallest and lightest man ever to win a world championship. The other was Jim Wilde – as the boxing writers said to avoid confusion – the Welsh Heavyweight Champion boxing out of Swansea. To everyone in Swansea, he was Jimmy Wilde though. During his fighting career (1932 to 1946) Wilde had some notable opponents, including a memorable draw with British and Empire Champion Tommy Farr and a rather shorter bout with Freddie Mills in 1941 when he was knocked out in the third round. Just as well Wilde didn't stay on his knees in front of Freddie Mills for long since in the early 1950s, Mills was suspected of murdering three prostitutes by choking them to death during oral sex!

Jimmy Wilde continued his boxing carer after the war but with ever-increasing defeats. But there was more to Jimmy than being a boxer. He was a very big, strong striking man – just the kind of Aryan specimen Moseley's Blackshirts were hoping to recruit in the 1930s. In 1936, the Blackshirts approached Jimmy before their rally at the Swansea Plaza about leading the march. Jimmy led the march all right – but the one that got stuck into the fascists outside the Plaza ensuring they never marched in Swansea again.

Later Jimmy ran a drinking club opposite High Street Station called The Alexandra Social Club but known by all as 'Jimmy Wilde's'. Wild it certainly was – being the club of choice for every low-lifer in town when the pubs closed – especially mid-afternoon. Sitting on hard railway waiting room pews, drinking rough – I mean rough! – cider trying to avoid eye contact with the psycho in the corner. Mass brawls were never far away. Jimmy would chuck all comers out through the doors. One day, a punter trying to open his bottle on the bottle opener attached to the wall – to avoid theft – pulled the whole wall down. Ladies of easy virtue were also alleged to frequent the club. Jimmy remained a towering presence in old age closing the club and popping over to the Labour Club at The Elysium for a couple of pints and bunging a few quid to the local anarchists and *Alarm*. A working-class hero is something to be.

Bash The Rich

SWANSEA 1965-1982

Most political and cultural histories of hippiedom
and punk all centre on London. But as every denizen
of a provincial city or small town will tell you,
there was a fuck sight more genuine bolshy rebellion
going on in one fucking pub in these shithouse towns
then you'd find in swinging fucking London. You know
the pubs — with geezers in denim jackets with 'Free
the Weed' on their backs and ACAB (All Coppers
Are Bastards) on their knuckle joints, drinking to
liver heaven in some backstreet boozer, not overly
concerned with their own longevity. Andrea Dunbar
— teenage playwright of *Rita, Sue and Bob Too* gave
a big Fuck Off to London and middle classdom and
stayed boozing in The Beacon on the Buttershaw in
Bradford. Cheers Andrea — you'd have fucking loved
Swansea. I did. I can't do it justice in prose. So
this page is for you lot who were there.

Peter Cowley, Peter Hunt, Kingo, Mickey Baker,
Stan Phifer, Kustard, Ian Hunter, Trigger, Paul
Durden, Ray Jones, Howard Griffiths, Viv Cory, Jeff
Gray, Jane Crawford, Kate Stacey, Pete Stacey, Kenny
Richards, Alfie Cooper, Finnselbach, Danny Gralton,
Josie O'Dwyer, Dido, Darryl Evans, John Jenkins,
Helen Crocker, Jill the Pill, Rita, Ben and Jackie,
Phil and Muff, Phil Thomas, Jack Harris, Hank Mac
Conkers, Snakey, Phil Williams, Dave Fresco, Mav,
Mamf, Ianto Bowen, Derek Manser, Dai Cannabis, Martin
Ace, Tommy Trumpet, Stan Autonome, Steve Mitchell,

Jay Jay, Steve Devine, Liz, Kerry, Ruthie Bennet, Keith Thomas, Dorian, Jock McVeigh Kym Burns, Reg Atherton, Gwyn Dawe, Vivienne, Jock Spence, Eve Spence, Jimmy Grimes, Carolynne Thomas, Lindsay Bruce and Pig, Wilbur O'Kelly, Cotters, Christine Orr, Mike Kenefick, Julian Ross, John Plant, Neil Bowman, Tony Levene, Mick Kidd, Wayne Jenkins, Boz Morris, Leonard from Pennard, Joan Smith, Rev Leon Atkin, Rose Barnes, Gaynor, Sandra, Jenny, Lynne, Peter Shore, Joan Evans, Pete Miller, Dick Chamberlain, Chris Proctor, Mike Synott, Jenny Synott, Louise Graham, Jan Green, Paul McCarthy, Richard Jones, Dave Lamb, Kevin, Gaynor, John Barker, Hilary Creek, Anna Mendelson, Reg Jones, Winky, Duncan Bush, Pete Crombie, Graham Larkeby, Ed and Gina, Andy Pandemonium, Steve Potter, Sarah and Amanda, Sue Patterson, Sheralee, Colwyn Williamson, Donna Kiley, Fred Fitton, Glen Evans, Dai Griffiths, Paul Elliott, Arthur and Margaret, Phil Henry Helen Griffin, Adele Crocker, Peter Edwards, Paula, Griff, Robbie James, Jimmy Wilde, Ralph the Books, Peter Singh, Mike Pany, Roger Forsythe, Bob Dumbleton, Mike Fleetwood, Manuel Mazzoriaga, Chris Leake, Cris Haines, Dickie Urge, Gerald Castle, Max Milburn, Christine Milburn, Paddy French, Dan Williams, Tim Mitchell, Dawn Mitchell, Jonathan Smyth-Murray, Gaggsy, Danny, Kelly, Jackie Sullivan, Terry Burgess, Sue Annette… and Swansea Jack — 'He's done it again!'

KIDNAPPED!

I walked across the green to Swansea Guildhall where Prince Charles was visiting with his new bride. I was mulling over his last visit after the investiture, when he'd declared Swansea a City and Lin, me and Chum the dog had been the first to be pulled by the city cops. Suddenly, I was windmilling my legs in mid air as I was well and truly lifted by a couple of burly cops and dumped in a car by Joe's Ice Cream Parlour on St Helen's Road.

'Am I nicked?'

'No, we're just keeping you out of the way like, until Charles leaves town. So sit quietly and be a good boy.'

They weren't Special Branch, just a couple of Rhondda cops seconded to the Royal protection squad for the night. An hour passed. I needed a pint.

'Fancy a drink?' I chanced to the bored twosome on the front seats.

'Shut up!' Silence.

They where just as much imprisoned, bored in the car as I was… and they knew it.

'Fancy a pint?' I asked again 30 minutes later.

They looked at each other.

'Where?' one of them asked.

'I dunno out of town somewhere.'

Cop two grabbed me by the neck. 'If you fuck us about, I'll fucking kill you!'

'Fair enough,' I replied. We motored off.

They couldn't be arsed to drive out of town so we stopped at the Cross Keys off Wind Street. I was still handcuffed to one of them.

'We can't go in the fucking pub in handcuffs,' I pleaded.

Handcuffs off and another threat to be on good behaviour. Two pints later, it was my round.

'I ain't buying cops a fucking drink.' They laughed. We was rabbiting about Paul Ringer's sending off against England. Six pints flowed. They looked at their watches. Well past Charles leaving town by now. But we was getting on like a house on fire. Two more pints. Off they went with waving promises to meet up when I was badge-selling outside the Arms Park.

I staggered home to Townhill. Two hours later there was a knock on the door. Some Welsh Republican friends had seen me get lifted.

'Did the cops beat you up?' they asked concernedly.

'Not exactly,' I slurred.

Chapter 12

THE AXEMAN COMETH

Until 1982, I hadn't left Swansea since 1965 apart from trips to London for the Grosvenor Square Vietnam demonstration in 1968, and to visit Hilary Creek and Anna Mendelson during the Angry Brigade trials. My political activities had all been localised and following the fashions of the day. Claimants' Unions, community activism, Men Against Sexism (aaargh! Don't EVER ask) and a brief flirtation with Welsh Republican Socialism in various forms.

I'd squatted an empty children's home in Sketty Park with homeless families, blocked the streets and got nicked with the Morriston Cross boys, been involved in five different community papers, worked with Paddy French's Cardiff-based *Rebecca* magazine exposing Labour Party corruption across South Wales, and even stood as a 'Community Control Yo Ho Ho' candidate in the May 1970 local elections for a laugh. I'd had an argument with the electoral registration officer about whether you could put 'Yo Ho Ho' on the ballot paper which finally ended up being quoted in *Hansard*! I'd even adopted a literal welsh translation of my name – Ieuan ab Asgwrn – for a couple of months.

We'd run an anarchist bookshop in the Uplands – Revolt Books – with full-on, metal, The Angry Brigade armed love machine gun sign just down from the gentility of Dylan Thomas' beloved Cwmdonkin Park. During 1981, some copies of *Xtra* had filtered down to Swansea. *Xtra* could certainly be seen as a precursor of *Class War* with its humour and support for anti-cop violence and I'd written an article for one issue on the holiday home arson attacks. Maybe *Xtra* was the type of national anarchist paper there should be – it was certainly a cut above *Freedom* and *Black Flag*. During the 1981 riots, I could only watch as an exhilarated TV spectator as every town and village in the country erupted apart from fucking Swansea. I'd tried to instigate a riot on The Kingsway but only legendary footie hooligan Hank had turned up. That was it. Swansea's failure to riot in 1981 was the last straw. I had to get out.

All the like-minded people from Swansea had gone to London long ago. In January 1982, I finally waved Swansea bye bye. Just before I left, I printed off 400 copies of my own little version of *Xtra* called *Fuck Off*, with the intention of flogging these to like minds in London. With two bin bags full of clothes, 400 *Fuck Offs*, I arrived in Ladbroke Grove. Ray Jones, singer with our one-time punk band Page 3, and veteran *Alarm* seller was living in Ladbroke Grove and had a vibrant social scene going in the Elgin and later in the Warwick Castle pubs in Portobello Road. Keith and Kevin Allen, and Tony Allen, were part of this and the Portobello bohemians made a dramatic change to life on a shitty Swansea council estate.

Tony Allen introduced me to the London situationists around Nick Brandt, and I got involved in a few wacky scams with them around the Greater London Council's (GLC) fare fight policies including 50 of us dressed up and bewigged as Lord Dennings taking over a routemaster bound for Westminster. There was also the *For a Dignified and Effective Demonstration* leaflet (see p147) – a witty bit of Brandt Situ-spoofery featuring Cliff Richard and a wolf on the cover handed out on a GLC demo where we persuaded and manhandled the Trots into ludicrously marching in alphabetical order. I never really understood what Nick was on about, but his perpetually pained expression at the behaviour of others was fun to watch. He continually produced leaflets 'critiquing' other members of his household, mostly around jealousy arising from who is fucking who. Aleks – situationist no. 2– eventually moved out of the Brandt household to Brixton where he shared a flat with Phil Gard of the London Workers' Group (LWG). The LWG was a discussion group of libertarians, council communists, workers councillists, who produced a regular bulletin (though hardly any of them were workers – apart from Printer Phil) quite correctly critiquing work as a no-no. Dave Morris of McLibel fame, and Paul Anderson, later to be deputy editor of the *New Statesman* were regulars. The group provided a forum for serious libertarian debate but lacked any serious oomph.

I'd met Lisa Ambalu while flogging *Fuck Off* at a University of London Union (ULU) gig and, during our brief romance, she introduced me to fellow ULU student Richard Parry who just happened to be the editor of the much-admired *Xtra*.

The Sits and the London Workers Group (LWG) were OK but where were the people who I might be able to spark something off with – something new and vibrant and not caught up in the perpetual London anarcho squabbles of the past. I was to find that person in a most peculiar way. Apart from trawling through the obscure anarcho-periodical section at Compendium and Housemans, Freedom Bookshop and 121 Railton Road were the anarchist bookshops where you might hope to pick up signs of any sentient life in the anarchist movement. The 1981 riots had spawned two interesting pamphlets *Summer of a Thousand Julys* and *We Want The Riot To Work*, both of which looked at ways in which a riot might be turned into insurrection as well as giving blow by blow accounts of the rioting. So there were some like-minded punters out there – it's just that I wasn't getting to meet them fast enough for my liking. Nick Brandt had produced a magazine called *Refuse* which contained some interestingly heretical analysis of long-held anarchist truths, as well as amusingly sticking the boot in to people he'd fallen out with. One such seemed to be an anarcho-psychopath called Martin Wright who'd played the piano at a party given by Brandt one night – with a sledgehammer! I got the full Brandt treatment of this 'nutter'. But I wanted to meet anarcho-nutters, wild men. What the fuck! An anarcho-psycho must be preferable to another Brandt 48-page analysis of his best friend's sexual jealousy. One Saturday afternoon, I went with Nick, Aleks and William down to 121 Bookshop in Railton Road for an afternoon discussion and meal in the 121 Cafe. We picked up Lisa on the way and tucked into a fine meal cooked by Cordon Red and Black chef Franco. The discussion was on Poland and Solidarity – typical of the 121-ers at the time who would spend hours discussing far away events which they could have fuck all influence while being oblivious to riots on their own doorstep. The discussion was pretty desultory when William nudged me. 'That's Andy Sutton – a friend of Martin Wright,' he whispered ominously as a leather-jacketed figure came late into the room. I was as hopeful as Nick was apprehensive that he might be followed by the dreaded psychotic himself, but Andy was alone.

We got talking to Andy afterwards – he seemed friendly enough to me – and Nick offered to drive him back to Islington. We stopped at some Firkin pub on the way and I downed a rapid six pints of Dogbolter. By now I was determined to meet Mr Wright that evening. Nick was prevailed upon to drive Andy back to the house he shared with Wright in Duncan Terrace, Islington and, on arrival, me and Lisa jumped out of the car with Andy and staggered into No. 19. We followed Andy into a sitting room. The introduction wasn't all that I might have wished in retrospect. 'This is a mate of Nick Brandt,' said Andy, waving me in the direction of the one I assumed must be Martin Wright. A twisted leer spread over the Wright visage as he rose from his seat – not out of politeness I think – and stood before me. 'And Brandt is in a car outside,' Andy added. 'What! Brandt's outside!' shrieked Martin disbelievingly to those in attendance on him.

They all raced from the house, followed by Lisa and me as interested spectators. Duncan Terrace was a cul-de-sac, and Nick had sped off in the wrong direction, necessitating a rapidly executed U-turn and return past No. 19. As he sped past, a hail of bricks, bottles, cans and street furniture smashed into the car. Nick kept his nerve and managed a squeaky tyre getaway. I wandered back into the house. Andy must have had second thoughts about the wisdom of his original introduction and was now explaining to a glazed-eyed Mr Wright that I was merely an acquaintance of comrade Brandt rather than a bosom pal. I was too rat-arsed to be scared.

After doing some air guitar with his knuckle-duster and filing his nails with a sheath knife, Mr Wright sat down. I seized my moment: 'Look, all this fucking about is no good,' I began. 'All this stupid fucking arguing and splits and slagging each other off. What is the fucking point of being so fucking inward looking when there's thousands of punters out there who we should be getting to. I haven't come up to London just to fuck about with a load of fucking idiots,' I continued – the megalomania count of my role as an anarchist of destiny rising by the minute. 'Now you seem like fucking someone with a bit of fucking oomph, so let's get things sorted out. We ain't gonna cause more fucking riots by having stupid fucking squabbles.' As you can see, the speech was a bit short on analysis, but not on the fuckings and passion. Mr Wright – the alleged psychopath – seemed to watch on with a look of bewildered amusement. Who the fuck was this drunken, long-haired hippie who barged into his front room late on a Sunday evening – having been driven there by the detested Brandt – and was delivering him a lecture on the future of the British anarchist movement. He remained silent as I strode about the room demanding anarchist unity now, that I had arrived in London, to get things sorted out.

Eventually Martin vanished upstairs for some reason. Suddenly I had to have a very urgent piss. I couldn't locate the toilet on the ground floor but I made it into the hallway where a rather fine, gleaming motorbike was standing. Whooosh! I weed all over the bike, amusing myself by hitting different bits of it with a hot vaporising stream of steam-driven Dogbolter piss rivulets cascading along the passage floor.

'Martin, the fucking hippie's pissing on the bike. He's pissing on the bike!' Another of the housemates, an astonished lean figure at the top of the stairs – presumably the owner of the bike – came flying down the stairs brandishing a meat cleaver! A fucking meat cleaver. Other figures poured out of rooms towards me. I turned tail with Lisa and fled to the street. The meat cleaver went flashing past my head. The mad fucker was trying to stick the cleaver in my head – just for a pissing bike. Adrenalin pumped the legs along faster. We turned from Duncan Terrace towards Upper Street and the cleaver stopped pursuing. We flagged down a cab and away. Fucking hell, Brandt was right. They were nutters!

I was still buzzing down to Swansea for the occasional weekend of boozing. A group calling itself the Workers Army of the Welsh Republic (WAWR) had been setting off small-scale explosive devices at government buildings for a year or so. The cops had finally got their act together and busted a load of people I knew from the Welsh Republican Socialist Movement (WRSM). A big show trial was coming up in the autumn – it seemed like overt state repression to smash the WRSM before it grew any bigger. One of those arrested was Dafydd Ladd, who'd previously been one of the defendants in the anarchist Persons Unknown trial before he'd skipped bail the day before the trial was due to start.

In mid-August, I had a drunken day out at the Pontardawe Folk Festival with my *Class War* founder-to-be mate Jimmy Grimes. We'd met some people from the WAWR defence campaign in the Pontardawe pubs, and I'd been particularly smitten with the feisty Brig Jones, a fiery Celt with a Bobby Sands fixation, a vitriolic sense of humour and a decent alcohol intake. One of the defendants in custody, Dafydd Burns, was going to stand as a Welsh Political Prisoner candidate in the Gower by-election. Help was needed. I zoomed up and the down the M4 by cheapo bus for a few weeks. An anarchist mate from Cardiff, Roland Cleaver, stuck a custard pie in Tony Benn's face at a Welsh miners' rally. I got drunk afterwards with Brig Jones. I fell into bed with Brig Jones. Fuck all was happening in London. I moved to Cardiff in time for the trial. I don't think Brig was overly impressed when I turned up on her doorstep with my perennial black bin bag.

Moving to Cardiff was a bit like admitting defeat with the bigger project of starting a national anarchist newspaper – but that would have to stay on the back burner while romance and conspiracy trials sorted

Bash The Rich

themselves out. The WAWR trial proved to be a conspiracy of duplicity and mistrust – and that was just among the defendants! I'd taken on Brig's analysis of the good guys and bad guys – who'd spilled the beans to the cops and who hadn't – but by the end of the trial, the whole thing was a sorry mess with splits and bitter division within the defence campaign.

Dafydd Ladd seemed to have a fixation with letting off small-scale explosive devices and drawing other people into his fantasies of non-existent republican workers' armies. I made a mental note to give him a wide berth when he prepared his next armed insurrectionary movement. He was an insurrectionist with a soft spot for squirrels, however, this proved his downfall. Dafydd had buried WAWR's entire stock of explosives in the grounds of Castell Coch – in the circumstances a suitably Ruritanian site for a Ruritanian terror cell. His co-defendant and girlfriend Jenny had lain awake at night worrying that squirrels might dig the explosives up and be blown to squirrel pieces. Dafydd was persuaded to go and dig the stuff up; unfortunately he was now being followed by the cops who observed him on his squirrel rescue mission. Though this was a farcical end to the trial there was no doubt the local cops had determined to frame some of the leading lights in the WSRM and effectively brought that movement to an end.

The WSRM had started to make some useful political links beyond the usual republican diaspora and in a way the Free Wales Army had never thought of – in particular with some striking workers at Duport steelworks in Llanelli. But, yet again, the fantastical armed struggle wing (two people and a squirrel) had fucked things up.

During the first week of the trial, a bomb had gone off at the Inland Revenue offices in Swansea – apparently to prove the defendants in the dock must be innocent. I was scuttling up and down between Swansea and Cardiff at the time, so was a prime suspect. Two months of ham-fisted, cock-eyed, cop surveillance followed during the trial with listening vans parked outside Brig's flat eavesdropping on hopefully conspiratorial bedroom conversations. They'd have heard more about a disintegrating relationship than bomb plantings. In Swansea, a telephoto lens projected from curtains opposite a house we regularly visited. Steve Edwards – a fellow WSRM supporter – spotted a white van parked permanently round the back of his flat. We raced round and forced the back doors open to find two sheepish coppers crouched over a bank of listening devices. 'TV Licence detection' they mumbled before haring off.

Brig's brother Rod was a council communist and despite relationship dysfunction, me, Brig, Rod and Jimmy Grimes decided to bring out a radical Welsh magazine called *The Scorcher* after the trial ended. It staggered on for four acerbic issues in my mistaken belief that there might be some Welsh radicalism left to ignite. There wasn't. Jimmy Grimes wrote a blistering front page piece slagging off the 'Dancing Dorises' of Greenham Common and *The Scorcher* collective disintegrated in the subsequent argy-bargy. *The Scorcher* and *Fuck Off* can both be seen as the smoking lava to *Class War*'s subsequent eruption. In the meantime, I'd moved into a shared house in Claude Place with a mixed bag of Cardiff anarchists, and reformed the Living Legends with Doc Whelan, Roland Cleaver, Dean Poole, Nicky Evans and Gareth Joseph. We played a few gigs with the Soldier Dolls, The Oppressed and Demented Are Go and took up residence in the Cardiff ex-Servicemen's Club.

Michael Roberts, the MP for Cardiff North, had dropped dead mid-speech in the House of Commons, so we knocked out our seminal track *Tory Funerals*, complete with photo opportunity on his newly dug grave and Roland doing a passable impersonation of George Thomas, speaker of the House of Commons. I wasn't sprinkled with the McClaren stardust, however, and no resulting 'disgusted of Cyncoed' publicity ensued. Abergavenny Town Hall was a laugh though.

After a gig where we'd gone down like the Belgrano brothers playing the Aldershot NAAFI, I was totally rat-arsed and, using all my keenest streetwise misjudgement, surmised that Abergavenny was ready for its first riot as we left the town hall. There was some minor stand-off

Bash The Rich

between a couple of cops with an Alsatian and some suited drunks. My brain whirred fast forward – a spark could ignite this into The Summer of 1,000 Julys, mark 2.

I'd clocked a posh antique shop on the way in – at least I thought I had. I raced back into the town hall, grabbed a chair, flew out into the street and hurled the chair through the shop window, right in front of the cops. In the ensuing scuffle, to arrest me would surely cause a riot. Not. Very definitely not. There was a deafening hush as I was pushed into the cop van. Subsequently fined £100 at Abergavenny Magistrates Court for inexplicably throwing a chair through the local hairdresser's window.

To describe my flatmates at Claude Place as 'a mixed bag' doesn't quite do them justice. Roland Cleaver used to drive an old ambulance round the town with a black flag flying proudly from its window. During the severe snow of winter 1981, he'd delivered milk and bread to pensioners who couldn't get out. Red Dragon radio announced repeatedly 'Get your milk and bread from the ambulance flying the black flag' making it sound like an NHS service. Roland was of the 'Act Now' brigade and I'd seen him bravely plant a custard pie in Phoney Benn's face at the South Wales miners' gala – which took a lotta bottle considering the hero worship the miners had for the phoney old aristo.

Cardiff anarchists were pretty action orientated at the time – if not always blessed with success. Some comrades had launched a petrol bomb attack on the army recruiting office in Cardiff during the Falklands War. The petrol bomb had bounced off the recruiting office window – leaving a few scorch marks – and set fire to one of their trouser legs. Undeterred, the scorched comrade had phoned in a communiqué to Red Dragon radio claiming responsibility for the attack in the name of 'The Peace Brigade'. After finishing reading out the, hopefully, anonymous communiqué, the Red dragon man taking the call said 'Cheers XXXXX, thanks for phoning that in, I'll pass it to the news desk'. XXXXX had got through to a nightime DJ covering incoming calls who recognised his voice! Whoops – the looks on the faces of his fellow Peace Brigaders was a picture!

There had been an earlier legendary petrol bomb attack – before my arrival in Cardiff – where a target had gone up with a mighty whoof sending burning petrol back under the door setting fire to the bomber's trousers! It was described to me as 'another Cardiff comedy classic' as the perpetrator cycled – yes, cycled! – off home with his inconspicuous corduroys glowing like fag ends as cop sirens and fire engines wailed past in the opposite direction. Cardiff anarchists were angrier than The Angry Brigade. They were the extremely fucking Angry Brigade and one was angrier than most.

Doc Whelan was in the Welsh Karate team but it was his fearsome nutting ability and famous short fuse that inspired awe. In me at least. We played a gig with The Oppressed who had a big skinhead following. A couple of them made racist remarks to Doc's Asian girlfriend as we were leaving. Doc nutted both of them to the floor before the peacemakers prevailed. He had a deep hatred of lefties – he had a deep hatred of most things including Roland occasionally – and composed the seminal Living Legends anthem *Trendy Leftie Drop Dead* complete with firing squad sound effects. He didn't like the Cardiff punks much either as he expressed in the anthemic *Motherfuckers* with the lines: 'Cardiiff punks, you're all like sheep, all you ever do is bleat bleat bleat'.

In fact, of all the incarnations of the Living Legends, the Cardiff one was the most talented, both musically and in the sharing around of song writing credits. A particular favourite of mine was Roland Cleaver's anti-Falklands War anthem *Island Wars* complete with the Phil Spector wall of sound drumming of Dean Poole. 'Boy' Dean was a quiet geezer compared to the rest of us, but put him behind a drum kit or on one of Cardiff backstreet pubs bowling alleys and he was a man possessed.

The household in Claude Place was *Citizen Smith* meets *The Young Ones* and exhilarating fun for a few months after the heavy-duty backstabbing of the WAWR trial. The other flatmate was indeed called

Bash The Rich

Neil – later of Reading supergroup *Cuckooland* – who used to hook up bottles of cider in wooden crates from the off-licence at the back of us with a fishing rod then take the empty bottles round the front for the deposit back! Oh yes – living on the frontline by The Claude pub was pretty edgy.

Thatcher visited Cardiff City Hall prior to the 1983 General Election. Cordoned off from, but pretty adjacent to, the front of the building, we were singing *Tory Funerals* to try to wind-up the Tories over Michael Robert's death when some CND twat with an X-ray skeleton – don't even ask – told us to shut up. Doc Whelan jotted his fearsomely effective nut into said CNDers face and possessed the skeleton on behalf of the Cardiff Working Class. Now we changed our tune. 'We've got Michael Roberts, we've got Michael Roberts,' we sang gleefully waving the skeleton about. Even the CNDers laughed. A flat-hatted copper came over, hands raised.

'Look, we've all got our points to make, but Mrs Roberts will be along in a minute so please desist or you'll be arrested.'

'Alright,' I said, 'give us a signal when she's coming and we'll shut up and put the skeleton down.'

'Thank you,' he said, imagining there was some common base of human sensibility between us, him and Mrs Roberts. The signal came. The mourning black Mrs Roberts came into view. 'We've got Michael Roberts' came the raucous cry louder than ever as the skeleton was even more gleefully thrust aloft. Exit Mrs Roberts in tears – a casualty of the class war on their side for once. We legged it. *Western Mail* next day reported: 'CND condemn anarchists blah blah.' This was a precursor of *Class War*'s proud stuntist days to come.

In March, the disparate remnants of the Cardiff anarchist scene held a conference under the auspices of Black Flag. Full of the usual deadwood CNT worshippers and armchair-armed struggle fetishists with no real or desired connection to the urban insurrectionists of the previous year. I was selling *The Scorcher* and came upon the one bright spark of the conference. Sean Mason was down from London with his accentuated Sarf London accent ('Well, quite frankly my son, we'll 'ave a result 'ere'), cultivated swagger and self-affirming head nodding a la Mussolini. He was about 5'3", full of mouthy self-confidence and derision for the assembled gathering of 'soap dodgers'. We hit it off right away – here was a good lad after my own heart at last.

We left the conference of anarcho-buffoons for a few pints of Brains SA. What was needed was a paper for the street rioters for the class struggle anarchists not the life-stylers. Sean's 'Yes, I'm well into that' was music to my big ears. At last, someone to work with. Sean told me he went to the LWG meetings but he was also a member of the London Anarchist Youth Group which met at 121 Railton Road the last Friday of the month – there were some like-minded others there he promised me. We bonded. I told him it was my plan to bring out an in-yer-face national anarchist paper soon, but still wasn't sure what it would look like, the content would be, or name or anything.

The conversation with Sean persuaded me that I'd have to consider moving back to London soon. There was fuck all going on in Cardiff for me, sexually or politically. But this time, I wanted to go back to London with a paper a bit better than the paltry *Fuck Off* had been. With Sean's help, we could pull in some of the better people from the Bullshit Conference and the London Anarchist Youth Group (LAYG) which Sean said included the impressive Ian Slaughter. I realised it was no good just talking about some vague plans – every fucking anarchist in London did that – only if you had some concrete product would you be able to pull people together. I arranged to meet Sean at a future LWG meeting and he zipped back to London facing a big SA hangover.

The Scorcher collective had fallen apart leaving me and Jimmy Grimes with the prospect of having to flog the 500 print run of issue 4 to get our desperately needed money back. But where? Jimmy's mum lived at Burghfield in Berkshire where a big CND demo was scheduled for Easter. We could stay there, flog *The Scorcher* and use the money for drink. Off we went. Burghfield was the usual mix of no hopers, religious pacifists, earnest good-willers and Jimmy's 'Dancing Dorises' tying tampons on the wire fences in the hope that this would lead to closure of the base. By humorously aggressive *Scorcher*-selling, our booze intake remained high. The protesters were barred from the Burghfield pubs but because Jimmy was a local – and we hid our subversive literature – we were OK.

On the last day, we were strolling round the perimeter fence trying to paper-sell our way to more alcohol when a sight beheld our eyes. A host of black flags hove into view. About 100 Crass-style black, ragged anarcho-punks were running around the base with dog handlers and security guards accompanying them on the other side of the fence. Excitement at last. We picked up our sodden carrier bags of *Scorchers* and trawled behind them. They looked fucking great. About 30 black flags – yes OK, I'm always a sentimental soft touch for a black flag. They chanted: 'Fight war, not wars – fight war, not wars. 1, 2, 3, 4, We don't want your fucking war, 5, 6, 7, 8, organise and smash the state. Fight war, not wars, fight war, not wars.'

Crass patches were everywhere and circled 'A', Poison Girls slogans, there was a brilliant selection of Mohican and crasstifarian locks. I was just struck by visually how good it all looked compared to the sodden drabness of the rest of the Burghfield protesters. It ended in some gate rattling and sit downs blocking the driveway. They didn't want to buy any 'radical welsh magazines', but I'd also brought the unsold remnants of *Fuck Off* with me and they sold – at cheapo discount rate of 10p – on the strength of the imaginative title. And that was it really. But something had at last stirred in the Bone brain.

Chapter 13

THE POPE GIVES US HOPE

The court case and our singer Ray Jones moving to London meant the end of Page 3. Just before I joined him in Portobello Road, at the end of 1981, the remnants of Page 3 went into a studio Cockett and recorded *The Pope Is A Dope* and *Dum Dum Bullets* for a Dumb Dumb Dummy with the help of Chris Leake's top work on saxophone and improvised vocals by the 14-year-old Stan from the Autonomes .

When I got to Ladbroke Grove, I dropped the tape off to Fuck Off Records on Portobello Road. Two weeks later, the geezer from Fuck Off said Upright Records in Westbourne Grove were interested so I should phone Upright supremo Bill Gilliam. I think Bill was expecting some punk-as-fuck geezer to turn up so when I breezed in with my long hair and market trader camel hair over-coat, he must of thought 'Why the fuck do I always get the weirdos'. Bill readily agreed to stick out the two tracks on Upright, not realising that meant providing me good naturedly with free booze all summer. The problem was that the Living Legends no longer existed as a band who could promote the record but through the Ladbroke Grove connection, I quickly recruited Keith Allen on drums, Mario from the Tesco Bombers on base and Glyn John from X-Ray Spex on the saxophone. A stellar line up compared to our previous Swansea incarnation. The punky sisters Sarah and Amanda came up from Swansea and were joined by Lisa Ambalu. We did a couple of well-received gigs at the Idiot Ballroom in Hammersmith and the Greyhound in Fulham Palace Road. Bill wangled a favourable write-up in *Sounds* from a novice reporter complete with photo. The three girls looked punky as fuck and great but I looked like Tiny Tim gone wrong! Whatever. Rock stardom beckoned! Bill got me to sign a contract – woaah! The *Pope is a Dope* was released just before the Papal Visit of the reactionary old bigot John Paul the Second. Bill was uneasy about the Papal gunsight cover and favoured the more light-hearted pope smoking dope approach but I steelily prevailed (what did I know for fuck sake).

Bazoom! Bloody bazoom! The record crashed straight into the indy charts at no. 28. I cut the charts out of *Sounds* and carried it round with me carefully folded up in my coat pocket. There was a newsagents in Notting Hill where you could pick up *Sounds* early on a Tuesday afternoon. The following week, I was feverish with anticipation waiting outside for *Sounds* to arrive to check out our indy chart position. I put my hand over the charts and slowly moved up the lists towards the number one slot. Got to number ten and still no sign of it! Maybe it was number one – palpitations pumped inside. Alas! Oh lack a day! It wasn't no. 1, it wasn't anywhere. It had ignominiously crashed at the charts.

In truth, sales were not going well. Many distributors where refusing to take the record because of the gunsight on the Pope's head. Bill had been proved right. We needed some shock horror publicity. I told Bill about my Page 3 front page lead on our not-dead exotic dancer. I had another idea which I convinced Bill – against his better judgement – to carry out. The pope was visiting London – the reason the record was out. Bill would pretend to have brought a copy of the record from a street vendor among the Papal welcoming crowd thinking it was called *The Pope Gives Us Hope*.

He gave it to his

daughters who burst into tears on hearing the vile lyrics. 'Something should be done to stop this record which is by the Living Legends on Upright records, distributed by Pinnacle and available from all good record stores!' Bill would phone up LBC radio to make his complaint. I watched over him as he nervously phoned the news room. Success! 'They want me to go down for a live interview,' he gasped. We punched the air. Bill had to go for it. He wasn't over keen but off he went. We tuned into LBC and then on it came. It went brilliantly with Bill embellishing on the story... 'Up from Cornwall with two daughters to see the Pope, trip ruined, girls in tears, something

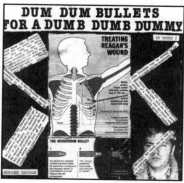

should be done, and full details of the record read out.' End. Brilliant. We waited in Upright Records in Westbourne Grove for a triumphant return... and waited... and waited. Eventually, a red-faced Bill crashed into the room. Oh, how we fucking laughed... including Bill eventually!

On concluding the interview, the LBC newsroom had told him that they'd contacted the police about the story for a comment and they where waiting to interview him about his complaint! Oh lordy lordy! Bill had to make a complaint about the record company he owned and the cops were sure to find out!

Bash The Rich

Somehow he'd managed to backtrack... maybe he'd over reacted, the girls where better now, the train to Cornwall... speedy exit. We headed for the pub after a few pints, Bill had regained his good humour. A woman came over to me and said she recognized me from some band. 'Look, it's fucking working already!' I screamed back-slapping Bill, 'It'll be back in the charts next week.' 'Aren't you the drummer from Deep Purple?' she inquired.

Exit. Stage left.

I spent the rest of the summer pinching free drinks from the Cherry Red Records fridge on the floor below Bill and forlornly trying to convince him a Living Legends album would be a winner. But by then Bad Brains and Serious Drinking where winning his interest away from potential chart toppers.

The Legends did the one last chaotic gig with Conflict at the 100 club in Oxford Street and that was it... for ten years anyway!

The Sounds Living Legends photo - Lisa, me, Sarah, Amanda on the brink of fame.

TORY FUNERALS

Sing-a-long - Living Legends
   There's some occasions, some special events
   You could say they were heaven sent
   They engrave the stones with Roman numerals
   My favourite ones… they're Tory Funerals

   Conservative Ministers or Tory MPs
   There's one sure way for them to please
   They can call me a bastard, call me a red
   In return… just drop dead
   Tory Funerals, Tory Funerals
   I want more of Tory Funerals
   Tory Funerals, Tory Funerals
   I want more of Tory Funerals

   ORDER! ORDER!
   The Speaker of the House of Commons
   'It is my painful duty to have to inform the
house that the Rt Hon member for Finchley, Mrs
Margaret Thatcher has dropped dead!'

   Cheers, laughter, party poppers, etc

   I couldn't care less, I couldn't give a toss
   At the sudden death of a factory boss
   The ruling class are really hated
   All I want… is them cremated

FUCK OFF!

PILOT ISSUE

HE MAG. FOR WELSH ARSONISTS, NARCHISTS, MUTANTS, REPUBLICANS, UNKS, PROSTITUTES, RIOTERS, HIPPIES, -A FANATICAL MAGAZINE FOR WALES

40P
RIP-OFF
CHEAP

A FUCK-OFF EXCLUSIVE:-

CONSPIRACY TRIALS ON THE WAY

Also in this issue:
Mutants
right to
wank
CND
slagged
POPE'S
visit off
first
daffs
of spring

plus →
WORKING
Class
stupid!!
SHOCK
HORROR
REPORT

Wales is currently in the enviable position of havin at least two freedom loving organisations at work. MEIBION GLYNDWR burning holiday homes in the North, and the WORKERS ARMY OF THE WELSH REPUBLIC planting firebombs along the route of the royal visit and at Tory party offices in the South.
Despite a huge amount of work the police continue to run around in circles.ROBERT GRIFFITHS,secretary of the Welsh Socialist Republican Movement,and JOHN JENKINS OF MAC,are regularly arrested after every bomb attack and just as regularly released.As with the bombing campaign in the late 60's the police are being exposed as the idiots they are - the amount of possible suspects so small,the police saturation coverage so great,yet no results.They resolved this in the 60's with the preposterous FWA conspiracy trial in Swansea....which got mammoth publicity, and three gaol sentences but had nothing to do with the bombing campaign it was supposed to stop.The answer to their complete failure now could there-fore be the same as in the 60'S - another consp-iracy trial.

,As in OPERATION FIRE,last year's massive police swoop in search of second home arsonists,in recent raids in search of the WAWR-bombers those arrested have not been questioned at all about the bomb incid ents - which is somewhat odd to put it mildly.Instea they have been asked about their political beliefs, their reading habits,their friends,and above all, their acquaintance with Robert Griffiths and John Jenkins.

CLASS WAR

MAY 20

'**WE** Must **DEVASTATE**
the **avenues** **WHERE**
the **wealthy Live !**'

LUCY PARSONS . 1e

er be quick about it as well, your t
is running out.

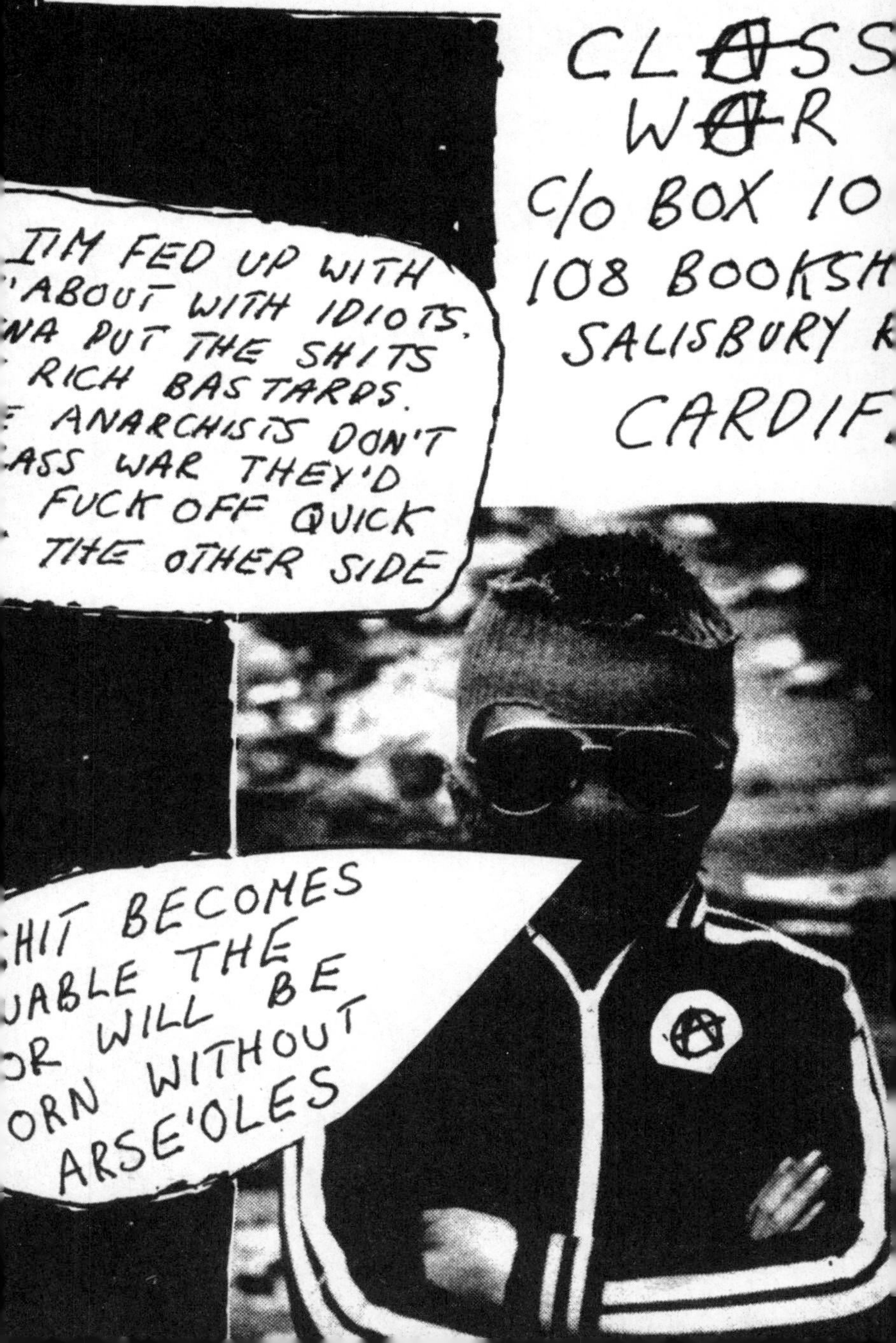

"GISSA TUXEDO.......
..I CAN WEAR THAT."

AUSTRALIAN MOTHER CLAIMS DINGO
TOOK BABY

Lindy Chamberlain, accused of
the killing of her son in the A
yer's ro

nti
ists o
amberl

WHERE WERE THE DINGOS
WHEN WE REALLY NEEDED
THEM?

40,000 join hands in
14-mile nukes demo

SECTION THREE

CLASS WAR

Chapter 14

LET US DESTROY THE AVENUES

Crass's first gig in Swansea with Poison Girls in 1979 had gone very well. I asked them to come back in 1981 to do a benefit for the Welsh Socialist Republican Movement with Dirt and our band the Living Legends – heirs of page 3 and a lot of Page 3's Vetch Field hooligan following turned up high with hate on the rumour that Crass 'were from Cardiff'!! This later transpired to be a rumour based on the fact they had once 'played in Cardiff'!! The Living Legends were first up. I was pissed and ranting and Crass thought I was winding the hooligans up even more as I started advocating the assassination of President Reagan during *Dum Dum Bullets*. In a totally surreal moment, our replacement 'exotic dancer' (Jock Negative was in gaol) leapt on stage dressed as the pope during the wrong song – *God Bless You Queen Mum*. Crass realised now that we weren't exactly in tune with their pacifism and pulled the plug on us. No doubt a few years later when they discovered *Class War* was started by that same purple-haired shit-stirrer, they'd met in Swansea it entrenched their views about us.

Mick Sinclair reviewed the gig in *Sounds*:

'The first group the Living Legends play an odd, uninviting brand of pantomime punk. Each song proceeds at a pedestrian pace and one The Pope is a Dope *features a walking caricature of the Vatican boss. Their grossness and the immature antics of the singer aggravates the more volatile sections of the crowd. The shaven heads of the local football fraternity bellow their rallying cry and seek rival mobs. This could be very ugly.'*

Let Us Destroy The Avenues

It was the political paradox of Crass that was causing me to scratch my bonce post-Burghfield, however, rather than our past dealings. It was later summed up by Jimmy Grimes in *Class War*, No. 2:

'*The only band to carry the musical-politics line forward was Crass. They have done more to spread anarchist ideas than Kropotkin, but like him the politics are up shit creek. Putting the stress on pacifism, they refuse the truth that in the cities, opposition means confrontation and violence if it were to get anywhere.*'

That was it. Crass had found a way of getting anarchist political ideas through to tens of thousands of youngsters. From the plastic As of Rotten's *Anarchy In the UK*, Crass had given the circle As real political meaning. They had created an embryonic political movement – I'd seen it at Burghfield. They'd reached punters in towns, villages and estates that no other anarchist messages could ever hope to reach. But now in 1982 – what were they doing with it? 1981 had changed everything. How could you tell the rioters of July 1981 to be pacifists? People were fighting back but Crass were still telling them to turn the other cheek. They'd achieved something much bigger than I'd previously recognised but now their influence was becoming reactionary, if they persisted in the ideological commitment to pacifism. But – and this was what had struck home to me – the Crass punks at Burghfield didn't behave like pacifists. They were stroppy, upfront, rattling the fence, looking they'd have liked to break through and have a rumble with the dog handlers, if not the dogs. Maybe things were changing. Maybe 1981 had had an effect on the Crass punks, if not Crass. Maybe they were still mouthing the pacifist slogans in their heads but their body language was telling them something else. Contradictions. Maybe Crass were changing – I couldn't know, I wasn't in touch with them following our Swansea fall out. Maybe it was a pivotal point for change which could do with a little push in the right direction. The Burghfield punks had received *Fuck Off* well enough with its incendiary exhortations to fight back. No-one had asked for their 10p back saying it was violent shit and they were pacifists. Maybe the time was right to produce a paper aimed at the Crass punk anarchists and ally them with the 1981 street rioters. You couldn't find the latter to flog the papers to but the former would be easy enough to find at gigs and on demonstrations. Then, when you'd built that up, you could make the riotous links. These were the jumble of thoughts in my head as I headed back to Cardiff after Burghfield – 1 April. By 29 April *Class War* No. 1 had hit the streets.

CLASS WAR NO. 1

Cardiff – The Printer's Tale

I went to see Alex Bird at Fingerprints when I got back to Cardiff. 'How much would 1,000 copies of 4-sided A3 black and white camera-ready artwork be,' I asked. '£75,' said Alex.

London – The Financier's Tale

I bumped into one of the Ladbroke Grove working girls. 'Give us £75 to start up an anarchist paper,' I whispered conspiratorially. She'd had a good weekend at Cynthia's and there was wadges of cash lying around amidst the dope. 'Yes, alright,' she said 'but it had better be fucking good. What is it called?'

'Dunno,' I said.

Swansea – The Class Warrior's Tale

I lugged every old radical magazine I had down to Swansea. Bought some black felt tips, a stencil, some sticky Prit and scissors. No Letraset – couldn't afford it. I arrived at Jimmy Grimes' place Friday evening. He lived with his girlfriend Carolynne and we went to the Mayhill offie to get loads of cans in. It was typical grey, slanting rain-in-for-the-weekend. Swansea weather. Inauspicious circumstances for the seminal breakthrough in radical publishing. We were both agreed – and Carolynne as well before she conked out – that we wanted to produce a newspaper which would put (1) class and (2) violence back at the top of the anarchist agenda. It would be big and tabloid brash, lots of short articles and graphics, no long boring shit. It would be fucking funny as fucking fuck. It would plagiarise and pinch like there was no yesterday. It

Flogging Class War No. 1 at Glastonbury with Jimmy Grimes

would be pro-action and violence. It would look like a punkoid fanzine mutated into a newspaper. It would have blood dripping circled As on the front to flag up our anarchist intentions and buy in those anarchists who only purchased any commodities with As on. It would hate the rich bastards and slag off CND and the Labour Party. It would be madly in-yer-face and up-for-it. No one would have seen anything like it before. We would produce the finished article by Sunday night. It would be called... what the fuck would it be called? Leave that to the end.

We started with no writing at all. We spent all of Friday night cutting pictures, headlines and graphics out of all my precious old mags I'd vowed never to take the scissors to. I'd remembered an old slogan from *Heatwave* magazine which I'd bought from Albert Meltzer's Wooden Shoe bookshop in 1966: 'When shit becomes valuable, the poor will be born without arse'oles'. We had a picture of the kiddie with ski-mask and shades on and had the slogan in a bubble coming out of his mouth. It was the favourite for the cover. Then we came up with this picture of Lady Di and baby William. It was the time of the Lindy Chamberlain 'the dingo took my baby' case. So we stuck a picture of a wolf next to Di and William with the caption 'Where were the dingoes when we really needed them?' That became the frontrunner for the cover at 3am Saturday morning. Then it came to me just like that. We were playing around with the Crass slogan 'Fight war, not wars': 'Fight war, which war, class war'. Class War. CLASS WAR. That's fucking it. CLASS WAR!

Me and comrade Grimes shook on it there and then. Saturday afternoon, we continued. Wrote most of the stuff about the unions, the Labour Party, fuck the right to work, fuck cops, fuck CND, single-issue wanks. Slagged off Yosser Hughs for crossing a picket line – Yosser is a tosser! Pinched some pictures for 'We want the riot to work'. Came up with a cracking picture of some middle-class CNDers holding hands round some base and stuck some bubbles in the mouths. Nice kiddie No. 1 is asking: 'Mummy, if we hold hands right round the base will it really stop the missiles going in?' Mummy: 'Of course darling'. Daddy: 'And the bosses will probably give all the money away to the poor'. Little Baby disagrees: 'Stupid wankers! Fuck the dead end of pacifism. Let's smash the place up!' We laughed for fucking hours at that. Sunday night, we were still fucking convulsed by it. Stomach aching hiccoughing laughter. We knew that it was good. We were fucking excited. Ecstatic. It looked fucking brilliant. Carolynne felt-tip penned in the stencil slogans. Pinched The Angry Brigade's 'If you want peace, prepare for war'. Stuck in Jimmy Heather-Hayes quote just before he died 'I hate the country and its fucking system. I hope Argentina beat Britain and sinks the whole fucking fleet. God rot those shits with their Britain, the Queen, courts, judges and palace. God burn those fucking po-faced shits with their tea and three-piece suites and their money'. RIP Jimmy.

Jimmy was a Teddington punk who'd chucked a petrol bomb into the local cop shop but committed suicide in Ashford Remand Centre. There was a big punk march through Teddington to protest at his death in custody. I'd gone to the inquest with his mum and sister Fran where Gareth Pierce, his solicitor, had secured a lack of care verdict against the governor who me and Fran had a right pop at. It was to the thousands of other Jimmy Heather-Hayes's we knew were out there we were addressing his words. By Sunday afternoon, we had pages two, three and four sorted. Jimmy Grimes had designed the classic *Class War* logo of blood dripping letters and circled As – he'd never drawn anything else before or since in his fucking life. But what to go on the cover? Lucy Parsons was one of my anarchist heroes and I wanted her quote: 'We must devastate the avenues where the wealthy live' to go on the front. Jimmy cut letters out of

Me and Stella flogging Class War

newspaper and stuck it on the front like a ransom demand. It still didn't work though without some threatening image to go with it. Nothing seemed to fit thought – all a bit lame and understated. Then we got lucky again. I'd brought down a copy of *City Limits* with me. In it was a still photo of some ghastly creature from the film *American Werewolf in London*. It was small but I could get it blown up at Fingerprints. It would look fucking great with the Parsons quote. That's it. Done. Not quite. There was still a bit of a gap between 'Class' and 'War' on the cover. I pulled out the skull and crossbones sticker I'd got from the Soldier Dolls in Cardiff. Stuck it on – fitted a treat. Cheers Dolls! The rain's stopped. I swear there was a rainbow over Morriston. We've been in all weekend. Let's get over the Rum Puncheon. Oh yes, and don't give me any fucking bollocks about magazines taking months to get ready. 48 hours had cracked it.

29 April 1983: *Class War* was delivered to an unexpectant world.

Alex printed it quick – he would, he wanted to get it off the premises pronto. I lugged the whole print run up to London on the National Express. It has to be said, initial reactions were not auspicious. I excitedly raced it over to Sean Mason and his girlfriend Stella Coyle at the London Workers Group Meeting in the Metropolitan in Clerkenwell. They burst out laughing – not because they thought it was funny funny, but because they thought it was funny peculiar. Stella couldn't stop laughing all night

– and she was the politically astute one of the twosome. I thought at least all the punters at the LWG meeting would buy a copy but only two did, and the silence was deafening. They seemed to think I was some kind of Trot paper-seller! Could I keep my nerve in the face of such a muted response. Sean kept saying it was 'alright' but 'alright' was not what I wanted. Where was the 'fucking brilliant me old chum'? Had me and Jimmy been laughing at an in-joke. No, I had faith. I knew what made for a good-selling magazine, even if the other anarchists didn't. People have got such a fucking lame idea of what makes good political propaganda – of what the punters want to read rather than what some anarcho with his head up his arse thinks they should want to read. *Class War* was the proof of that pudding! On 7 May, there was to be a Youth CND march to Brockwell Park. Comrade Grimes was coming up from Swansea. Sean and Stella were going to help us sell *Class War* at the Embankment. We'd soon fucking see if I was right or not.

Thank fuck – sunny day. I lugged 600 issues of *Class War* down to the march start. Sean and Stella were waiting. Embarrassed timed wasting while we nervously talk rather than get on with the selling. Whooop! Here we go.

'*Class War* – new anarchist paper – *Class War* – new violent anarchist paper'. We quickly sussed it was the '*Class War* – extremely violent anarchist paper' which was provoking the most interest from the Youth CNDers. People coming up staring perplexedly at the cover. People laughing at the three of us shouting out '*Class War* – new extremely violent anarchist paper' on a peace march. Good humoured reaction, lots of laughs and looking, but no one has actually bought one yet. Someone asks to look at one then hands it back saying it's not worth 20p – in comparison to the size of the leftie papers, *Class War* did not in fact look like 20p well spent. Fucking hang on – someone's buying one off Sean. Only 599 to go. Four or five others step forward. It always happens – once people see someone else buying, they're all up for it. Stella has suddenly got a queue of people clutching 20ps in front of her. People are taking it back to show their friends then they're coming over to buy. We're snowed under – stuck for change. Bingo – they're flying out. Sean and Stella can hardly believe it. We rip open another carrier bag full – as the march goes by we sell about 300. 'Well fucking good!' says Sean. Give the march a miss, tube it to Brixton. Flog the other 300 in Brockwell Park. All fucking gone...

Sean Mason

Sell a load more the following day at a May Day rally in Victoria Park – all the Brixton anarchos buy some – word's got out already from the day before. Drop a load off at Compendium, Freedom, 121, Collets, Housemans. Head back to Cardiff and flog the rest at the Miners' Gala in Bute Park, where a peculiar event occurred. Yorkie and Ian Minton – another flatmate – were waving a copy at Neil Kinnock who was guest speaker. Kinnock thought they were waving the paper to be autographed, grabbed it and signed it before giving it back to a nonplussed Yorkie! Little did Kinnokio know but he'd be seeing us again very soon.

On 29 April, *Class War* No. 1 came out. 13 May sold out. 27 May, got a reprint of another 1,000 done. Ecstatic, back to London, to tell the financier how incorrect her analysis is. She is happier – doesn't want the money back now – just as well as I've spent it on the reprint.

Me and Jimmy go to Glastonbury Festival with the *Class War* reprint, flog the fucking lot and piss away the sales fees. The Ladbroke Grove girls offer to front money for Class War No. 2 – after all we can't go on forever flogging reprints. But we'd never ever thought about No. 2 or whether

Bash The Rich

Class War was to become a regular paper. It was just a one-off, throw the pebble in the pond, light the blue touch paper and wait for the effects. We'd hoped *Class War* might be a catalyst for something – for bringing like-minded class-struggle anarchists together – but it hadn't dawned on us that *Class War* might be a regular newspaper. Anyway, maybe we'd used all the good stuff in issue one – was there anything else besides to say. Jimmy had said at Glastonbury that he wouldn't be involved in any more than a second issue, even if we could cobble stuff together for that. While he was in Swansea and me in Cardiff, it had been easy enough but now I'd decided to move back to London permanently. So the *Class War* train waved founder Jimmy Grimes goodbye.

LONDON CLASS WAR IS BORN

Sean and Stella took me down one Friday to meet the rest of the London Anarchist Youth Group (LAYG) at 121. Ian Slaughter, who I'd met at the Bullshit conference, Ron, Gareth, Paul Pethard from Reading (representing the Thames Valley Partisans), Errol and Franco, the 121 chef. Sean had made sure they'd all seen *Class War* by now. Sean had flogged a load to his mates up Kingsbury who'd never normally buy anarchist papers – 'Gone down a treat mate'. Sean was now well – 'well my son' – into *Class War*. It had to keep going to be a second issue. The first issue was now not just 'alright' but 'fucking brilliant'. Stella was on the case as well – 'got to be another one Bonehead,' she told me. So fucking disrespectful these young pups. The tide of enthusiasm from the LAYG was torrential. Best paper ever. Ian Slaughter nodded his more restrained approval 'Yes, not bad'. But Jimmy had dropped out. I told them I couldn't do it on my own. 'No problem,' says Sean. 'I propose the London Anarchist Youth Group is disbanded and we become London Class War'. Unanimously agreed. The sun streamed down on us as we danced down Railton Road to get sloshed in the Atlantic and make future plans. Things were moving at a right old pace – we had the making of a good little mob already. Full steam ahead through the shit! It was a delicious fucking night in the Atlantic with the promise of much more to come.

Sean and Stella agreed to help me get *Class War* No. 2 out. The Tories had won the 1983 election since *Class War* No. 1, so we led on 'Five More Years of this Shit – No Fucking Way', and the classic Crass lyric over Thatcher's photo 'Birds Put the Turd in Custard But Who Put The Shit in No. 10'. Jimmy Grimes contributed an article on punk and 'oi', while Ian Slaughter provided us with the lyrics of *Pigs for Slaughter* by The Apostles which was a pretty good take on Crass pacifism. I got another of my Lucy Parsons quotes on the cover: 'Now is the time for every dirty lousy tramp to lie in wait outside the palaces of the rich and shout to stab them to death as they come out', with suitable illustration of toffs heading for a cheese wire. Stella was a member of Red Action and Sean a close sympathiser so they contributed a Provisional IRA cheerleader piece 'I. I. IRA – Fuck the Queen and the U.D.A.' It was the last time a pro-republican piece was to appear in the paper since our collective view was to become as opposed to Catholic nationalism as we were to Protestant unionism. Stella and Sean invited me to a Red Action meeting in Tottenham Court Road one night – but were gutted when I turned up wearing pink corduroy trousers as they'd promised Red Action a proletarian hard nut. *Class War* No. 2 had a good response from Red Action who wrote a short supportive piece in the next issue of the paper. It looked for a very short while as if some regular joint action, if not an eventual merger might take place. It wouldn't survive their realisation that we weren't cheerleaders for the Provos after all.

Class War No.2 hit the streets on 24 June. Sean had also produced a load of definitive *Class War* stickers. 'Beer first – business later', besides an illustration of foaming pint. 'Bash the rich – but first, where's my pint', with a double illustration of winged Doc Marten boot and foaming pint! Others included: 'Fuck the revolution – where's my beer', 'Our lives will be better when all the rich are dead', 'Buy *Class War* or Fuck Off' and 'Class War: 9 out of 10 rich bastards said their slaves preferred it'.

They perfectly encapsulated the exciting feel and spirit of the paper and those involved. We were serious revolutionaries but not of the martyr kind – we were going to have a fucking good laugh while we smashed the state. The humour of *Class War*'s early days was what was to make it stand out from the ultra-seriousness of the other anarchist and leftie papers with their whining and victim martyr posturings. Since we were now London Class War, as well as a paper, we decided to hold our first ever 'conference' in the Colville pub in Portobello Road on 27 August 1983 – the Saturday of the Notting Hill Carnival weekend. To be honest, I doubt if anyone who was there can really remember what the fuck happened.

We had an all-afternoon lock-in, with even the landlord joining in the political arguments. In attendance were Sean's mob from Kingsbury and some Red Actionists with Stella. The LAYG and a couple of Brixton anarchos, the West London sex workers, assorted Ladbroke Grove bohemians, Alex the situationist, a couple of LWGers, Ray Jones, an old Swansea mate Viv Cory, and Portobello drinking cronies. The 'conference' started at 11am and Sean and co. were well pissed on arrival. There was no chair or agenda. So far as I can recall, there were three very pissed and animated areas of discussion: Stonehenge, IRA, sexual politics.

Kate was a big advocate of the Stonehenge free festival and a regular attendee every year. She said we should all go to the festival, take our clothes off, have group sex and then make a revolution. A fairly simplistic revolutionary programme but not without its attractions. Sean thought everyone who went to Stonehenge – he'd never been himself and neither had I – was a middle-class, life-stylist, soap dodger, crusty, dog on a string, smelly hippie and poured scorn on the Stonehenge proposal, promptly eliciting the first pint being thrown at him by Kate who adopted her disdainful lip-curling posture every time she looked at him and referred to him as a 'proletarian dwarf'. Sean and Ian Slaughter were part of a strong current in *Class War* from the early days who liked dressing 'smart but casual' and contrasting their appearances with the 'soap dodgers'. They then added their own class analysis saying the soap dodgers were all middle class while the smart boys were working class. This led them to the belief that the Stonehenge festival was just a gathering of middle-class life-stylists to be mocked and abused.

It was a sort of proletarian cultural ghettoism – 'we know what working-class people look like and they don't fucking look like that crusty over there'.

It was a position that was to paint *Class War* into a corner, divorced from a lot of its natural allies by a comically narrow version of what working-class behaviour was and was not. It would periodically erupt into disagreements throughout our subsequent history. As opposed to the Mason/Slaughter casuals, Kate was an anarcho-hedonist who didn't give a fuck for the revolutionary potential of the proletariat. On the contrary, she was quite happy to describe them as ignorant pigfuckers – citing comrade Mason as a proof positive of her arguments. I didn't think we should abuse the crusty/hippie/punkoids because they were some of the very people our politics were likely to appeal to in the short term. But I didn't think the Stonehenge festival was the salvation for the working class either.

The next eight hours of the 'conference' meandered in a ramshackle fashion from monogamy to the provos to prostitution and back again. Viv Cory, who'd only just come out of the nick after serving a 12-year sentence for trying to run a comically inept protection racket from my flat in Swansea, collapsed with acute alcohol poisoning towards early evening. From there, the gathering ended in shambles, with the true-Brit pub landlord trying to strangle the Provo activist Sean Mason in a neck-crunching headlock. The whole meeting had been conducted in front of a good crew of Colville regulars drinking with us during the afternoon lock-in. So much for secret conspiratorial meetings! I can truly say with the benefit of acute political hindsight that the conference achieved absolutely fuck all but that the process of achieving fuck all was hugely enjoyable.

Kate decided that her flat would do for the after-conference love-in since Stonehenge was ruled out. I had other plans. On the Saturday before the Notting Hill Carnival, the Ladbroke Grove shops all get boarded up after trading in case of Monday night rioting. I'd decided that these boards would make ideal platforms for a *Class War* graffiti campaign – in view of the half million punters who'd be pouring through the area in the next two days. I loaded up with my spray cans and graffitied the whole of Ladbroke Grove and Portobello Road. Move over Dr Alimantado. Anything that wasn't boarded up, I sprayed as well – banks, shops, the fucking lot – in full view of crowds of punters.

They still stick the same boards up now, so my faded red paint graffiti still gets its annual airing, while the newly-gentrified Colville awaits the erection of the *Class War* heritage trail blue plaque.

SEXPOL!

Class War was somewhat unusual in its composition in that sex workers made up a significant section of its early London membership. There was a group of feisty, proselytising, articulate and up for it girls from Paddington and Ladbroke Grove — 'The Class Whores' who weren't on the game full time but would supplement their income by occasionally working at Cynthia Payne's 'Luncheon Voucher' parties in

Streatham. They were upfront about where the cash came from and generous about splashing it about in the Portobello pubs. Since anyone who sold their labour power was a prostitute you'd be mad not too maximise your earning power when you had the chance. Wouldn't ya!

Some of them also occasionally linked up with Tuppy Owens — publisher of The Sex Maniacs Diary and organiser of 'Sex for the disabled' parties. By way of contrast to the services provided by Cynthia Payne, Tuppy Owens did provide a much needed service in providing sex for severely disabled people who would otherwise never get the opportunity. A service much more appreciated by the users than an endless push around horrid luncheon clubs and looming Patricia Hewitt faces asking 'how are we today dear?'. In contrast to Cynthia Payne's traditional views that men were 'the superior of the species' and that 'women are either hard or scatter brained' Tuppy Owens had the air of the genuine sexual liberationist.

Their work was giving them a fairly unique slant on sexual politics running against the anarcha-feminist of the time. Most women in the anarchist movement were organising separately as anarcha-feminists but they didn't buy into 'sisterhood'. The early Class War issue 'One From The Girls' was pointedly subtitled 'For all the Women Who Fuck Us Over' - a line made easier by the fact that Thatcher was Prime Minister. Class War naturally put class consciousness not gender consciousness as the way to fight back so this line slotted neatly

Bash The Rich

into our class analysis. Class War's 'class not gender' line estranged itself from the anarcha-feminist separatist women but early Class War was distinguished by having a strong presence of women in it. The pro-pornography and pro-prostitution line was always going to be called into question by other Class War women at some time — but not just yet.

There were some bizarre forays into the politics of prostitution after linking up with Helen Buckingham — the 'Prostitutes Rights Campaigner' as it said on her calling card and second only to Cynthia Payne in the notoriety stakes. They're in ideological battle with the Kings Cross Wimmins Centre for the soul of the prostitutes politics movement. XXXX has been to hear Selma James talk about Wages for Housework. XXXX is not in favour of either! Selma James and Wilmette Brown are running all sorts of campaigns from the Kings Cross Centre — Wages for Housework, Wages due lesbians, Payday (paid housework for homosexuals!) — and are very much held in awe by the gullible. One of Selma's many front organisations is the English Collective of Prostitutes. 'Wrong on all counts,' says XXXX at Selma's public meeting. 'They're not English, they're not a collective, and their not prostitutes'. That is to say they are all Selma's pre-programmed transatlantic pals, there's no collective decision making 'cos they do what Selma and Wilmette tell them, and none of them are prostitutes — they're just self-appointed spokeswomen for prostitutes trying to hoover up the media franchise thinking actual working girls are too dumb to do it for themselves. Disagreeing with Selma and Wilmette was shock enough for the Wimmins Centre 'lets play whores' but the lip curling, cheek v-signing, parting remark of 'who'd pay to fuck her anyway' caused a collective swoon among the sisters.

Helen had a bit of a Mary Magdalene fixation so they dream up a plan to occupy a church in Kings Cross as a prostitutes' base. In the event they persuade the ECP to make up the numbers and occupy the church. A perfect photo of Helen appears in the Evening Standard holding her baby Jesus baby, looking pleadingly up at the altar and looking a dead ringer for Madonna and child. Highly offensive!

It's not all bad taste though — oh by no means — another Class War supporting working girl with a flat in Paddington had as a punter an aristocratic Scottish lord (no I couldn't get his name out of her — very ethical they were) who liked to be abused while he was whipped. 'You rich fucking bastard!' she screamed as his blood flecked buttocks turned beetroot. 'You rich fucking scumbag!' He always gave her a big tip. 'Sounds like you really mean it' he used to say. She donated the fees to Class War and if the Scottish lord had ever looked under her bed he'd have discovered the Class War banners she was sewing in the dead time between punters ready for October 23rd.

A rich brew was Class War. Funny as fuck.

Chapter 15

CND OCTOBER 1983

Having no place of my own to live was getting a bit on the debilitating side, so I squatted a flat on the Ashburton Estate in Putney with my old Cardiff flatmate Paul Pritchard, a vegetarian who survived solely on a diet of rich tea biscuits. Four weeks later, some scumbag broke in and stole my sleeping bag and my two binbags of clothes. They also broke my only plastic spoon! At this point in life, September 1983, I did not have a single possession in the world apart from the clothes I wore. I had no money in the bank, no savings, no cash apart from a fortnightly giro, no toothbrush, no change of socks. I was fucked. I was absolutely, comprehensively fucked.

I moved into the Leinster Hotel just off Westbourne Grove. They charged £75 a week for bed and breakfast but the DHSS paid and it was quite flash, not the dossers' hostel I feared. A room of my own with telephone, late bar until 2am, laundry and TV lounge. It give me a stable base, at least for a few months to look after my body a bit better, cut down on the boozing, and relax a bit in my own space after a frenetic summer and not have to spend money walking the streets all day. Anyway, signing on at Lisson Grove always had its absurdist moments of quiet desperation to look forward to every week.

We'd started work on *Class War* No. 3 at Sean's place in Kingsbury. The idea was to get it out in time for the October CND demo in Hyde Park. We came up with a cracking cover – picture of miles and miles of gravestone crosses with the caption: 'We have found new homes for the rich'. The CND rally was going to be our big push forward. We were going to have our first physical presence as *Class War*. Brenda was making loads of black and red *Class War* banners between punters and stashing them under the bed she worked on.

News suddenly came through of a big CND rally at Islington Town Hall. Full *Class War* mobilisation – that meant 20 people – and Ian Slaughter said Martin Wright and a few others would join us. All well pissed, we occupied two rows of seats in the middle of the hall and did some aggressive paper-selling. Martin's brother Danny got into about

jerking off in Islington town hall as the BUAV bureaucrats wanted.

KINNOCK PELTED

LABOUR leader Neil Kinnock was pelted with cans and bottles as he spoke at Britain's biggest ever ban-the-bomb rally yesterday.

He was the target of a mob of flag-waving anarchists who had surged to the front of a crowd of more than 200,000 in London's Hyde Park. After shouting "Liar, liar" repeatedly, they showered missiles on to the stage from which Mr Kinnock was speaking.

Police pounced on the 100-strong anarchist faction and dragged away youths and girls, three of them bleeding from cut heads.

They then drove the group back into the crowd before forming a three-deep guard on the stage.

ANSWER

Mr Kinnock did not appear to have been hit by any of the missiles and continued his speech unruffled.

Earlier another group of anarchists in studded black leather jackets tried to take over the stage while Liberal MP Paddy Ashdown spoke. Six were arrested.

While he was at his oratory, black flags unfurled in front of him. Half an hour before there had been 18 of them. As he spoke, the number of flags grew to 30 or so, sticks and a shoe were hurled through the air, the police moved in, and four men, that I saw, were dragged out of the crowd. By the time Mr Kinnock was quoting Tennyson on a thousand years of peace, quite an active little riot was in progress

But earlier I had bought for 10p, a news-sheet called Class War. Plainly it had nothing to do with CND, Under a headline, "Rich Bastards Beware"

So why do we have this unity of the anarchist establishment, the pacifists and the aspiring bureaucrats of the animal liberation movement against us? BECAUSE THEY'RE SHIT SCARED OF THE SUCCESS WE'RE HAVING..because we do not water down our class hatred or our commitment to class violence as the only way to get rid of the rich scumbags and politicians who run our lives..... because we are commited to the building of a fighting, combative, anarchist movement.....because we believe that revolutionary change is still on the agenda unlike the anarchist establishment which happily accepts its status as the 'permanent minority voice of reason'. Because the pacifists are seeing the coll-apse of their CND/Peace camps strategy as its impotence becomes obvious to their troops who they have led to the top of th the hill and led down again as they did in the 60s.They fear a turn to violent action by those disillusioned with holding hands and singing.Similarly the bureaucrats of the BUAV fear the growing militancy of the animal liberation movement, the increased daring of its attacks on property and confrontations with the police.On the contrary we warmly welcome the increased ferocity of these attacks and will do our best to extend them into

POLICE ATTACKS ON ANIMAL LIBERATION MARCHES, AS AT CARSHALTON ABOVE, ARE DESCRIBED AS "UNFORTUNATE" BY THE B.U.A.

At the same time approximately 50 people at the front decided to sit down in the road. Mingling amongst these were the agitators. After a while this protest became more aggressive, with insults and taunts were thrown at the police who up until then had handled things quietly.

Added to this BUAV organisers were aware that a small infiltration of National Front type agitators masquerading as Anarchists were present distributing leaflets which were crude, insulting violent and speciesist.

The atmosphere became more aggressive, and police from behind unfortunately chose to charge in as the tail end of the demo filed past. Scuffles broke out and arrests were made

135

three push-and-shove fights in the first five minutes. I'm not sure he's over keen on me either – he keeps asking Martin if we're on the same side. The idea was to wait until main men Tony Benn and Bruce Kent speak, but, as always, we're always too rat-arsed and excitable to keep any self-discipline. Poor old Leon Rosselson gets a volley of underserved abuse. Heckling, chanting, a stream of insults hits every speaker. Every mention of peace is met with chants of 'Class War, Class War'. It's very fucking enjoyable, we're in our element – the meeting is brought to a standstill. We're demanding to have a speaker from the stage. They grant our wish hoping it will shut us up. The honour falls on me. I stand in front of Bruce Kent ready for my first ever speech to a big London audience. I'm too drunk. I gesture bewilderedly at Bruce Kent with my thumb 'See 'im – 'e's a fucking vicar – 'e is, 'es a fucking vicar'. That was it. It still gets wild acclaim from the Class Warriors. The cops are called – more argy-bargy fracas without any real spilt blood. A good bit of bonding with Martin and Co, all well pleased. The hatchet seems buried at last – and not in my head!

'Anarchists Wreck CND Meeting,' screamed the *Islington Gazette*. We have moved beyond talk to ACTION. A week later, we go down to a Newham Seven demo. The Revolutionary Communist Party are being self-importantly pissy with the organisers demanding their banner heads the march. We shove them out the way. The RCP say we're acting like fascists. We say they're acting like the middle-class plonkers they are. The two skirmishes set us in good heart for the big one. We gather our forces in an Islington boozer the night before the Hyde Park rally to discuss tactics – but as always its 'beer first, business later,' and fuzzy alcoholic brains and fatty livers only produce wild threats and over-hyped aspirations.

Blinking into the sunlight of Embankment Station are me, Doc Whelan, Lloyd and Brenda with eight split carriers bags jammed full of *Class Wars*, six banner poles and flags and, amazingly, no fucking hangover. There are loads of leftie paper-sellers but none of our lot.

CND October 1983

Nothing for it but to get stuck in to the paper-selling right away. We out shout the lefties and *Class War* flies out like fuck. The sales pitch acts as a meeting place for the rest. By 11.30am, we're mostly together – Martin, Ian, Charlie, Ron, Phil, Steve, Sean, Stella. We feel confident we'll be up for it. The CND stewards are starting to form the front of the march for the usual CND VIPs – Joan Ruddock, Bruce Kent, Tony Benn, various dog-collared radicals. Adrenalin rush as we stop the papers sales, get our smart as fuck *Class War* Brenda-stitched black and red flags hoisted up and move into the VIP space at the front. We kick the crash barriers over and take the head of the march. The CND stewards politely tell us the march won't move off until Ruddock and Co are allowed at the front of the CND foot sloggers. So fucking what – we couldn't give a fuck if the march moves off or not. Mason starts his singing, jabbing his finger at the astonished mass of assembling CNDers:

'Fuck off back to Hampstead – la, la, la, la'
'Where's my soup with croutons – la, la, la, la'
'I drink in wine bars – la, la, la, la'
'Where's my poodle salon – la, la, la la.'

Sean's equation of the CND middle class with poodle salons always seemed a bit odd – I thought it rather spoilt an otherwise outstanding song. Altogether now. 'Fuck off back to Hampstead – la, la, la, la.'

Most people were totally bemused, but we were in full throttle – our flags and general buzz bringing all the anarchos with us. The stewards made several half-hearted attempts to physically shove us out the way, but we stood our ground and shoved back. Only a small thing but it was good to see people standing up and not bottling out of what they'd agreed to do in the pub the night before. Gradually we got by-passed as Ruddock and Co gave up the idea of a VIP-led march and the police pushed other sections of the march past us. Sean Mason was just launching into his 26th chorus of *Fuck Off Back to Hampstead* into

Bash The Rich

the bemused faces of Stoke Poges Ex-Servicemen's CND Group when he's lifted from within our midst and nicked by the cops before any of us noticed it was happening. Our cheerleader arrested, we decide to move off before we end up at the back of the march unable to execute the more ambitious storming of the Hyde Park stage.

Ron gets nicked en route for shouting 'jump, jump' at some filming estate agents on a rooftop, but apart from that, we were all in Hyde Park by 1.30pm. Papers sales until 3pm, then we'll go for it. The delayed onset hangover starts to hit me after half an hour of hectic selling and I slump down in the sunshine alongside some teenage Crass punks.

Although the head's pounding I liked the imagined image of myself with shiny shaved head, leather jacket ,black shirt and trousers and the day's going pretty good so far.

'Hello Ian, are these all your followers?' It's Adrienne smiling wryly as she gently goads me. I'd known Adrienne from Swansea 1978 punk days. I'd conspicuously failed to get off with her then and she'd always been pretty sarcastic about my 'revolutionary' activities in the past. But we'd bumped into each other at the Notting Hill carnival in August and enjoyed winding each other up with some flirty bantering. I'd been a bit vexed afterwards that I hadn't got her phone number when she left. Anyway here she was, in typical well-organised Adrienne fashion, sharing her tuna sandwiches with me when I whinged that I was starving. I mean who'd bring tuna sandwiches on a march? Ha! Ha! My turn to take the piss. I told her we were going to storm the stage at 3pm. 'Oh well I'll watch out for that then,' she said with a more than willing suspension of disbelief. She flounced off with her pals leaving me with her last tuna sandwich – 'you'll need the energy' – and her phone number!

Time to get up for the mob forming at Speakers' Corner. We'd spread the word when paper-selling and there's about 80 of us at 3pm – including the young dervish himself Sean Mason who's already been charged and bailed by the cops. I've often wondered what it must have looked like from elsewhere as we set off on our bee-line from Speakers Corner to take the stage 400 yards away. The flags attracted the rag tag and bobtail anarchists and 200 yards from the thronged stage, we were about 150 strong.

Then opposition! A single police inspector came forward hand upraised bringing our on-rush to a halt. We all stop. It's a defining moment. Unless

Adrienne shares her tuna sandwich

someone's up for it, *Class War* will be stillborn. Cometh the hour, cometh the man. Step forward unlikely *Class War* superhero Paul Pritchard, my old flat mate from Cardiff. Biff bang, a solid right to the coppers' face – the most laconic but precious solid right I've ever seen – and Inspector Fuckface eats Hyde Park dirt. The onrush is resurrected. The crowds cleave before us but we're too fucking early. No Kinnock. The plan is to storm the stage with Kinnockio speaking. Deferred gratification was never a *Class War* virtue, and how to keep our hyped-up mob happy while waiting for an hour for Kinnockio is a major problem.

There are now about 300 of us and the CNDers pull back leaving us facing a load of coppers who are pouring in to protect the front of the stage. Surprise has gone. Spasmodic clumps of mud and grass fly towards the cops. They charge forwards 20 yards then retreat, pushing, shoving, shouting, spitting. A few cans go on stage, just missing the warbling Leon Rosselson (nothing personal honest Leon!).

Next up is silver-mained EP Thompson, author of *The Making of the English Working Class*, a book we all hold in great esteem and whose mob traditions we even feel we're part of. But no matter – Doc Whelan's limited patience threshold has been well and truly breached. He has a glass cider flagon which he was reserving for Kinnockio but decided 'some fucking professor' will do just as well for a target. He has a sighting heave with a piece of concrete which whistles past EP Thompson's locks on a still rising trajectory. He starts to spin like a hammer thrower with the flagon as the hammer. E P Thompson's health is seriously at risk, and I'm doing fuck all to protect one of my favourite authors from decapitation. Thankfully, others aren't so paralysed. A firm arm grabs Doc's wrist – a move usually likely to incur the dreaded Whelan forehead crunching down on the bridge of your nose. Happily, Doc recognises the owner of the arm as Penny Rimbaud. 'He's not the one who deserves that,' says Penny, 'save it for later'. Wise words and Doc concurs.

We don't have long to wait. Kinnockio takes the stage. We surge forwards and a quite vicious ruck begins. The delayed cider flagon missile zooms just over Kinnockio's head looking as if it will still be rising when it hits the moon. One foot lower and Doc would have changed

the course of Labour history! Clods of earth, cans, banner poles, reign down on the stage. A group of about a dozen break through the cops lines and clamber over the crash barriers at the edge of the stage before being forced back. Dick's Pompey footie mob are well to the fore as are the Roseberry Avenue Peace Squat Punks. 'Peace Punks'? This is really the day things start to change from 'Peace Punks' to 'Class War Punks'. Our aim from Burghfield onwards is playing out before us. The cops charge into the crowd and we charge back. Several cops are isolated and given a good kicking. Kinnockio's speech stumbles as the wider crowd is drawn in. CNDers beg us to stop fighting – we're destroying the rally. Who are we, they ask incredulously. One burly proletarian comes up to Martin and gives him a fiver for the 'boys and girls'. All Brenda's hard

Class War storm the Kinnock stage – the pivotal moment when the anarcho-punks abandoned Crass pacifism

work on the banners is lost as they're grabbed by the cops. The ruck lasts 20 minutes before the rally comes to a premature end. Comedian Tony Allen comes up to me and shouts that he hopes I'm fucking proud of myself. 'Yes, I fucking am Tony. Fucking brilliant. We're on our fucking way'. He shakes his head and later produces a very funny cartoon (see page 144) mocking our ferocity, which we've put on for the TV cameras as he sees it.

But we're pleased as punch. Everyone's acquitted themselves well. We've made our first mark outside the anarcho-ghetto. The shit has hit the fan. The CND wankers and Kinnochio got what was coming and we didn't allow any arrests. Brenda, Suzie, Martin, Steve, Ian, Doc and me head for the nearest boozers on Edgware Road. Suzie tells me she fancies a fuck. A strange thought entered my head. I am 36 years old and I'd never had sex with a woman who isn't from Swansea (including the Neath Valley). 'You're not from Swansea are you, Suzie?' I blurted out. She looked at me simple like.

Then we head to the Burn It Down Ballroom – a squatted venue miles away in Finchley where the old Cardiff Living Legends are to perform a shambolic drunken set in the evening. Swamped by beer showers, falling arse-over-head on alcohol-drenched floors and throwing and spitting beer back at Martin, Steve, Sean and the rest of the 'audience'. A *Class War* bonding session to seal the day. Kate turns up – heads off home with Martin, Suzie and the rest. Me and Brenda taxi it back to Paddington and drink ourselves to euphoric sleep. We're up early for the Sunday papers to read about ourselves. Have we made it onto the front page? YES! 'Kinnock Flees Anarchist Mob' and 'Leather Jacketed Youths Storm Stage'. We're delirious. Fucking euphorically fucking delirious. We stay in bed all day – hangovers clearing for a late afternoon giggling attempted fuck. Then off to Kings Cross for the Sunday night *Class War* meeting. Should be a good one.

Class War met every Sunday night at the Prince Albert just off York Way in Kings Cross. Attendance was small, but the hard work since issue 1 in May was paying off. Regular attendees were the London Autonomists (Martin, Steve and Ian Slaughter), London Anarchist Youth Group (Ron, Sean Mason and Gareth), the Red Actionists (Stella and Tim), the Albany Street Squatters (Tim Paine and Spike), the London Workers' Group (Phil Gard and Andy Walker), the Situationists (Alex and Leah) and the Ladbroke Grove Sex Workers.

We'd managed to pull in most of the London Anarchists who had similar politics to ours. We had a viable base in numbers at least, though most of those attending would not as yet consider themselves as part of *Class War*. Martin considered that *Class War* was one part of a 'current', but not the only part, and was keen to continue the separate existence of the London Autonomists. I was more of a build the organisation person and was keen for everyone to be part of *Class War* and leave their separate identities behind. That Sunday was a good step in building that shared identity out of the euphoria of the previous day and that morning's headlines. It was the biggest meeting we'd had. The politics were easy: keep the momentum going to the next event which was the Animal Liberation March on the Biorex laboratories in Islington in two weeks' time.

Some of us weren't particularly committed to animal liberation at the time but we knew that was where the action was to be had and that our future recruits were going to come from the activists in that broad movement. There were lots of jokes about lentils and sandals and a quick chorus of 'Meat means dinner' as opposed to the Animal Rights' Movement's 'Meat means murder'. Tim Paine and Spike, who were Animal Liberationists, were gamely not put off by our beefy posturings. We'd lost most of the issues of *Class War* we hadn't sold in the rucking at Hyde Park. We couldn't get a new *Class War* out in time so we decided to rush out a leaflet – *Vermin in Ermine* – which I was to write. We reckoned 1,000 would do and scraped together the £30 we needed thanks to generous donations from the Ladbroke Grove girls..

Illustration of Class War at the CND demo by Tony Allen

THE TIGERS OF WRATH
THAT THIS IS A PEACEFU
EVEN IF THEY ARE WISER THAN

Chapter 16

BIOREX

The march on Biorex was organized by the British Union for the Abolition of Vivisection (BUAV). We'd already picked up on their annoyance with Animal Liberation Front (ALF) militant-type activities and could see they were a reformist Labour Party-like group and that it might be possible to deepen the divide between them and the ALF. We didn't want to recruit the ALFers in to Class War but we did want to establish a common base of direct action militancy with them. Biorex would show that we meant business, the same as they did.

Adrienne had expressed an interest in coming on the Biorex march and had invited me over to her flat in Clapton for a meal the night before. I presumed it would just be me and her but to my surprise, and mucho fucking annoyance, a third plate was laid for Stewart, her boyfriend! She'd failed to mention her fucking boyfriend! I took it badly and got very drunk down the pub after dinner, insulted everyone including Adrienne and fell off my chair before crashing out on her living room floor whilst she cosied up with Stewart in the bedroom. That was it, I thought, but the following morning Stewart mega fucked up over breakfast by repeatedly moaning about the quality of the porridge Adrienne had made for us. Me? I lapped it up: 'Delicious... please may I have some more' and piled on the compliments as Adrienne got visibly fed up with Stewart's moans. Much to my surprise, she decided to come to Biorex with me gamely choosing to ignore the previous nights abuse.

We gathered at the Cock and Hen pub in Highbury but quickly moved off to dish out our *Vermin in Ermine* leaflet, which bombed badly. I wasn't used to writing leaflets for animal liberationists and besides I'd used the word 'rats' as a term of abuse. We were roundly condemned for 'Speciesism' which put us into a decidedly 'what a load of wankers' mood leading to a heartening rendition of 'meat means dinner' as we

FOR A DIGNIFIED AND EFFECTIVE DEMONSTRATION

Brought to you by the ALL-LONDON UNITED ALLIANCE OF SOCIALIST AUCUSES to whom the following are signatories: G.L.C., London Labour Party, T.U.C., W.P., W.R.P., I.M.G., C.N.D., Ecology Party, Y.C.L., and B.F.

CORRECT

INCORRECT

e welcome everyone to today's demonstration, which we hope will be amongst the ggest London has seen for many years. We are confident that the vast majority of you ll keep intact your dignity. A disciplined rally is essential if we are to avoid discrediting rselves in the eyes of the public and losing the approval of the police. We want to give e media no reason to condemn our campaign by pointing to any over-imaginative acts. this end, we call on everyone to obey the dictates of the stewards who will be found ongside the police. They will be acting in your interests. They are sensible people — ease be sensible with them. Beware of troublemakers — some may be in the crowd with u. If you see any do not hesitate to summon stewards or the police, who, we must member, are our brothers in work. Comrades! Even in a socialist society we shall still ed Specialists-In-Order to combat hooligans and deviants. While it's true that nowadays e police are occasionally over-zealous in their protection of privilege, property, and the olence of the world market, the best way of dealing with this is by demanding public countability through elected local government or some other representation of sub- issive community. In the meantime we should recognize that they will only listen to our mplaints if we conduct ourselves in the correct manner.

Bash The Rich

Tim Paine

passed the butchers' shops in Essex Road. Outside Biorex, things took a sharp turn for the better. The BUAV were anxious for us to pause briefly outside the laboratory gates then move quickly on to a hot air rally of labourites at Islington town hall. Fuck that, we thought, let's stop the march outside the gates - trouble would then surely follow. The ALFers sat down, blocking the road while we hovered on the fringe of the sit-down urging others to stay put and not go to the town hall. Sitting down was never our cup of tea since – it smacked of passive resistance and we had something more active in mind. People often wondered why so few of us ever got nicked on demonstrations when we were rucking with the police. Basically, if you use your wits, anyone with half a brain can keep mobile, clock the movements of the cops, and spot escape routes.

If you're sitting down, you're at the mercy of whatever the cops do and end up getting nicked or clouted. Also, sitting down is often the pre-cursor of the dreaded music and juggling which is the kiss of death for any hope of trouble. Still, we welcomed the ALF sit-downers since the fighting would surely start when the cops tried to clear the road. Cops asked us to clear the road over their megaphone and were met with a shower of sticks and stones. Cops charged sit-downers and we fought cops hand-to-hand punching, kicking and barging them over. Cops retreat whilst we urge the sit-downers to stand up and fight. Many do but some leg it to the town hall. We spot additional cops preparing to charge our rear and block our major escape route. We move to the other side to continue fighting and to be nearer another escape route. Shit! Some cops we hadn't spotted charge from the back and about 20 of us get pushed to the ground over a low wall. The cops are clinging on to try to make arrests. Adrienne is knocked to the floor. I grab her hand and pull her from the struggling melee and we leg it down a side road.

Four hundred yards later, I'm still holding her hand. I'm conscious I no longer need to because the cops our nowhere near us. I'm conscious she knows I no longer need to hold her hand but she shows no signs of wanting to let go either. Fucking hell, love on the barricades. Romantic or what? We make it to the town hall where all our mob are reforming outside. Susie's been nicked but everyone else got away. The BUAV bureaucrats try to bar our entry to the town hall but we barge past them and occupy seats to the side of the stage. We interrupt the speaker: 'Why are the BUAV continuing with this meeting when the cops are battering people outside Biorex? Why did BUAV not defend the direct actionists but insist on moving to this waste of space rally at the town hall?'

The chair threatens to call the cops to have us thrown out. Brilliant! What could expose the collaborationist nature of the BUAV more than that? We demand a speaker and get one. Ron takes the stage mandated to attack BUAV, support direct action and plug *Class War*. He says five words with a leery smile on his face: 'Hitler was a fucking vegetarian' and lurches drunkenly off stage, oh dear. That's not done a lot to articulate our position, but fuck it, time to get to the boozer for the after-match analysis. Everyone is pleased – another result! Two punch ups in three weeks with us at the centre, only a couple of arrests and the reformists fucked over. Even Aleks, the doubting situationist, was upbeat. Some of the ALFers from the anarchist squats in Wood Green join us. Martin did his side of the mouth conspiratorial whisper to me that Tim Paine would make 'an excellent bureaucrat' which he subsequently did in answering the *Class War* mail, keeping subscription lists and filing back issues.

I was more interested in Adrienne than Tim's bureaucratic potential, but my style was cramped by Susie (released from Islington nick) sitting on my knee all night. But we both knew we'd end up at Adrienne's at the end of the night, this time with me cosied up and Stewart locked out in the cold. These Saturdays were getting better and better.

Chapter 17

AUTONOMANIA

By the end of 1983, some political differences were already emerging in the Class War group which couldn't be wished away in favour of 'action'. Aleks was our last remaining situationist, adherent with his Italian autonomist girlfriend Leah. Unlike his ex-mate Nick Brandt, who could only grimace with horror at the very mention of the vulgar *Class War*, Aleks saw some positive things in *Class War*. He was however a wary critiquer of Sean Mason's 'working-classism' – that is Sean's belief that anything working class was intrinsically good. This wasn't just used to dismiss any objections to out-of-order behaviour as 'middle class' but glorified what was in fact some of the worst aspects of working-class culture.

Aleks and Leah volunteered to produce *Class War* No. 4. At this time, anyone who was associated with the group could just go off and write the next issue. There was no discussion of articles at meetings or desire for editorial control by the group as a whole. Me, Sean and Stella had effectively produced No. 3 and were quite happy to have a rest and let Aleks and Leah produce the next one.

Class War No. 4 is totally unlike any other issue of the paper. Aleks and Leah produced a paper which contained a sustained and cogent intellectual attack on the Mason position but which had none of the populism or propaganda values of the earlier issues. It was more of an internal discussion document than a newspaper and proved extremely hard to sell with its perplexing 'We have our own idea of time and motion' cover. You pays your money and you makes your choice – it was either one of the best *Class Wars* ever, or one of the worst.

I didn't really understand its content at the time and just thought Aleks had no fucking idea of how to produce a populist paper. Looking back now, the article had a lot going for it and should have led to a wider and more careful discussion leading to a more rigorous analysis of our future actions. Anyway, here's what Aleks and Leah wrote:

'You cannot separate class from struggle. Class warfare creates the class. Single-issue campaigns only produce single-issue groups. Without struggle, 'class' just means your background. And the world's full of people of working-class origin who survive by arse-licking, conformity, working for the nation. Some admire the rich, some vote Tory. Until they do something to combat the system, they'll continue to promote individual interests over class interests. Coming from a working-class background isn't enough: many cops come from there as well.

Britain has got the oldest working class in the world. The pride of this class in its distinctive character, its culture, language and traditions has a useless as well as a positive side.

Positive: self assertion and confidence, and a healthy suspicion of middle-class trendies and political parties who claim to speak on our behalf.

Useless: inverted snobbery which boasts such miserable compensations for impotent poverty like machismo, tepid beer, football, ignorance, dignity of labour… in political terms, this snobbery was exploited by Labourism. Labour politicos and Trade Union bureaucrats are class traitors.

It's not enough just to defend the class as it is today, class liberation has got to be the goal of struggle. So let's hear less about how the class is sexist, racist, submissive, and so ignorant it can only understand The Sun, and more about how the class transforms itself, how individual and social change actually happens. It's not simply the system that brainwashes the passive masses, rather it's the active antagonists (which include most of the people some of the time and some of the people most of the time) who by their actions force the system to change. Capitalism

CLASS WAR

WE HAVE OUR OWN IDEA

OF TIME AND MOTION

152

*would never have altered since the 19th century if everyone had
merely co-operated. But the class doesn't co-operate – it refuses to
work on the bosses' terms, it refuses to obey the laws of property.*

*Self organisation and class transformation also means getting
away from habitual and pathetic aspirations, like being satisfied
with an extra pound in your pocket or trading your birthright for
a bag of chips. The wealth we produce is immense, the desires we
could make real are legion. At least we can aspire to take ALL the
good things in life from the rich. The working class is antagonistic
or it is nothing.'*

The whole paper was a brave exposition of Marx's dictum that a
class is only a class when 'it's a class for itself', that is class conscious.
For a paper called *Class War,* it was important to be clear on this but the
composition of London Class War at the time was not given to careful
discussion. Sean Mason was fuming. He saw it as a personal attack. Leah
was told to: 'Fuck off back to Italy' and the Masonists burned a large
number of issue No. 4 in the back garden in Kingsbury while they danced
cider-bottle naked around the burning pyre with black flags. Sales in our
usual London outlets were poor and our previous buyers perplexed to
say the least. The unrelenting negative feedback and abuse from Sean
Mason led to Aleks and Leah quitting the Class War group and 'working
classism' was left unchallenged. 'We're all racist and sexist but so what?'
Sean had written once. 'But what the fuck – we're working class.'

WILD IN THE CITY

Two other events towards the end of 1983 led us to believe that *Class
War* was reflecting a change in attitude away from pacifism towards the
creation of a more combative social movement. On 29 September, the
first Stop The City action had taken place outside the Mansion House.

Bash The Rich

In many ways, it seemed like the dying embers of pacifism, non-violent direct action and the peace camps, to be followed only a few weeks later by the fighting in Hyde Park and six months later by the second Stop The City full-scale riot.

I'd written in an article entitled *Wreck the City!* in *Class War* No. 5 disparaging the pacifist Stop The City thus:

> *'Standing outside the Mansion House at the Stop The City action on 29 September, things were looking well good. About 300 anarchists were chanting 'fuck off!' as the toe rag of a Lady Lord Mayor was installed. The chances of inflicting some severe damage on the Old Bill and the rich brat stockbrokers they were protecting were looking very rosy. But then the dreaded 'Upper Heyford disease,' signs of which I had diagnosed earlier in the day, proved it was still at epidemic proportions among those present.*
>
> *The main symptom of this wasting disease, which is 100% fatal, is a complete paralysis which makes resistance to the police impossible even when they are heavily outnumbered. The paralysis also attacks the brain resulting in its victims patting police horses, chatting to the filth and voluntarily getting themselves arrested in the absurd delusion that this constitutes 'direct action' of some kind. As sufferers of this dread disease were taken away for treatment, fellow sufferers made no attempt to pull them back or to attack the vans taking them to the treatment centres. At the end of the day, there was one broken window, no police or stockbrokers put in hospital, and 203 arrests! 203 arrests for one fucking broken window!*
>
> *This was naturally hailed as a great success in the anarchist press, considered to be a far greater triumph than the Oxford Street fiasco the previous year when 48 anarchists were arrested for causing even less damage. Join the Class War mob at Stop The City on 29 March. If you want peace, prepare for war.'*

Shortly afterwards, a big punk squat was opened up as a peace centre in Roseberry Avenue in Islington. Martin, Ian and me had gone along to argue for a united anarchist mob to storm the stage at the CND rally. Though we encountered a lot of opposition we were able to pick out quite a few potential class warriors and the Roseberry Avenue punks had been right at the forefront of the fighting in Hyde Park.

In particular, we'd come across two lively and articulate anarchists in Tim Paine and his mate Spike who subsequently opened up a squatted bookshop on Albany Street. Their conversion from pacifism was so rapid that the two of them produced *Class War* No. 6 early in 1984. There is no doubt that the six months from October 1983 – March 1984 marked just the kind of shift towards combative street action we had been hoping to encourage. Many of the key players for *Class War* over the next two years were now in place. Phil Gard (Alex and Leah's flatmate), who I'd met at the London Workers' Group, worked as a printer at Calverts North Star Press and had taken on the printing of Class War. Phil's commitment to printing *Class War* was a boon to us. It meant we could get the printing at cost price and steadily increase the print run. Phil was one of the better balanced common-sensical comrades in Class War. He was an avid political reader, well-versed in anarchist history and theory, a Chelsea fan, and unafraid to tell the rest of us we were talking bollocks when no one else had the bottle to.

Steve Sutton was just about to produce Class War's gay newspaper *The Wolverine* with its coruscating analysis of gay sexual politics. Martin and Steve's analysis was that everyone should be bisexual. Those who weren't were sexually repressed might have to be forced to be 'free'!

Fabian Thompsett and Dave Sparks – a printer from the Little A press at Wapping Wharf – came into Class War with Martin (those perplexed by the recent revelations that UB40 were on MI5's subversives list cans trace it back to a benefit they'd done for the Autonomy Centre at Wapping). Dave's Danish activist girlfriend Tina was one of the first anarchist women to join Class War along with Lin, a New Zealander from the Roseberry Avenue squat. With this hardcore of about 20 people, we entered the new year with considerable optimism, when a comically bizarre event intruded.

Richard Parry, the ex-editor of *Xtra!* had produced a one-off magazine called *Logo!* which ripped the piss out of the London anarchist movement. Class War was not spared. In an article entitled *The alcoholic road to anarchism,* he echoed some of Alex and Leah's criticisms of 'working classism' in *Class War* No. 4 and criticised Class War's 'macho beery posturings'. We took it on the chin. Parry was never part of Class War but we regarded him as a political ally and *Logo!* was generally both pretty accurate and acutely funny. The rest of the London anarchist scene, however, was suffering a pompous sense of humour by-pass. In particular a paragraph entitled 'the dead generations' mocking the holy trinity of Stuart Christie, Albert Meltzer and Ronan Bennett incensed the armed struggle fantasists. Copies of *Logo!* were seized from bookshops and destroyed. The editors of *Anarchy* magazine issued a ludicrous call to arms: 'Whatever our differences comrades, we must respond to this threat from within'. For fuck's sake! Parry thought he was about to be physically attacked. Martin knew the *Anarchy* editors and we resolved to throw our weight behind Parry and against the anarcho-censors who backed down when confronted at a meeting at Freedom Press but the episode showed the London Anarchist scene in its fully-inflated ridiculously fragile ego glory.

Class War No. 4 had been a sales and political disaster. It was important to get the show back on the road with an effective issue 5. So I decided to write it myself. Adrienne, who I was still romancing, had, by now, got involved with *Class War* and, besides contributing an article called *Class War Macho? You Must Be Joking!',* she also helped me design the cover. One of the most simply effective ever. A blown-up photo of a huntsman cut out of the Tatler was stuck on the front with the felt-tipped accompanying headline 'You Rich Fucking Scumbag – We're

Gonna Get You!' and the lesser 'Join the Class War Spring Offensive Against The Rich'. As soon as we'd done it, we knew it was a winner. The Spring Offensive was an important political decision by the London group to start organising our own events rather than just disrupting other people's. We decided to concentrate on the social events of the rich. Starting with the annual Rose Ball at the Dorchester Hotel and the rest of their social calendar from Henley to Cowes week. It was basic core Class War stuff.

The early evening of 1 March saw us gathering our forces in a pub near Marble Arch. The Rose Ball was due to start at the Dorchester at 8pm. We'd made banner out of one of sex worker Kate's semen stained sheets, a truly offensive weapon – 'Behold Your Future Executioners'. The threatening and deliberately intimidating posture was backed up by the wearing of ski-masks. It must have made a bizarre sight to the early evening car drivers and bus passengers in Park Lane as we infiltrated our way down to the Dorchester. No cops, no security, no-one expecting us. 'Us' comprised the Class War hardcore, plus a good turnout of Red Actionists. This eye witness account appeared in *Class War* No. 6:

> *'Our protest began in earnest when we unfurled our large banner reading 'Behold Your Future Executioners'. We're not people who play about with words. Soon the rich filth began arriving in droves with their top hats and their 'pinks' with their high society cinderellas on their arms. Jostling, well-placed kicks, and one outstandingly well-placed smack in the gob contrived to ruin many an evening.'*

Class War No. 5 appeared just before the Rose Ball in time for a big student demonstration to Battersea Park. Sales on this march went ballistic as people stared incredulously at the 'rich fucking scumbag' cover before gleefully handing over their 20ps. Ron, Gareth, Adrienne, Charlie and myself sold the entire print run of 1,000 in three hours. We were ecstatic. Weighed down with change we did a jig of delight at the march's end, and treated ourselves to a jolly decent meal in Kings Road! My idea of what the paper need to be like to get big sales was more than confirmed.

There was limited time for self-congratulation though, as Stop The City No. 2 beckoned on 29 March. We knew this could be an important turning point for our movement and we played an active role in a series of meetings to plan the momentous event – with the usual violence versus pacifism debates to the fore. Subsequently Class War was often credited (or blamed) in the press with organising this Stop The City. This was far from the truth and, for once, we never played up our organising role. The real credit goes to London Greenpeace, Dave Morris, the Roseberry punks and countless unsung others. It was a fucking brilliant day when all our movement in its disparate forms was united in action for once.

I'd stayed at Adrienne's the night before and when I suggested bussing it down to the city at 9am, she expressed doubts that the anarchists could get up so early! It must be admitted it was odds on nothing much starting at an anarchist demo until mid-afternoon. We were on the bus into the city at 10am with no sign of anything at all to suggest Stop The City was happening. Adrienne was giving me the 'I Told you so' look when wham bam! A fucking huge forest of black flags legs it out of an alleyway in front of us hotly pursued by the cops in a pall of orange smoke. Fucking hell! Whoa, off the bus, let's get stuck in. I can't beat the general descriptions of the day written by me and Martin in *Class War* No. 6. But other memories of little incidents were just as vital in gaining the feel of the events.

Roland, my old flatmate from Cardiff walking around, briefcase in hand, looking like a City yuppy. He gleefully opened his briefcase however to reveal a small arsenal – distress flares, smoke bombs, stink bombs, spray paint, glue.

Crass splattering the cops with red paint bombs. Nuns splattering the cops with red paint bombs – Crass nuns or nuns on the run? I get stuck in some static rucks outside the Royal Exchange. Ruck caves in on me and Attila the Stockbroker heaves me out with a happy Harlow grin on his face. A yuppy is chased into a wine bar by a gang of punks, one of whom throws a waste paper bin through the wine bar window.

There's hardly any sign of most of the Class War mob – Sean Mason couldn't take the day off work! The rest are about getting stuck in but we don't operate as a cohesive unit. Me and Adrienne dive into a cafe midday for a coffee. A mohicanned punk is explaining to three gobsmacked young punkettes that things are going to get much livelier in the afternoon: 'Yeah, Class War are coming down – they're fucking psychos, they're fucking mad, they've got machetes and guns, there's going to be fucking carnage everywhere.' We keep a low profile as we don't really look like the psychotic Class Warriors he's expecting.

Autonomous groups are causing grief everywhere. The mob from Llandeilo, who stayed with us the night before, are heading up to Fleet Street to go on a window trashing spree. We survey their splintered handiwork with pride later.

The Jethros – a well tasty mob of old hippies from Exeter – are going up the West End to start trashing Oxford Street, waterfalls of glass cascading everywhere. The Jethros had some idea about crashing a load of cars together at the junction of Oxford Street and Tottenham Court Road and torching them but they're talked out of it in case innocent bystanders get blown away. One of them mutters Emile Henri's famous 'There are no innocents!' The Jethros line was either fight with us or get what's coming to you. Oxford Street is duly trashed. All the out-of-towners act the same, forming little hit squads with their mates, coalescing, melting away and striking again. The cops are ill-prepared for the diversity of the actions and completely taken by surprise.

Charlie's brick is my outstanding memory of the day. We're part of a mob charging down Fenchurch Street with black flags flying like a Makhnovist column – unfortunately, unlike the Makhnovists, we ain't got any weapons. There's not many weapons that come to hand in the City, and the cops have taken care to remove street furniture and builders' rubble. But look! I kid you not – a fucking lorry load of bricks hones into view. A swarm of anarcho-locusts strip it bare within minutes, windows caving in like dominoes along the street. There's some fucking huge bank windows about 50 foot high, but some proletarian typists are sitting just behind them, blissfully ignorant that they're about to be guillotined by huge shards of glass. Charlie does his Marcel Marceau bit, bangs in window to get typists' attention, points to brick in his hand, steps back and mimes throwing brick through window. Typists scarper sharpish. Charlie's brick arcs its mime through the window. A fucking huge whoop at such ethical brick-throwing and we're off.

Smoke everywhere. We meet some fucking giant wearing full Spanish republican military uniform, coughing his guts up. He gets a flask of milky coffee out from his knapsack that his mum had made for him. He takes size 16 shoes his name is Juan Zapata, he carries a small CNT pennant on a stick. Style or what. He is well impressed we're from Class War and we're quite impressed with him. We'll meet again.

Stop the City completed the transformation from pacifism. Things would never be the same again until the fluffies reared their heads in the 1990s. Crass and every other fucker were well up for it. We'd fucking won for once. The miners' strike was only a month away, and we had the wind in our sales.

The next big set piece was the Animal Liberation March organised by BUAV on 12 May. We saw this not as another potential ruck but as a paper-selling exercise. We reprinted *Class War* No. 5 which was the perfect example of using the paper to feed back the image of ourselves we wanted to create – pictures of the 22 October CND, and accounts and press cuttings of the Biorex and Islington town Hall actions. And an 'image' of ourselves that was true – we had instigated the trouble at both events. We had also used the paper as an 'organiser' to get people to join with us at Stop The City and the 12 May march. In these two ways, *Class War* No. 5 is a classic issue of the paper. We quoted back what the liberal anarchists of *Freedom* and *Peace News* had been saying perplexedly about this new phenomenon in their midst. We defied BUAV to keep us off the march as they'd intended.

On 12 May, we just concentrated on paper sales. My daughters, Josie and Jenny, who were in their early teens at the time and well into animal welfare issues wanted to come to London for the march. Two days before 12 May, Josie had injured her leg so arrived off the train from Newcastle in a wheelchair. So me, Adrienne and Jenny pushed her around on the march and I combined wheelchair duties with some paper-selling. The sight of the wheelchair arriving at Hyde Park threw the BUAV leadership into panic. They were convinced it must be some cunning plan to take over the front of the march, and Josie and Jenny were accompanied everywhere by a phalanx of BUAV stewards and cops. The march passed off uneventfully. Just as we were heading for home, I was approached by a couple of Americans saying they wanted to start up Class War in the States. We arranged to meet. That was a big mistake.

The current issue of the BUAV's paper *The Liberator* had contained the following account of the Biorex march: 'The BUAV organisers were aware that a small infiltration of NF-type agitators masquerading as anarchists were present distributing leaflets which were crude, insulting, violent and speciesist'. When me and Adrienne met the two Americans in the National Gallery cafe they certainly seemed to have been taken in by *The Liberator's* view. After enthusing about *Class War*, the *Anarchist Cookbook*, and 'the Poor Man's James Bond', they produced a sort of do-it-yourself crudely typewritten terrorist's manual – a redneck survivalist guide to poisoning people and reservoirs, blowing up buildings, making pipe bombs etc.

Now, I'd always been impressed with the sections in the *Anarchist Cookbook* on how to turn your garden hose into a rocket launcher and the other bit where you stick a hatpin into someone's brain through their ear while you sit behind them in the cinema! However, it was obvious to anyone who read *Class War* that we were into mass street action and disavowed individual acts of terrorism. But these guys weren't interested in our political arguments. They just kept insisting that we print the document for them. We said 'You've got our politics all wrong' and left. End of story – or so we thought.

FALL OF THE HOUSE OF MASON

I really had a lot of time and affection for Sean Mason, but he was starting to seriously grate on my nerves. From the 'Well good my son' fellow spirit I'd recognised in Cardiff in 1982, Sean was turning into a caricature of himself. His contempt for middle-class lefties had endeared him to me but since then he'd used 'middle class' to put down any argument he disagreed with. So it was middle class to object to him calling women 'birds' and so on and so on. His comment: 'We're all racist and sexist but so what?' in an early *Class War* was a hostage to fortune which would be bound to come back to haunt us.

On the coach on the way back from the Coventry CND demo Sean's stock in-trade jokes were like something out of the 1970s show *The Comedians*. Adrienne was the only woman with us and seriously had the hump with Sean by the time we made an uncomfortable arrival at Victoria Coach Station. The lack of anyone else telling Sean to shut the fuck up didn't help either. At Victoria, we'd picked up the *The Sunday People* expose of me which Sean and Charlie thought was hilarious while I was seriously worried.

It wasn't so much the piss taking but the lack of any solidarity. I had the feeling that if I'd been sent down for 12 years for incitement, Sean would have been laughing: 'Old Bonehead — got 12 years — stupid cunt — middle class'.

On the way back from a CND rally in Cardiff, Martin and Co had dumped Sean at the services because he'd become so irksome — and you had to generate a lot of irk to be dumped by that crew of desperados. The real dumping that got to Sean was by his girlfriend Stella. To describe Stella as simply Sean's girlfriend was to do her an injustice. She had shit-hot politics and sat across that Red Action/Class War divide which was still possible in the early days. She was a working-class woman who any political group would have been proud to have as a member. She was passionate, funny, sharp, committed and a pretty decent pint swigger. If she'd had enough of Sean, it was not hard to imagine how the other women in Class War felt about him. It was obvious that while Sean continued talking bollocks we'd never attract any women into Class War.

Sean seemed content with his small group of acolytes as he snarled: 'Get yer leg warmers off darling!' at anyone who he might consider a feminist. Building a political movement seemed to have vanished from his flightplan. There was even a bizarre temporary alliance with the Ladbroke Grove girls because of their joint dislike of feminism. It couldn't maintain its unity once the Stonehenge question reared its regular head and Kate's disdain of Sean — 'the proletarian dwarf' — reappeared. For once, he was at a complete loss. He could hardly describe her as a middle-class feminist because she'd taken the piss out of 'the leg warmer brigade' long before him.

I still had a residual loyalty to Sean because of his early involvement with Class War and it did seem possible he might one day just shut up and wise up. But Sean just continued his wind-ups with a small group of mates who'd ape his behaviour. After Stella split with him, he was really cut up and we saw less of him. 'What the fuck did you expect her to do?' I asked him. 'Keep putting up with all that shit you're coming out with?' He shrugged his shoulders as if it was a feminist conspiracy. He pulled a stupid stunt on Red Action which nearly got his head caved in and caused friction between our two organisations. He gradually stopped coming to meetings and I never saw him again.

We'd managed to lose both the Masonite 'classist' wing of Class War and their opposites the Aleks/Leah 'class consciousness' wing in 18 months. Still, a thousand other flowers were blooming and it wouldn't be long before other protagonists were battling over the same ground. 'What is class?' might be an interesting question but as Sean Mason would have said in his heyday 'Good question Bonehead. But first… where's my pint?'

Chapter 18

THE URGE TO DESTROY

After our initial machete 'misunderstanding' I hadn't seen Martin Wright again (thank the lord!) until the 'Beyond the Bullshit' conference in Harrow Road in 1983. Unfortunately, I was walking up the road with situationist Nick Brandt's crone Aleks, so a lairy smile spread over the Wright visage. Being seen with the situationists was getting to be a problem I didn't need. However, the conference passed off without incident and I got on quite well with Ian Slaughter – Martin's right hand man. Ian had been at the London Anarchist Youth Group (LAYG) meeting at 121 Railton Road when I'd first brought *Class War* along. He must have fed copies back to Martin at Duncan Terrace, and a thaw in relations set in. I met Ian a couple of times over on Portobello Road where he closely questioned me about my politics and gave nodding approbation to the name *Class War*. I was beginning to see how both were essential to the creation of some kind of street level violent anarchist mob.

Ian was well respected in the punk scene with his fanzine *Pigs for Slaughter* and links to Andy Martin of The Apostles. Ian had an acerbic wit, smart-casual contempt for soap dodgers and a Machiavellian style. He had been trying to bring the punks into violent confrontation with the cops for some time including a none-too-ethical attempt to set them up against each other after the 'Beyond the Bullshit' conference.

A year earlier there had been the arrest of 48 anarchists in Oxford Street after a Hyde Park demonstration. At the end of the Hyde Park rally, someone announced that anarcho punk favourites The Mob were playing a gig down Jubilee Gardens, and the punks were moving away to the gig. Ian jumped up and shouted a withering verbal attack: 'Go on, slope away, and see your fucking stupid anarcho-band while we smash up Oxford Street' (but rather better put, as I recall). It had the desired effect and most of the punks came with us instead of going for the easy-listening option.

In the event, the Oxford Street action was a fiasco but it was an impressive bit of mob oratory and I clocked it. It also coincided with my view that anarcho-punk music, far from helping the struggle, got in the way of it by diverting the punks away from street action and into the anarcho-ghetto of endless squat gigs.

Ian Slaughter and Martin Wright were a sort of Danton and Robespierre double act. Of all the people who came into Class War in 1983, Martin was the most influential. Bringing Martin on board meant we also got Ian, Dave Sparks, Fabian, and Steve Sutton – who was to edit two very fine issues of *The Wolverine* – *Class War*'s gay newspaper – though not exactly a touchy-feely pink-paper production. But it also meant you got Martin himself with all his political experience, his street sussedness and his pure gutter-level rage, class anger and knowledge of the London anarchist scene. Coming up from Swansea, I had no idea what had been happening in the anarchist movement in London, so hooking up with people who did was vital.

Martin and I were moving closer together after some initial wariness post-machete incident. We came from completely different backgrounds but had ended up sharing views on what tactically needed to be done to create a combative anarchist movement as well as a visceral class hatred and contempt for middle-class lefties.

Martin came from an Irish working-class background and was a street sweeper for Islington council. He'd been heavily involved in the Lewisham riots against the National Front and had assembled a sort of street-fighting crew of mates who became the nucleus of the 'Monday Group'. Through the Lewisham and Southall riots, they'd developed a nodding acquaintance with the Socialist Workers Party (SWP) 'squaddists' who were to form Red Action, sharing a belief in the efficacy of physically critiquing the Nazis. Martin also had a withering and contemptuous analysis of the twin pillars of English anarchism – *Freedom* and *Black Flag* and their respective gurus Albert Meltzer and Vernon Richards. The labyrinthine feuding between the two stretching back over 30 years had been a major factor in rendering the English anarchist movement impotent. *Freedom* was a fucking boring, awful liberal irrelevance of a newspaper, apart from around 1968 when it was edited by John Rety. *Black Flag* had a fixation with international terrorism and worshipping at the shrine of the Spanish Syndicalists. Not content with falling out with these Martin and others – under the guise of the Kronstadt Kids – had produced a devastatingly funny critique of *Anarchy* magazine called *Authority*. This dealt British anarchism's obsession with the past a hammerblow by printing a hitherto unseen map of the Gulf of Finland in 1920 showing irrefutably that the island fortress of Kronstadt did not in fact exist! It was greeted by the usual humour by-pass which was a defining characteristic of London anarchism. Allying with Martin meant you had to take on all his feuds and enmities – *Black Flag*, 121 Railton Road, the Sits, *Freedom*, – but it was a price I never doubted was worth paying.

Martin was a rumbustious street mob orator as well as a coruscatingly erudite observer of the British anarchist and leftist milieu. I lost count of the number of times SWPers would flee pubs after Martin had conclusively demonstrated their party was in fact a family business rather than a political organisation – hereditary leadership principles from the Harmans and Glucksteins. We were selling papers outside some particularly turgid leftist gathering when Martin hailed a passing ambulance... 'There's people dying of torpor in there,' he motioned.

Martin's violent notoriety among London's anarchists was achieved, not by his malevolent and lairy grimace, but by the Conway Hall incident of 1981. Crass had been playing an anarchist benefit when 40 British Movement (BM) supporters intruded into the hall and began systematically attacking robbing and bullying the anarcho-punks. Crass played blithely on adhering to their pacifist straitjacket. While the BM lot ran amok – like shooting fish in a barrel. A phonecall alerted Martin and the Monday Club who raced to the scene of the carnage. Assessing the odds, Martin in turn called out the Red Action squaddists and the bloody fight back began. Suddenly the BM were confronted not by pushover pacifists but by knuckle-dustered, cosh-waving, iron bar-wielding (and that was just Martin) nutters who weren't setting any parameters to their level of violent response.

Time Out reported: 'Their attack took the form of a flying wedge, bottles and iron bars reinforcing the point. Several of the BM were on their knees crying, others ran through the rear exit only to fall upon more of the knife-wielding enemy. A bloody scene! Several people I talked to said they were amazed no one was killed. It was a blow to the heart of the BM's self assuredness that they could 'smash the Reds! Crass were far from happy. They issued a statement condemning both sides as 'fascists' for using violence.

Years later, the penny still hadn't dropped for Rimbaud who was describing the Conway Hall incident thus: 'The resulting carnage was ugly, unnecessary and utterly indefensible' and peddling a spun version of history that 'leftists had attacked a Crass audience looking for Nazis! Well, they certainly found some!

The scene was set for the battle to move the Crass anarcho-punks away from pacifism to violent street rioting. It was to take less time than we thought. I was well pleased with Martin's notorious propensity for violence – apart from when it was directed at me, of course! What was the point of creating a paper committed to violence if the people selling it all looked like Clark Kent weaklings – there had to be a unity of theory and practice!

In May 1985, there was an 'alternative' rally at the Friends Meeting House addressed by Tony Benn and 'Red' Ted Knight, Leader of Lambeth Council. The week before, Knight had evicted the squatters from Effra Parade in Brixton using baton-wielding riot police. Errol, Franco and other Class War supporters had been involved in resisting the eviction and considered it a fucking disgrace for Ted Knight to be passing himself off as some kind of radical only a week later. About 20 of us turned up demanding Benn remove Knight from chairing the meeting and the Effra squatters got a chance to speak. Benn, the aristocratic phoney whose hero status on the British left for decades speaks volumes about the poverty of radicalism in the UK, denounced us as 'fascists' and said the miners present would 'sort us out'. Unfortunately, these horny-handed sons of toil and aristocrats of the proletariat were all sitting alongside us reading *Class War*! Knight mobilised a load of billowy-trousered 'healers' (yes it was a fucking odd audience!) to surround us singing peace songs to remove our bad karma violent vibes. It was a bizarre sight seeing this old school tankie and ex-Workers Revolutionary Party (WRP) hack enlisting the help of the crystal therapy brigade to sort us out. This might have worked with the usual anarchists but not with us! Charlie hurled an apple at Ted Knight – which was caught by a Green Party type on the platform and eaten – well stylish! Then we rushed the stage. The tables went flying, microphones used as weapons, and Ian Slaughter pulled out his steel comb which glinting in the sunlight may well have looked like a knife. Either way the platform fled, the squatters said a few words, and we legged it over to the Eliza Doolittle pub opposite to sit in the sun watching the wailing cop cars arrive.

Action was what made us different from the other anarchists and kept our disparate support together. Martin had written famously in *Class War:* 'Without action, you're just posing. Action is the lifeblood'. The blood was certainly flowing.

Tribune ran a story the following week denouncing us and seeking further information under the headline 'Who Are Those Guys?' Neither the left nor the anarchists were quite sure who we were. Albert Meltzer in his autobiography *I Could Paint Golden Angels* describes *Class War* as a 'culture shock'. We didn't seem to behave like 'proper anarchists' wailed *Freedom* – i.e. sit in your armchair and do fuck-all.

Bash The Rich

Our paper, despite the blood dripping circled As on the cover, bore no resemblance to other anarchist papers. Something new was stirring and Martin Wright and I were right in the middle of it. We were seeking to break with the past and get *Class War* to be relevant to the present – to the concerns of the street rioters not the anarcho-archivist worshippers. The reformist organisations couldn't work us out because of the way we looked – short cropped hair, bald heads, tattoos, smart-casual clothes – was the way they thought fascists looked! And we were working class to look at and by the way we talked and they weren't used to working class people taking part in political movements.

Two other recent proletarian cockney recruits to Class War were Angie and Andy, two council gardeners from Hackney. Hackney was increasingly home to a lot of Class Warriors and Mare Street was festooned with Class War graffiti and a couple of local pubs were unofficial Class War gathering spots. Angie spotted that Tom Watt and Susan Tully (Lofty and Michelle from *EastEnders*) were to be opening a yuppy housing development at Watermint Quay one Sunday. They were playing at being salt of the earth knees-up-mother-Brown Eastenders on TV whilst selling out real Eastenders by colluding with gentrifying property developers. We rolled up and chased them down the road where they were barricaded into a show house by security guards. The *Daily Mirror* headlined the story the following day and the episode added one more layer to Class Wars violent reputation.

To be fair, Tom Watt later wrote us a letter apologising for his actions and saying he'd like to come to a Class War meeting. Turned out he was a great admirer of Proudhon – which is more than we were!

We were playing a dangerous game of brinkmanship in order to build up *Class War*'s reputation. Perceived violence but, in reality, more threat and gesture than anything we were likely to get serious grief for. We weren't going to be martyrs or get done for a one-off action. We had bigger plans – to create a revolutionary movement that would sweep all these fucking wankers away for good. There might be casualties along the way (but if you boxed clever) not too many. There was nothing more anarchists liked than Defence Campaigns that would give them something to do for a year or so in their otherwise clueless approach to politics. We didn't want to waste time on traditional anarchist defence campaigns. We wanted offensive campaigns – as fucking offensive as fucking possible!

Chapter 19

A FACE LIKE HIMMLER

We'd been on a bit of a damp-squib CND demo in Coventry in May 1894, highlighted only by a long suffering Monsignor Bruce Kent giving about 15 of us a lift back into the city after we'd been heckling him all afternoon. We asked him a couple of smart-arsed questions to get a few smirks from each other but he knew who we were and gave as good as he got. I grudgingly quite liked the Monsignor after that – genuine bloke or what!

On arrival back at Victoria station (with Sean behaving all journey like a complete fucking twat), the last thing we expected (or wanted) was a grinning Charlie and Sean to come rushing back over to us waving

A Face Like Himmler

The Sunday People as if it was the most hilarious thing in the fucking world. To Sean's delight, I was exposed as the crazed anarchist behind 'shadowy hate group Class War'.

'He's got a degree in sociology, a face like Himmler... and a heart over-flowing with hate'.

So ran the *The People's* headline on 27 May s1984 under the headline 'Un-masked... the evil man who preaches hate to children'. Blimey! I mean it's not exactly the press cutting you want to send home to your mum. 'Evil man' and 'children' have a kind of Gary Glitter feel about it rather than your Che Guevara 'dangerous revolutionary' kind of tag. It got worse. A supportive comrade told me the accompanying photo didn't look like Himmler alive at all, but was in fact a dead ringer for Himmler's corpse! I could hardly raise the matter with the Press Complaints Commission could I? 'That should read a face like Himmler's corpse... if you could just print that clarification'. The article continued 'If bristle-headed Bone had his way, the blanks fired at the Queen in the Mall would have been real bullets. And the attempt on the life of President Reagan would have succeeded'. The latter acccusation was taken from the lyrics of the Living Legends song *Dum Dum Bullets*. Where the fuck did they get that from? I instantly wondered.

Alongside the text was a photo of me and my daughter Jenny taken on the 12 May BUAV animal rights demonstration a couple of weeks earlier. The children I was allegedly peddling hate to were my own daughters but *The People* had failed to mention that minor detail. I was completely fucking shocked. It wasn't expected or something I'd even thought might happen. I'd never been in the paper since winning third place in the miniature garden competition at Goudhurst Village Show! What a follow up! Then there was the shock and worry at seeing Jenny's photo in the paper. What would her mum say?

Me and Adrienne made our way back to Hackney white-faced with worry. A shitty day had just got shittier. My stomach clenched and I was hit by stomach cramps the next day. At the same time I was struck by the absurdity of worrying so much about an expose in a paper where revolutionaries elsewhere were being shot and imprisoned. The thought failed to alleviate the cramps though.

The next day, my dad phoned. They didn't get *The People* but some kind neighbour had pointed the story out to them. My mum was (understandably) not too keen on being the mother of 'the most evil man in Britain'. In fact she was sick with worry and had stomach cramps all day. Why the fuck do we have such weak stomachs in our family? My dad rarely got annoyed with me and I could hear he was trying not to but: 'Could I not think about other people for once? How could I drag Jenny into it?'

Gloom. I now wished our movement didn't have the wind in its sails after all. But after a week or so, things didn't look so bad. The world hadn't caved in. Mum's stomach cramps had stopped. Crowds of fiery brand-waving hooded vigilantes hadn't appeared outside Adrienne's council flat. Josie and Jenny's photo had past unnoticed back home in Newcastle. Tim Paine and Phil Gard had been very supportive. Tim reported a huge increase in mail to our box number and comrades round the country were positive and excited about the coverage. We were seen as a threat not a fucking joke. I started to feel a bit jaunty about the whole thing. 'No I hadn't been worried... it was a sign of our success... only to be expected... if you can't stand the heat... etc etc' (liar! liar!).

The People and then the *Sunday Mirror* ran almost identical stories the following year but with a photo of Adrienne in full throttle at the Coventry CND demo. I'd realized by now that journalists are lazy bastards who just go to the clippings files so that once a lie is printed, it gets endlessly repeated. There was some barking story that I'd become a militant animal liberationist after vivisectors stole my cat! David Henshaw in his book on the Animal Liberation Front ran it there so it has hung around ever since. Just before the *Sunday Mirror* article I'd been coming out of Adrienne's Hackney council flat one Sunday morning, sleepy-eyed and hungover, to get the papers. I caught a glimpse ahead

EXCLUSIVE
THE ENEMY W

Terror plan to 'smash the rich scum and their lackeys'

Ian Bone—the driving force behind the Class War anarchist group, with his girlfriend Adrienne.

NGER and NIGEL NELSON

The ruthless anarchists who brought a decade ago are manipulating an es into bloodbaths.

al anarchists are motivated solely by a o sabotage.

mer punk musician Ian Bone, 38.

Their charter states: "Together we can do our bit to smash the rich scum and their state, courts armies and lackeys."

Class War has close ties with **VIRUS,** a communist-anarchist group who publish a paper called The Enemy Within.

The winter issue says: "Virus gives a welcome to the burning and looting . . . take it, it's yours! Burn it, it's rotten!"

Sabotage

A journal called CROW-BAR in Brixton, South London, offers advice on how to commit sabotage.

And BLACK FLAG, also based in Brixton, are thought to be linked with a Belgian terror group.

The Bristol-based group ACAB —which stands for All Coppers Are Bastards — call on their followers to attack expensive cars.

Their leaders often visit Ian Bone at his council flat in Hackney, North-East London.

This is the main way that informal links are made between British anarchist cells.

Intelligence chiefs know that most of the groups were active during the riots last year in Brixton and Tottenham.

These are likely to be the flashpoints again this year.

One police officer

The magazine

vered their plot rces in a cam-olence.

eve Angry Bri-an guerillas are sinister behind-role in the plot.

ve close links groups abroad.

are also closely the shadowy ritish anarchists.

t active of the s is Class War ing force is for-

ER DEAD N WED

HATE

ion and with -Left French n Direct.

ce services are ned that Euro-lse will lead to n Britain be-ore and more d.

r police chief, Angry Brigade

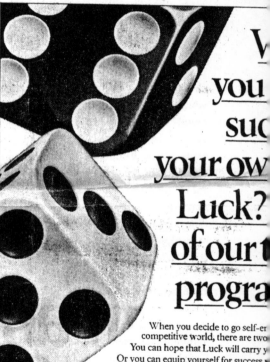

V
you
suc
your ow
Luck?
of our t
progra

When you decide to go self-e competitive world, there are two
You can hope that Luck will carry y
Or you can equip yourself for success combining your own talent and enterprise programmes – *at no cost to yourself.*

We've got together with experts who know all abo training. Together we've worked out what essential know-how people need most when they start work

The result is hundreds of very practical and very us the country, at all levels, at times to suit you best.

The result is also hundreds of people nationwide w are now: with a bright idea and a market to go for. V for Enterprise programme, they're now running sor business ventures in Britain.

Put yourself on course to succeed. Fill in the coupon

of some bloke wearing a baseball cap seemingly adopting the classic shoot to kill position and aiming at me from about 50 yards away. Eye message reached the brain synapses and I hurled myself behind a van. I crawled to the side and saw him run off with a zoom lens camera rather than the handgun. The photo that appeared in the *Sunday Mirror* shows a swivel-eyed loon in abject terror trying to execute a Fosbury Flop! If only I'd stood my ground and given it the old black gloved clenched fist salute with jutting jaw. Bastards!

British anarchists had for years avoided publicity hiding behind box numbers and anonymous publications. Partly through not wanting to be 'exposed' as anarchists to their next door neighbours, partly because any collaboration with the capitalist press would be seen as a sell out and partly because most of them where hobbyists who didn't want too many people to join their club. This had always annoyed me. The anarchist movement was, in fact, guilty of hero worship the likes of Durrutti and Makhno more than most. Ask any anarchists to name any other member of Durrutti or Makhno's revolutionary armies rather than the leaders and they'd be stumped. If you where to build a revolutionary movement people would want to relate to real, living, vibrant, exciting human beings not anonymous balaclava wearers or people too scared to give their views a public airing. One of my favourite revolutionary images is of Lenin arriving at the Finland station (Heresy!). The anarchist version would consist of the same hissing steaming train with a placard on the front reading: 'FFI contact Box 2, 84b Whitechapel High Street.'

In fact, most anarchists kept their private lives completely divorced from their anarchist activities and would have been horrified if their neighbours had known about their hobby!

More to the point, I thought not talking to the media was missing out on major opportunities to spread our ideas. Yes of course we'd been misrepresented... blah blah... but still, however deformed, our ideas and existence would be read about by far more people in the *News of the World* (ciculation 5,000,000) than a piece in *Class War* (circulation 15,000). After all, I'd first found out about anarchism in *Punch*. So when Andrew Tyler contacted us about doing a piece in *Time Out* about *Class War* in May 1985, me and Martin Wright decided to brave the cries of 'sell-out!' and go for it. If we were going to be exposed anyway, we might at least get a few good quotes in.

The *Time Out* piece was better than we could have dreamed of. Tyler had grasped the difference between us and the stultifying torpor that was British anarchism and written a coruscating piece that gave *Class War* an electrifying jolt. The oxygen of publicity resulted in a packed Class War conference two weeks later. The predicted criticism of our sell-out in *Time Out* came early in the day. 'Yes, I am sorry we appeared in *Time Out*,' I grovelled, 'I'm sorry, it wasn't on the front page of the *News of the World*. Tumultuous applause (well so it seems 20 years later). The case for talking to the press was won and has always been vindicated in my view. I was subsequently exposed in the *Sunday Mirror, Today* and the *News of the World* ('Dangerous lunatics who want to kill the entire cast of *EastEnders*' – don't ask!) and despite the vilification we got, our post bag was always rammed full the following week with people who'd never heard of us before but wanted to get involved now.

Bash The Rich

In particular, the quotation from the Living Legends lyric *God Bless You Queen Mum* appearing in the *Sunday Mirror* and wishing her an early death was especially popular. The key, of course, is not to believe your own publicity and the oxygen certainly went to my head in those intoxicating months in 1985. At the conference I had argued for '500 people with sledgehammers attacking the bridge at Henley'. By the time of that year's anarchist bookfare in Conway Hall, I was well away. Having sold shit loads of *Class Wars* with Martin I took the stage at the end of the day. Well, actually, there was already someone on the stage so I had to push him off it first. Unfortunately, that person was Donald Rooum – a veteran comrade I have a lot of respect for going back to his framing by the police for intending to throw a brick at the queen of Greece in the 1960s. However, it wasn't really Donald I was shoving off the stage but the old anarchist movement. Drunk as fuck I declared:

'You liberals and pacifists have had our movement for too long, now it's our turn. If we haven't reduced the place to ruins in five years you can have it back!'

Quite why I wanted to reduce the venerable Conway Hall to ruins was unclear. But what the fuck. I might have paraphrased Durrutti, but the point was clear. We were on a fucking roll.

Chapter 20

THE PAPER

Central to all our activities was the paper itself. By the end of 1984 thanks to our increasing notoriety, circulation was up to 6,000.These were virtually all direct street sales done by our ever expanding network of bulk order takers all over the country. The on-going miners' strike had enabled us to break through into big sales in South Yorkshire and in the big northern towns of Liverpool, Manchester, Leeds, Sheffield and Bradford. The network of sellers also fed back information, stories and articles for the paper which got rid of its London bias. Although Alarm had sold 5,000 a week in Swansea alone, whereas CW was selling 6,000 countrywide only every two or three months, the informal network that fed news stories back to the paper had a similar feel to it. Bumping up the circulation as rapidly as possible was a priority. We were lucky on two fronts. Phil Gard's endless commitment to printing the paper at Calverts for cost price enabled us to increase the print run each issue with no undue financial burden. Watching Phil come alive as he clambered smudgily over the big Calverts presses for hours on end was one of the wonders of the CW world. Secondly we had in Tim Paine an excellent punk bureaucrat who sorted out the subscriptions, bulk orders, and replied endlessly to scraps of paper from 'Psycho of Leeds' or 'Scuzzo of Merthyr' or 'Animal' or the hundreds of others who were now writing to our box number.

The paper kept pretty much to its original, if unstated, founding principles established by me and Jimmy Grimes doing the first issue. Make no demands of anyone, no victimhood bleating about how terrible the cops were, don't defend what we don't want like the GLC, don't defend anything – offend, no appeal to the concept of rights, no overseas coverage, ferocious class anger, lots of laughs, lots of swearing, tabloid style lay-out, set our own agenda.

Bash The Rich

Within those parameters people could do what they liked, though the freelance production of each issue was now brought to an end following the production of a hilariously awful issue by Tim and Spike from the depths of the Albany Street squat. Articles for each issue were now discussed at the weekly London meeting which took on editorial responsibility for each issue. Myself, Martin, and Tim Paine remained the main writers, but a mass of new faces was now contributing as well and setting the political direction for 1985.

Our ever popular 'Hospitalised Copper' feature managed to marry that difficult trick of combining violence with humour and alliteration 'Brixton PC Basil Bastard bashed on the bonce by a boulder in the bloody battle of the barrier block' or 'PC Arthur Arsehole attacked with a 'arf brick' and 'PC Billy Bollock bashed bruised and beaten in Bristol bundle'. It became almost like a syndicated feature. Loads of people would buy Class War off me 'just for hospitalised copper'. When we missed it out one issue we were deluged with complaints. Eventually it had to have a yearly calendar of its own.

There also started to be some pretty decent quality writing in *Class War* – way above the usual standard agitprop bollocks beloved of the Left and anarchists. We'd lost Jimmy Grimes but Jake, Martin, Pete, Kate, Tim and Chris could all knock out a bit of magical writing.

Editorial meetings were now up to 40 strong and there was a significant influx of new attenders, most of whom came as part of an already existing small group either local, interest or friendship based. The Class War collective now included:

Pompey Footie Crew: 30-year-old Pompey hooligan Dick, the white van man, and his group of Pompey lads were a regular fixture on *CW* outings.

Tufnell Park Militia: Organised by Seamus the TPM formed an autonomous unit within CW. Seamus' girlfriend was known as 'The Tufnell Park Melissa'. Composed mainly of Sunday afternoon footballers from Finsbury Park

Streatham Action Group: Punky serious animal liberationists led by pink-haired vegan Chris with autonomous Asian girl posse.

Wood Green Squatters: Squatted bookshop in Wood Green and animal liberationists. Gary was telling me he'd freed some rats from a laboratory but accidently stood on one and killed it. 'He had to die to be free' I consoled Gary. He nodded sagely.

Molly's Café Squatters: Tim Paine and Spike brought a load more punky squatters into the group including a smattering of anarcha-feminists.

John Underhay and Jake from Brixton: Wise old commonsensical political heads not afraid to tell us we were talking wish fulfilment bollocks. Jake was in the band 'Nocturnal Emissions' and would periodically blow up at the idiocy of our proposals and bring us back to Planet Earth! Jake wrote some of the best and most visionary articles in Class War including the famous '*What do we do when the cops fuck off!*' with its purple – and often quoted – apocalyptic prose: '*By 1999 the urban war will be a permanent feature of everyday life in every benighted city on this sceptic isle. There will be guns and deaths on both sides, as the cops mutate into daleks and a host of scrapheap geniuses become the weaponsmiths of the ghettos.*' You won't get that in *Socialist Worker*!

Chris Evans aka 'Tall Chris': Shoot first ask questions later fire from the hip let'em 'ave it spontaneist! He got an office job working at the TGWU. His first act was to call Michael Meacher a 'fucking cunt' when he got into the lift! His second, from his job in the mail room, was to mail a huge box of free copier paper to Martin's house. A dozy Steve Sutton refused to sign for it and it was returned to the TGWU where Chris's act of 'liberation' was discovered! He somehow survived!

Ron: Brixton based Wolverhampton Wanderers fan. Typical of the white working class young proletarians coming into Class War and politics for the first time. Used to act like he was my minder during mammoth drinking sessions in The George Canning.

Brendan and the legendary Hengai from Kilburn: The baby faced assassins!

Angie Wardle from Hackney and her boyfriend Andy: Angie was like Class War's trump card. A well good cockney no-nonsense proletarian she didn't come from an anarchist background like lots of us old timers but was politicised by Thatcher. An excellent and passionate speaker she was the well-grounded commonsense antidote to me and Martin's rantings.

Black Section: Big Dave Braithwaite, Matt and Gary from Norwood.

Foreign Anarchist Women Section: Tina (Denmark), Lin (New Zealand) and an American skinhead woman who's name we never knew! The anarchist women from overseas had less problem with CW's 'macho image' than did many of the home grown anarcha-feminists.

Add to this lot the London Autonomists, Red Actionists, Situationists, London Anarchist Youth Group, Kingsbury Mob, Danny Gralton, Ladbroke Grove Sex Workers and Bohemians, the in-house loonies (Mark, Vicky, Nick) plus the already existing hard core and you can see CW in all its early highly combustible glory!

MANSFIELD MINERS' RALLY

Up until June 1984 Class War had only ever been sold within the anarchist milieu. The miners' strike gave us the chance to break out of the much discussed 'anarchist ghetto' and sell to some horny handed sons of proletarian toil who didn't know an anarchist from an aardvark – and didn't want to fucking know either.

Adrienne and me were definitely a bit nervy as we got our *Class Wars* out to begin flogging in some Mansfield car park at 10am. We had a good miners' cover – a picture of some miner grabbing NCB Coal Chief Ian McGregor by the throat and the felt-tipped caption underneath 'We should have finished the fucking bastard off there and then'. But this wasn't going to be like flogging to some in-house anarchos on a CND rally. Here we would have proof whether the paper could reach out beyond the anarchist ghetto or just become an in-house journal. All those ideas going back to Alarm days in Swansea were going to be validated or not this very morning in a Mansfield car park. I had a lot invested in these next few minutes. Maybe I was wrong – maybe the horny handed proletarians wouldn't like the swearing on the cover – they might rip the copies from us to prevent their wives and offspring from reading such metropolitan filth. Alarm was different – we'd had time to build up a relationship with our own buyers at a local level. Here we were stone-cold selling to the punters. Also, we were going to have to contend with a mass of Trotskyist paper sellers who'd pinched all the best sales pitches at the car park entrance – there were fucking hundreds of them. I was reassured by the fact that the miners were steaming past their usual piss-poor 'Recall the TUC' garbage without a second glance. Our fucking cover stood out a mile from the rest. Right, let's drag our six bag-loads over here, form into a back-to-back defensive corral to stymie attack from behind and go for it.

'*Class War* – 20p!' My dry throat wouldn't croak out any more imaginative sales pitch. Even as I was shouting it I was thinking that is fucking stupid – no-one here has ever heard of Class War, so why the fuck are they going to buy one just because you shout the name out. Come on fuckwit – think of something more gobsmacking to get the attention. '*Class War* – 20p!' it came out again. But not so loud this time. My crisis of confidence is spreading to Adrienne who's giving me a look that says: 'What idiot persuaded me to get up at 6am and carry six bags full of paper we can't sell to a Midlands car park.'

A miner walks past and interjects. 'We're on strike mate, we can't afford to buy bloody papers'. Oh shit. He did have a point. Maybe we'll just have to give the lot away – if they'll even take them for nothing! Two miners have been staring fixedly at the cover for a minute. They're edging nearer. My faith in my ability to produce a popular proletarian paper is about to disappear down the shit chute of history. 'That's Cully, that is' they say 'That's our mate Cully'. Oh shit. Adrienne and I freeze. The geezer grabbing Macgregor by the collar on our front cover is apparently their mate Cully. 'He's over there. Oi Cully! You're on the front of the fucking paper'. Oh shit! Bollocks! Fuck! What if Cully in a big way objects to being stuck on our front cover? 'Does he know about it?' asks one of the miners as Cully – for indeed it is he – approaches. 'Er, not exactly' I thought to myself. Cully stares at the cover – reads the felt-tipped inscription under his photo – and laughs. Laughs! He fucking laughs!

'Ay, I fucking should've done,' he twinkles at us. 'How much is that'.

'20p – but free to you since you're on the cover.'

'No,' he says. 'I know it costs you to make these papers. I'll pay 20p – here's a quid for five'.

I love Cully – he's a proletarian saint. The others miners buy their copies and go off to flash the cover around to their mates. Pointing in our direction, a steady trickle of miners come over to buy copies. Oh sweet-sainted Bakunin! Cully is now posing for photographers with Class War stuck on his chest. I see a copy stuck onto a Socialist Worker placard. The trickle is starting to be a rush. Another bare-chested miner has got one stuck directly onto his chest. Suddenly the covers are on placards everywhere. The CWs are flying out – people laughing and joking as they buy them. We're under siege – every fucker is wanting one. Some of the miners have read the inside bits and are asking when the next Stop The City is, they'll come down. It sounded fucking great, they say. Miners are asking about STC! This is a Citizen Smith wet dream come true. If only the rest of the class warriors were here to see it – to see what is clearly possible now if we can keep at it – and stop all that fucking stupid bitching that's pulling us under at the same time. It was the best of times, it was the worst of times. But this morning was the fucking best of times.

The march moved off. We flogged CWs as we went, childishly thrilled to see our covers covering the front of SWP placards. A woman was sitting in the window above a shop. 'Get yer tits out for the lads'. She obliges to huge cheers. We don't bother to debate this. Vanessa Redgrave with her sensible brown brogues and chiffon headscarf is demanding the TUC call a General Strike in a plum home counties accent. She fails to get her tits out for the lads. Her Workers' Revolutionary Party group (herself apart) are all self-consciously wearing proletarian donkey jackets but looking like extras from Brideshead Revisited. We meet some of the Doncaster and Nottingham anarchists to take bundles of CWs off us to sell. End of march we sell all the fucking papers. Miners all around talking about Stop the City, telling us about other demos and actions. It's 2pm. We collapse with a couple of cans in the sunshine as the strikers set off to drink Mansfield dry. At 4pm miners coming back to coaches start to skirmish with the cops. At 4.15 a superbly executed flying drop kick takes an ITN camera crew out of the action. By 4.30, a full-scale riot going on in front of us. We don't join, just watch contentedly from the grass verge with our lager cans. The cops take a pasting but snatch squads make lots of arrests. Our last train back from Nottingham is at 6.30. We count our pockets laden with change as we jangle back to London.

Chapter 21

CLASS WAR – HEAL THYSELF

The aftermath of the Coventry CND demo and *The Sunday People* article showed that all was not as well as might have been hoped within Class War There were a number of personal and political problems, as ever intertwined, which were threatening our future development if not our very existence. Personal animosities and tensions were bubbling to the surface and despite the bravado of the paper and the immense political opportunities before us, by August I was close to jacking the lot in. We were, in fact, just one meeting away from folding.

The basic political problem was still the unresolved 'current' issue. Many people saw Class War still as one 'current' of a libertarian movement not the whole cake. Thus the London Autonomists and others wanted to retain their separate identities. OK but the problem was they were coming to Class War meetings and making decisions for Class War. Decisions were being made with very few of us to implement them. Half the people making decisions about what we should do never had the idea they should be involved in implementing that decision! Hence the poor Class War turnout on the first Stop the City and the May 12th BUAV march. The real nettle to be grasped was whether we could build a single, powerful class war anarchist movement which could go beyond the beloved 'networking' or linking autonomous groups. There'd been plenty of these in the past going back to the Anarchist Federation of Britain and no evidence that such lack lustre networks were capable of ever packing a punch to cause a dent in a powder puff! At the present it didn't look promising.

Class War - Heal Thyself

In addition the Sean Mason faction made a of of noise at meetings but their delivery was fuck all. In fact, Sean's arrest on October 22nd seemed to have traumatised him from going on further actions, so we were getting the worst of both worlds out of him.

The other problem was conflicting views over whether prostitution was a liberatory lifestyle or not! This had been an interesting debate within the sexual politics discussions but now during the miners' strike the advocacy of prostitution was verging on the absurd. In truth, it had always been absurd but being a small group there had been no urgency to challenge it before. Now there was. We were telling miners' wives that the liberation of prostitution was the way forward! After battling the overtime cash-rich cops all day on the picket lines they should go off and suck their cocks in the evening! This argument had got opportunistically ntwined with the Masonite attack on feminism as middle class.

So now it was that anarcha-feminism wasn't just wrong-headed but that by definition every anarcha-feminist had to be 'middle class'. 'Middle- classism' had become the refuge of the scoundrel so the influx of new women into Class War arguing against prostitution were 'middle class'. This was getting seriously fucking absurd. Personal scores were being settled by proxy 'political' argument and this was all entwined with bitching around personal and sexual relationships. The controls seemed set on self-destruct. It was my neck that seemed to be on the line post People and I wasn't inclined to leave it there on behalf of a movement riddled with backbiting and loathing.

Fuck it. We'd had enough. Me and Adrienne upped off to John Preston's place in Llandeilo for respite care for a week. Decision time by the banks of the River Towy as the darting swallows scudded under Llandeilo Bridge. 'Class War: Born Swansea: Died Llandeilo. Hasn't got far,' I moped. Enough is E-Fucking-nough! Get it sorted – warts 'n' all. Sort out Stonehenge, sex, middle class and collective effort at the next meeting or we'll call it a fucking day. Return to London for the big bust up – August 18 1984.

Chapter 22

CLASS WAR
CONFERENCE 2

The second Class War conference was considerably better organised than the previous year's piss-up in the Portobello Road. For once we'd deserted the pub and met at Caxton Hall in North London on August 18 and 19. There was an agenda and rotating chairperson, and representation from beyond London. Despite existing tensions there was a full London CW turn out including the sex workers, Aleks and Leah and The Situationists, the London Autonomists, Sean M's mob, the Brixton anarchists, Tim and Spike the Albany Street mob, myself and Adrienne, Phil Gard and some of the LWGers, Ron, Charlie, Gareth, Ian Slaughter and a few others. In addition there were anarchists from Exeter, Bristol, Bradford, Doncaster, Edinburgh, Sheffield, Manchester, Southampton, Swansea and Cardiff – about 40 in all. Many of these were from independent local newspapers with similar politics to Class War. Pride of place was given to Dave Douglas, an actual striking miner and NUM official from Hatfield Main Colliery near Doncaster. There were 6 items on the agenda:

(1) Miners' Strike
(2) Sexual Politics
(3) Local reports
(4) Stop The City and beyond
(5) The Paper
(6) Why the Conference?

One attender was Mike Vallance from Counter Information in Edinburgh. Mike was representative of a lot of the organised groups or papers outside London. Like Martin he saw CW as part of a 'current'. He didn't want to join CW but he was pleased an initiative had been taken to form a network where all the differing strands of the 'current' could meet up. The 'current' being broadly defined as 'council communist, autonomist, workers' councillists, libertarian socialists, class struggle anarchists'. Many people would use these terms as interchangeable to describe their politics at different times – to the horror of the purists who knew their Anton Bordiga from their Toni Negri. In the event some of us were pushing for the conference to be more of a build-the-class movement and I think Mike and some others felt let down by us. A shame really, Mike Vallance being one of the few anarchists I've met who could be genuinely at home doing the shitwork in an anarchist society rather than bitching about capitalism and plotting and scheming within it.

Dave Douglas gave his analysis of the miners' strike and its potential for genuine change and prospects for victory. He said *Class War* was the only paper that had been well received in the coalfields. That the rest of the leftie paper sellers were regarded as parasitic scum who'd rather sell papers than get stuck into the cops. He praised CW's attempts to develop links between strikes and inner city rioters. Out of this came our Open Up The Second Front strategy. The idea that the best way we could help the striking miners was not to tail end the picketing and demonstrations but to ferment unrest in the inner cities. We had encouraging reports from Bristol of more trouble in the St Paul's area simmering away. If riots erupted in the cities then the cops would be pulled away from the mining areas giving the strike a better chance of success. In view of the fast emerging miners' hit squads and increasing levels of violence in the strike we decided to pursue such a strategy in the next few months. Significant outbreaks in a couple of towns could stretch police manpower and morale to breaking point.

The most significant discussions – and most heated – came up under the sexual politics debate. The main thrust of her argument was that: (1) Everyone was bi-sexual (2) Coupledom and monogamy was shit (3) Prostitution was the way forward for working class and CW women

(4) All social workers should be shot (5) Middle class feminism was a wank and sisterhood was a middle class illusion (6) Everyone should go to Stonehenge and not to fucking Glastonbury (7) Pornography was a good thing.

Items (1) and (2) were accepted as a pretty good basis for autonomous sexual politics. There were significant for and against views on pornography which were reflected in for and against articles in the paper. Class War didn't aim to have 'positions' on everything and debate was encouraged and diversity of views well tolerated. The pornography debate was dominated in the main by Zeno Evil's contribution from Exeter on how he used to wank off to his mum's corset catalogues. Not the kind of debate you'd get at other anarchist conferences I suspected, but one men of a certain age might have some empathy with!

However, Steve Sutton seized the opportunity of the bi-sexuality debate to amplify his rather unique position on 'compulsory bi-sexuality', on how some comrades would have to be 'forced to be free'. I can remember feeling distinctly awkward at this stage. Steve's line was this: 'People were too conditioned by repressive influences to acknowledge their bi-sexual nature and even if they did acknowledge it they were too inhibited and repressed to act upon it.'

In other words to have a genuine revolutionary sexual politics you had to be actively bisexual. If you weren't sexually active in this way then your comrades who were would have to give you some assistance to achieve true sexual emancipation. This seemed only to apply to heterosexual men though since Steve Sutton apparently shared no interest in girls and didn't appear to be suggesting that he should be forcibly fucked by one. I'm sure a lot of comrades will be pleasantly surprised that CW should have devoted so much of its annual conference to a discussion on whether compulsory bisexuality should be a pre-requisite for joining CW. In fact, for those who thought we were all numbingly macho sexist pigfuckers (no, pigfucking wasn't discussed), I can point out that both our first two conferences were dominated by radical discussions on sexual politics. As I squirmed uneasily in my seat with my hands clasped defensively over my groin, I was wondering if this compulsory deflowering might even happen then and there that very afternoon in Caxton Hall. Who but a wet liberal could object to such gratification?

Fuck knows what Dave Douglas was thinking. It all smacked of some anarcho-maoist collective discussion in the early 70s interlinked with a Brian Rix farce. Meanwhile, out there was a miners' strike raging while we contemplated our belly buttons and below. Funnily enough none of the miners at Mansfield had asked me if I was bisexual before buying a paper off me. I wished I was somewhere else. The discussion dribbled away at the frayed edges in the late afternoon sunshine. I can't remember what happened the following day – I can't even recall being bi-sexualised by anyone.

The meeting was inconclusive. A lot of shouting – a non-meeting of minds – aggressive posturings and heated denials. I threatened to leave CW and start a local Hackney paper like *Alarm*. Unfortunately, for my ego no-one seemed unduly bothered at this threat. Most people seemed too tired to raise the necessary vitriol to the required levels for a major bust-up – it just meandered through irritable pettiness. I didn't leave. I didn't really know what to do. It had been a crabby waste of a day but where else was there to go without throwing away all the political opportunities we had going for us. At the end of the meeting I suggested that from now on Class War meetings should be for people who considered themselves to be part of Class War only. How many people there thought they were part of Class War I asked. Five hands went up out of about 30. But the logic was unassailable. From now on CW meetings were for class warriors. The other flotsam and jetsam would have to find another audience for their views. It looked like our next meeting would be a small one.

On Sunday night Martin Wright phoned up to say the London Autonomists would join CW.

PEACE AT LAST

Martin's decision to join CW after the bust-up meeting was followed by practically everyone else there joining as well. Maybe he sensed the incongruity of CW meetings being full of non-CWers and decided to get stuck in. Maybe not. I really don't know what accounted for the change of atmosphere but the bickering and backbiting faded away.

Despite the tensions and vicissitudes of the last year, me and Martin's political relationship had born up well. We sensed some oomph and imagination and commitment in each other. Martin's favourite line at meetings was 'the train's leaving the station to you'd better get on fucking board'. Well, now we were both for the next year to build the movement free from the tiresome backbiting.

With this aim in mind, we went to a Discussion on Sexuality at the Roseberry Avenue Peace Centre. This was a mixed meeting organised by the anarcha-feminist punks – most of whom detested CW's real commitment to violence, our 'alleged' macho posturings and the pro-prostitution, anti-feminist line contained in the 'One For the Girls Issue'. By the end of the day their low opinion of us had sunk even lower. We'd taken Juan Zapata with us, the Spanish Republican hormonally induced giant, we'd met at STC and found out that the affable colossus was in fact only 16 years old.

Juan's two genuinely honest answers to questions posed by the chairwoman sealed CW's fate with the anarcha-feminists. The gentle giant had mentioned he took his washing home for his mum to do.

'Why do you take your washing home for your mum to do?'

Zapata answered disarmingly: 'Because she likes doing it.'

Uproar from affronted anarcha-feminists and outbursts of spontaneous laughter at the honest naivety of his answers were seen as compliancy with his crimes.

Zapata had also said he was a sadist. This made a refreshingly honest change from the parade of men displaying their non-sexist credentials. 'Why do you think you're a sadist?' asked a Patricia Hewiit voice. 'Cos I like hurting people,' replied the gentle giant.

We exited. Stage Left. Pronto.

WE VISIT CRASS

After STC2 when Crass had put themselves about to such good effect, myself, Ron, Charlie, Gareth and Sean paid a visit to the legendary North Weald farmhouse to smooth over any remaining differences or past misunderstandings between us. It has to be admitted that the make-up of our high powered negotiating team left something to be desired – no women and three paid up members of the Masonite tendency. The Masonite leader himself was cracking jokes about black rags hanging on the washing line and lentil stew for tea. Charlie was prevailed upon to leave his bar of soap (which he wielded like a cross at Dracula) on the train. Andy Palmer picked us up from the station and sure enough as we neared the house we could see black uniforms flapping in the wind and on entry – a bubbling cauldron of lentil stew to sniggers from the Masonites. This could be far from a meeting of minds I thought looking imploringly to Gareth the Mr. Sensible of our party. However, things turned out rather well.

We were warmly and hospitably received by the full crew. There was no doubt that some members of the band had dramatically changed away from pacifism during the last two years – their support for the striking miners and STC being indicative of this. Phil Free, Andy Palmer, Penny Rimbaud, Steve Ignorant and Gee Vaucher spent the whole day nutting the violence/non-violence issue out with us. Penny seemed to be starting on the long road towards support for Angry Brigade-style tactics. We encouraged Crass to come to our conferences, the Bash the Rich marches and Henley Regatta. Once Sean Mason and the others had got into long and genuine political discussion with Crass attitudes changed on both sides with respect for each others commitment. Sean refused to eat the lentil stew on ethical grounds but we squeezed a grudging: 'Their music's shit, their clothes are shit and they're dirt crustie hippies, but...' out of him on the train back to civilisation. And things flowed from there onwards. Phil Free came to our Big Caxton Hall rally and some plans were developed by Crass for the Henley Regatta which never quite came to fruition but which would have been fairly spectacular.

Penny and Gee in particular dealt with the reasons the band was ending in 1984 as long promised. The real problem to them was the contradiction between being a band encouraging people to think for themselves resulting in the creation of hundreds of Crass clones saying 'we must think for ourselves.'

'Why did the Crass Punk cross the road?Because Crass told him to' had got too close to reality and they honourably kept to their finish date. I went up from Swansea with Mamf to their last gig at the Colosseum in Aberdare during the miners' strike. It had been arranged by my old mate Paul Pritchard from Cardiff and I'd wondered if Aberdare would take the expected punk influx better than Maesteg had an influx of hippies 20 years earlier! We arrived about 4.30 and dived into the pub next door to the closed doors of The Colosseum. The landlord was staring out of the windows at the punks as if they'd arrived from Planet Zarg!

'Look at that lot' he said to me confidentially like I was his new best friend. 'I ain't letting them in.' None of the locals seemed to know anything about it being a miners' benefit . It was just another gig – could've been Man from Swansea or Budgie from Cardiff for all they knew. We told him it was a benefit for the miners and the punks would drink lots of cider... He relented. By the time the gig was due to start the pub was awash with punks, miners and the locals getting on in storming fashion. I remember one miner greasing up his hair into a Mohican! 'Our class in all its diverse glory' I whispered sentimentally to Mamf.

The gig was a stormer. I went backstage to congratulate them. They were understandably subdued. It was their last ever gig so they weren't in backslapping mode. On the way back to Swansea I wondered what would happen if Crass were to publicly throw in their lot with Class War and unite our two armies. Maybe I should phone them in the morning. Maybe not. They'd determined their path and it wasn't for us to hijack it. In the event apart from one ludicrous plan to march round the country from Sellafield (hurriedly abandoned in case it got out of hand) the Crass army was like the German fleet after Jutland – never trusted to go out to battle. Still, it was their army. We'd have to create our own.

In the winter of 1984 we had the idea to knock out a Class War single in support of the miners strike entitled Victory to The Hit Squads. It was a Chas 'n' Dave type singalong ditty penned by myself.

And it's victory to the Hit Squads
Victory to our class
We will make McGregor
Kiss Arthur Scargill's arse
From Maltby down to Orgreave
We'll leave out calling cards
In overturned police cars
And burnt out colliers' yards.

(To the same tune as *Better Dead than Wed* which we did release as a single later to commemorate the Royal Wedding).

Ian Slaughter knew Andy Martin, once of the Apostles, so had the idea that Andy might be able to help us out on the music side. We traipsed over to Andy's place near Victoria Park where Hackney punk legend crusties Eat Shit were bashing about and volunteered their backing band services to the CW ....

We did some posing about on a nearby building sight with ski-masks and scaffolding poles as a cover photo opportunity for the record sleeve.

Bash The Rich

The actual day of the recording had to be postponed due to an all too usual fuck-up about access to the studio. In the meantime, Colin Jerwood from Conflict had been on to me about a possible miners' benefit gig at the 100 Club. Yes please, and I added the names of the Living Legends and Eat Shit as support bands. Two meetings were arranged with Colin to sort the details out but he didn't show up either time. In the event there was a complete information fuck-up between us. I arrived at the 100 Club to find Eat Shit furious on the Oxford Street pavement. Colin had said they couldn't play and Eat Shit blamed me. In the ensuing bad vibes the world of music missed out on the Eat Shit/Class War miners' strike single and who knows what success might have followed!

Although Colin had an annoying-as-fuck tendency not to turn up to meetings I had a lot of time for Colin, Paco and Biffa. They at least seemed to inhabit the same world as the rest of us and were always up for it whenever we suggested something to them.

There were a rash of punk squats in London at the time. The Burn It Down Ballroom in Finchley, The Bingo Hall in Kilburn, Dickie Dirts in Camberwell, the Ambulance Station in Old Kent Road, all of which provided CW with good regular paper sales outlets. Spike and Tim Paine, two of the first anarcho-punks to get involved with CW, opened up a squat in Albany Street which served as both an anarchist bookshop and CW's contact address. Napoleon, an associate of Eat Shit, used to hang out there sitting in front of a TV with a smashed up screen all day – that's real situationism! He never ever washed or changed his clothes 'cos he had the theory that if you didn't wash for three months the body's natural oils took over and washed away all your spots and scabs. Maybe they did, he was engaging company anyway. Hospitable as well. Trouble was he used to offer you bread out of bins with his tell-tale black as soot paw marks all over it.

Mr
Bone

Charlie and Ian Slaughter used to wave bars of soap at him every time he entered the room like they were warding off Dracula with a silver cross. Napoleon wasn't flummoxed by the 'dirty crustie squatter' talk. He was last seen planning to squat the derelict Brighton West Pier. The proletarian donkey-jacketed cloth capped CW leadership might have wanted to lead a spick-and-span working class army but the reality was that as of 1984 most of our troops looked more like Napoleon.

We went down to Brighton for the TUC annual congress during the miners' strike, flogged shitloads of papers, got pissed with the miners, met a couple of sound jack-the-lad Red Action types from the Pembury Estate in Hackney, and linked up with the Brighton mob. Ron knocked some papers out of the hands of a World Revolution paper seller resulting in their next issue's full page article about the incident 'A warning to the revolutionary milieu'. This failed to credit Ron with the attack but warned revolutionaries from Korea to Kamchatka to beware of us!

When I was in Swansea I used to buy *The Worker* the occasionally Maoist paper of The Communist Party of Britain Marxist-Leninist from their lone Swansea adherent – called 'Scotch egg' for some reason! For sectarian know-alls this was 'Reg Birch's lot' but otherwise they were Maoists for a bit then aligned with that delightful socialist Enver Hoxha of Albania who funded their paper. One week there was a photo of the Paris Commune on one page – dead horses, pikes, barricades – and of the glorious Central Committee of the Communist Party of Albania on the other. Unfortunately, the captions had been mixed up giving the impression the central committee was made up of blokes with beards, bedsocks on their heads and a penchant for killing horses with pikes! The next issue the whole paper thundered 'A warning to the revolutionary milieu' denouncing imperialist sabotage at the printers! In the evening we stuck Coal not Dole stickers on our chests and blagged our way into the TUC reception for bigwigs

197

Mr
Wright

in The Grand Hotel for a late night drinking session. Phil Gard had come prepared for some soporific TUC speeches and brought a 'Black Bomber' to keep himself awake. As he was about to take the bomber it rolled from his hand across the floor. We hadn't noticed but then saw Phil crawling desperately among the ankles of the TUC Titans of Labour looking for his amphetamine hit. The Brighton Bomber had struck early!

RIOT AGAINST RONNIE

After Stop the City, Class War's reputation had grown rapidly. We were in contact with a lot of other like-minded anarchist groups and papers outside London, many of whom came down to a big Reagan demo organising meeting we had in the Roebuck in Tottenham Court Road.

Most of the movement outside London was still anarcho-punkville, and the CW meeting at the Roebuck was a culture shock for many of them. The Bristol anarchist magazine *Stuff It* described their impressions: 'Going to a CW meeting is like going to Albania – men with short hair in short sleeved shirts'. The hammer-headed way the meeting was conducted – with a chair, hands up if you want to speak etc – was also alien to those used to the loosely disorganised meetings of punk squatdom. It was the biggest CW meeting to date, with 70-80 people, and the first time we'd managed to organise beyond London. We met Lee Groves and Fran from the Bristol Anarchists – ex punkers soon to become Sean Masonite middle class-hating class warriors. Lee was to produce his own one man version of Class War – *ACAB* – in time for the Reagan demo before throwing in his lot with us and becoming the leading spokesman for the workerist faction. To the donkey jacketed, flat cap wearing short sleeved, cropped haired London CW hard core though he still looked like a fucking punker. The meeting, despite fashion discordance, however was 'a big step forward comrades'.

The Reagan day itself was oddly mixed. We couldn't get anywhere near Lancaster House and tail-ended a whooping it up anarcho-punk mob running round central London – ending up at a rally in Trafalgar Square (the opposite of what we'd intended). We had to rescue something from the day's disappointment. Thinking on our feet we decided to trash the Savoy just up the Strand. The word was spread furtively out of the corners of many mouths and about 100 black flag carriers sidled away from the rally at 4pm and self-consciously drifted up towards the Savoy. Down the side of the Savoy towards the Embankment there was a lorry full of scaffolding poles.

Whoop! Go for it! The poles came off the lorry. Red Rick – an old brick shithouse builder mate from Swansea – caves the first windows in with the poles. Crash, every Savoy glass window in sight goes in. Up and away and leg it down to the river. Five minutes and still no sign of the cops coming. OK, let's have another pop. 4.30pm. Covent Garden: disperse, mingle and meet up there, and we'll start with the big bank on the corner. Covent Garden – no black flags now – the distant sound of belated cops getting to the Savoy. People have picked up ammunition on the way. 4.40pm we'll go for it. Trash everything in sight. Self-conscious adrenalin pumping five minutes. All that talking in meetings and this is what its all about. Red Rick leads the way again. Two bricks straight through the bank windows. Shoppers scatter screaming. We run through Covent Garden trashing everything in sight. The sound of smashing glass cascading after us. A two minute rampage around the streets – an American skinhead girl gets pulled for trashing one restaurant window too many. She'll be fucked if she's charged with all that damage. We've done just about enough – but only just about enough.

Chapter 24

KENSINGTON BASH THE RICH MARCH

Bone added, with a sneering attempt at humour, that 'they would not necessarily bash the rich areas completely flat.'
Sunday People, 8 February 1984

Emboldened by our Park Lane Rose and Hunt Ball actions, we decided to organise a Bash The Rich (BTR) march in Kensington on 11 May 1984. We'd start off from our strongholds in Ladbroke Grove (well, the Warwick Castle pub in Portobello Road) and march to the mansions of Holland Park. The simplicity of the Bash The Rich concept was outstanding. No demands, no 'what do we wants – when do we do its', no misery, no victimhood: just the chance to vent a splenetic class hatred on the rich, and give them verbal grief in their own muses.

It would be like a football away-day crew. Neat little stickers printed up: 'Bash The Rich: attitude hostile, balaclavas optional'. The idea was to end up back in Meanwhile Gardens for a bit of a rally where we could pump up our great victory. As this was the first ever BTR march we weren't yet promising to leave Kensington a 'smouldering ruin' as we were later to do at Hampstead!

This was very much 'let the first frissons of fear cross their cosseted lives' and 'this is just a start wankers, we'll be back'. The idea was to make them jumpy, to worry about their cars, to say 'we ain't far away, it's just down the fucking road, the cops can't look after you full time.' As far as we knew this was the first time people had marched on a rich area to say 'We have no demands to make of you, there are no concessions you can make to get rid of us. Our banners read only 'Behold Your Future

Executioners'. Plus it sounded as funny as fuck! People were bewildered and perplexed 'Can you just do that?' someone asked. 'Are you allowed?'

'Yes we fucking can,' we answered, well sure of ourselves my son. In reality, we didn't know what the fuck would happen, or what the police response would be. I don't think they did either.

BASH THE
RICH MARCH
LONDON MAY 11th 2Pm.
LADBROKE GROVE TO KENSINGTON
CLASS WAR BOX CW84b WHITECHAPEL HIGH ST,E1
(ATTITUDE HOSTILE)

Sometimes there's just a minute when things go wrong when you could say, if only this or that had happened. The start of the Kensington Bash The Rich march was one such moment. We had absolutely no idea how many people would show up. We'd had 30 at our Rose and Hunt Ball actions in Park Lane, but this was a more publicised affair, where we'd taken a chance and could fall flat on our faces.

The cure to calm down first night nerves was as always to get to the pub early on so me, Martin, Matt, Adrienne and Steve could all be found in the Warwick Castle knocking 'em back. The Warwick Castle was Class War's de facto west London HQ thanks to Ray Jones' paper-selling abilities in the pub and the vibrant bohemian social scene he'd created in there graced by such luminaries as Jock Scot, Bernie, Rogue Mayhem, Roadent, Pete from Rough Trade, Tony Allen, Kevin Allen, John the Hat, Heathcote Williams and Labour Councillor for Golbourne ward Maxwell Worrall – all presided over by legendary landlord Seamus.

On the dot of 1.57pm, we left with Steve Sutton and Fabian holding proudly aloft our very fine Bash The Rich banner. We rounded the corner into Ladbroke Grove and there was about 100 people there with homemade banners, placards and the occasional balaclava. Not bad at all. Me heart gladdened and my step quickened. Now as any demo veteran knows if you advertise a march for 2pm, you don't leave until 3pm, to allow your forces to muster and very few turn up on the dot of

Bash The Rich

2pm, plus on this occasion, there were lots of lurkers in surrounding streets waiting to be emboldened by the sight of a decent turnout. So naturally, we thought we'd wait at Ladbroke Grove for an hour. But what's this? The march is moving off too fucking soon.

Steve and Fabian, our banner carriers, had been asked by the cops to move off and headed off down Ladbroke Grove without even consulting the rest of us. The Class War invisible leadership – and the other 100 – head off after the banner, and they're walking fast as well. We later learn there were three separate marches. Our early starters, another lot who turned up after we'd left and set off an hour later, and a third lot gathered in Meanwhile Gardens with Crass and co. waiting for the march to arrive at its advertised finish. That was the minute we really lost the opportunity for a big impressive march, once Steve and Fabian had jumped the starting gun.

Still, we were cock-a-hoop as we moved off down Ladbroke Grove. We were actually fucking doing it – what we said – marching to a rich area with a full-on cop escort. The lurking doubters in the side streets straggled after us. We hadn't all been nicked at the start after all. We were pulling it fucking off.

There was a church fete going on halfway down Ladbroke Grove. Bewildered church goers were treated to a rendition of 'Burn it down, burn it down, burn it down' followed by 'We'll be back, we'll be back, we'll be back'. I looked back excitedly at the sight of our Class War mob about 200 strong. I'd have been even more excited if I'd known there was another 300 or so still trying to find us. We had no idea where we were going apart from a vague general direction of doing a circular loop through Holland Park and back through Notting Hill. In the event, the cops directed us – they certainly didn't force us – into Holland Park where we held our rally. In front of our banner, we announced our arrival on the political map. In dark glasses, flat cap and megaphone in hand Martin looked the part, and I waded in with the soon to be familiar troop rousing rhetoric followed by Pete Mastin and others. 'This is only the start... today for the first time... the rich cower behind their curtains... police to protect them... we'll be back... anarchist movement on the streets... smouldering ruins.'

And that was it – anti-climactic, a missed opportunity because of the early start, many people thought we'd never even marched, but it didn't feel like that to me. We'd been bold, we'd done what we said we would while others doubted and back slid. We had a mob, we had arrived, and we were in the fucking pub.

OPEN UP THE SECOND FRONT

Throughout the Autumn of 1984, we made better and better links with the miners. Besides Dave Douglas's Hatfield Main lot, we struck up a strong bond with miners from the Fitzwilliam pit in West Yorkshire. Copies of *Class War* were widely circulating throughout the coalfield areas of the People's Republic of South Yorkshire. CW groups close to the coalfields – Bradford, Doncaster, Sheffield in particular – were getting stuck into the picket lines and day-to-day guerrilla warfare on a regular basis. Disorder was spilling over from the pit villages like Maltby and Grimethorpe into sporadic anti-cop violence in these nearby cities of a kind that hadn't been seen since the summer of 1981. The paramilitary hit squads that suddenly appeared trashing NCB property in the autumn spurred us on to take action, based on our August conference discussions.

We'd heard reports from Dave Douglas and the Fitzwilliam mob that miners fleeing from police baton charges at Orgreave had been faced with lefties trying to flog papers to them. We had no wish to tail end such parasitic behaviour – our strength was in the inner cities which were stubbornly refusing to erupt on cue just when the miners needed them. Our line was clear – it was our duty to open up a Second Front of inner-city rioting to pull the cops away from the mining areas. In a

Bash The Rich

clear incitement to violence and riot, Martin wrote a very strong article in *Class War*, almost as if it were an internal discussion document rather than one for public consumption, advocating just such a course of action 'the next time the lights go out'. It was quite breathtaking in its openness and disregard of any consequences.

'So as the strike enters the winter months with the possibility of power cuts, we put forward these as yet rough suggestions to genuine revolutionaries and anarchists who aren't of the wally variety!

To organise from within the movement, as we've done in the past, by word of mouth and the usual informal contacts meetings involving delegates from as many trustworthy anarchist groups as possible.

Planning deliberate spectacular mini-riots as soon as the power cuts arrive. Or, failing that, late afternoon darkness. The aim being to spark off trouble in the major urban areas, thus drawing police out of the mining areas.

As proved on the July anti-Reagan demo, we can cause thousands of pounds worth of damage without suffering a single arrest, if well planned and co-ordinated. Judging by Stop the City turnouts and our own interventions, we can raise a force of at least 200 in London alone. This may be a conservative estimate. Obviously, we don't intend squandering people in a face-to-face confrontation, as we may need to repeat the performance. Besides, we're not of the martyr material. In case the sceptical reader may wonder how such a plan could be achieved, here's a brief scenario. Of course it's only by comrades working together that we can oil out the mechanics of the operation.

Thanks to the Electricity Board publicising where blackouts occur, we could assemble in a certain area at a pre-arranged time. Any sign of abnormal police presence would mean postponement.

Kensington Bash The Rich March

The ideal area would be a shopping area such as a high street. The crowds providing perfect cover when assembling our teams. Plenty of escape routes would be necessary. Gloves, scarves and balaclavas wouldn't arouse suspicion during the winter.

At a pre-arranged signal upon the advent of lights-out, the mob could condense within seconds, swinging into action. Parked cars should be dragged across the road, turned over, or even set alight, forming barricades, and causing traffic chaos there by making police access more difficult. Windows must be smashed, looting encouraged. Those police first on the scene, if small in number, could be resisted with bricks and other throwable material. Before they can gather sufficient strength, again at a pre-arranged signal, we'd disperse into the darkness.

Headlines captured, it wouldn't take long for the example to spread. Against the background we'd blend, time to add our political dimension.

Propaganda urging the opening of a second front, with the attendant looting and rioting, must appear beforehand. It should be made clear that these actions are a deliberate effort to spread class conflict as opened by the miners' strike. While the spreading of propaganda is an important task, we can't afford to dilute our numbers by having some engaging in their own individual actions simultaneously as has happened in recent times. Not only do they draw numbers away but these alternative actions mysteriously fail to appear. As a side interest, this would show who really meant business and who was all mouth. No one group should lead it, this is our common task. We've just contributed with this suggestion, now's the time to discuss the matter seriously.

There is no alternative as far as we can see. It's all right to sloganise about setting up factory committees or community councils and call for a general strike. As these don't seem to be materialising it all remains a comfortable abstraction. We're not

Bash The Rich

the vanguard but as a tiny fraction of the class, the plan mapped out above is the only realistic action we can indulge ourselves in, gain results for the miners AND ourselves.'

Guy Fawkes night was always going to be a good bet for some direct action with its usual lawlessness and fire raising. In addition, there was a big fair and firework display at Alexandra Palace which had attracted some anti-cop violence in the past. Nearby was Wood Green Shopping City – a palace of plate glass and consumerism. There was a well-established group of anarchist and Class War supporters there who could be relied on. Several meetings of our London wide contacts were held at Molly's squatted anarchist cafe in Cross Street, Islington. Autonomous groups such as the Tufnell Park Militia and Streatham Action Group were tied into our planning. The strategy was thus: We could start some anti-cop trouble up at Alexandra Palace and try to drag it sporadically down to Wood Green Shopping City. Avoiding arrests, hit and run but trying to drag in a much wider mob than just ourselves. We could smash the shops in Wood Green High Street, encouraging looting and then stand our ground and fight the cops.

Portable market stalls lined part of the road and these could be dragged on to the roads to block traffic and hold up police reinforcements. After that we'd have to think on our feet. If it worked we could hope for copy cat violence in other cities if it made headlines. There were the CW groups in the North – Liverpool, Manchester, Bradford, Newcastle, Doncaster, Sheffield, Leeds – who would be on standby to do the same. Meet outside Wood Green Tube Station at 6pm.

It's as cold as fuck in the Guy Fawkes smoke haze. With a frosty clarity of purpose, I bus it up to Wood Green. I don't trust the Tube for fear of being pulled by the cops. Word of the target should NOT have got out but our discussions and communications methods ain't exactly watertight. How right I fucking am! Outside the Tube station, there's about 20 14-year-olds running round saying there's going to be a riot. One kid comes up to me and asks if I've come for the riot. 'Of course I fucking have,' I reply to his glee. I ain't paranoid. This was quite likely to happen – I ain't seeing spooks or grasses everywhere.

We'd asked the Wood Green lot to spread the general time and date around to any locals who might get stuck in. And they'd done so. It wouldn't stop the plan – didn't mean the cops knew all we were up to – a bit of fine tuning with the time maybe. Scout for the arrivals and tell them to sit in pub opposite. Shit, I see Spike arriving on the up escalator. He doesn't exactly look inconspicuous in full black ragged anarcho-punk outfit. He's pulled by the cops inside the station. Smoke flares pulled from his knapsack and promptly nicked. Still, it's firework night – he should be able to talk his way out of that one.

The rest of us retreat to the pub for a pow wow. Kick off was going to be 8pm but that's out now with the amount of cops crawling about. We walk up to Ally Pally but no joy there either with all the cop vans snaking around. It wouldn't allow us to get enough of a build up to drag people back to Wood Green. A distinct lack of attackable targets also. Retreat to pub in Wood Green. We'll have to kick it off after closing time and hope for the best. I shove the pints down my throat in rapid succession. Whether the cops are there or not, there's no way we can back out of this one. I have the usual panics about whether we'll just get nicked for the criminal damage or done for conspiracy. 11.10pm – we can delay no longer. We rush out of the pub across the road, not a fucking cop in sight. XXXXX kicks it off with a litter bin through some shop window. Whoop! Go for it! 'Keep Wood Green Tidy' bins make effective ammunition as one after the other flies through the air. There are about 40 of us now. Everyone's up for it, spread out along the High Street, window after window going through. Cars screech to a halt. We've passed the main shopping centre and trashed everything down towards Turnpike Lane. Every window goes in, including Oxfam and Cancer Research we discover later, but you ain't selective in these circumstances. Builders' street lamps, benches, rubble, shop signs are through the air. We grab some loose scaffolding poles and crash window after window with our jabbing lances. We're suddenly among the market stalls. We push them in the road as planned to halt the traffic. Scared shitless drivers motor straight over them or crash up round on the pavements. Now we're supposed to stand and wait for the cops to arrive – that was the plan in Molly's anyway.

A quick shifty shows we've not attracted anyone but ourselves to the rampage. The hoped for Ally Pally street gangs, the chucking out time drinkers, the 14-year-old kids, there's none of them around. No freelancers getting stuck in inspired by our example, no autonomist activists creeping out to do the dirty deeds. Just the same 40 we left the pub with. Fuck it, to stand and fight on our own with that fuckload of damage behind us is going to cop us all years. The first sirens in the distance. No discussions needed, no group discussion on the street. Instinctively we split away in twos and threes and head for home down the backways. Even then we can hear windows going as the sirens get nearer – some late arriving freelancers after all. There's a fuck sight lot of cop action running just parallel to where we are heading heart fast beating home. Two cop vans top and tail the street peering through windows and their riot visors at us. Keep calm, walk normal, don't look at the fucking vans, keep talking about any old bollocks. The cops speed up and off. We make it home to Hackney. Drunk and chuffed as fuck we'd done it and got away. The morning after things looked a little different.

Five of the Wood Green anarchists had done some late trashing after we'd fucked off. Got nicked, charged with the whole lot of damage and remanded in custody. Fuck all in the papers – just a 'Punks in wrecking spree' in the *Daily Mirror*.

Just like the Reagan demo, we'd caused enough damage to keep our honour satisfied and we'd acted as we'd promised each other we could. No one bottled it. Good for building CW group solidarity. But, the damage done had made no connection with the causes they were done for. Mystified shop keepers blamed mindless vandalism. There were no 'anti-Reagan mob trash Covent Garden', headlines, nothing about 'miners supporters trash Wood Green'. We'd conspicuously failed to drag in others to join in our wrecking spree. Maybe we should have kicked it off earlier on when there were still lots of kids about.

What next? Learn from Robert the Bruce...

Chapter 25

THATCHER

'The Best Cut Of All'... The meat cleaver slicing through Thatcher's cranium with livid red blood splooshing across a startled face. Unfortunately, not a reality but *Class War*'s most popular cover. It turned up on T-shirts and a full-on Trade Union-type banner from Newcastle held proudly aloft by a gang of pissed-up miners on the razzle in Jubilee Gardens. Our follow-up during the BSE crisis of Thatcher picture with 'Mad Cow' underneath was another winner.

OK, let's tell it like it was. Without Thatcher, there wouldn't have been Class War. Straight up. No messing. You couldn't have felt that level of bitterness, anger, loathing, hate, violence towards Ted Heath or Callaghan. Thatcher was a class warrior – just on the other side to us. She was set to wage an unrelenting and pitiless war on our class and Class War was spawned as a result.

Thatcher wanted to obliterate the working class in the sense of destroying its knowledge of itself as a class with its own interests. Wherever there was some collective experience of life as a class in work (steelworkers, dockers, miners), in leisure (standing terraces at football, free festivals, Notting Hill Carnival) or place (inner cities, front lines, council estates) they were privatised, policed or gentrified out of existence. Her calculatedly softly spoken compassionate promise 'we must do something about the inner cities' on election night wasn't a promise of better things to come but a threat to the Labour-voting heartlands. 'Doing something' meant 'decanting' the inhabitants out to Basildon where they would hopefully become Tory voting home-owners and turning the homes they'd been 'decanted' from into loft apartments for Tory-voting yuppies.

It was 'policing by design' as the Thatcherite copper Chief Inspector Pearman of Notting Hill archly summed it up. The troublesome front lines of Railton Road, All Saints Road and Sandringham Road weren't to be policed to death, they were to be picture framed out of existence. It was a policy of 'spatial decomposition' in posh words but 'class cleansing' summed it up better. No wonder we were fucking livid!

Class War could never have taken off the way it did from 1983 to 1985 without Thatcher. Class War didn't bleat about how nasty Thatcher was – we just said 'come on then you fucker, we know what you're up to, we're up for a fight'. If you read the *Socialist Worker* of the time, they're a fucking laugh. I'm surprised they didn't hand out a free onion with every issue so we could sob about how wicked Thatcher was. Unlike the left, we didn't just react to her agenda with the mind-numbing banalities of 'defend this... we demand that... what do we want?' We trailed after one SWPer and his loud hailer chanting: 'What do we want... SOMETHING!... When do we want it... WHEN YOU CAN GET ROUND TO GIVING IT TO US'. He told us we were infantile.

We went on the offensive. They attack us, we'll attack them – Henley, Rose Ball, Bash The Rich marches. In the 1960s, the back drop of the Vietnam War on our daily TV bulletins politicised us. In 1984 and 1985, it was the bitter class war of the miners' strike that daily intruded into our brain stems and sustained a level of political consciousness and hate unparalleled since.

Our links with the miners developed rapidly. In particular in South Yorkshire where whole mining communities were on the verge of insurrection. In the People's Republic of South Yorkshire, villages such as Grimethorpe and Maltby were at permanent war with the police. We'd developed especially good links with Fitzwilliam and Hatfield Main miners. Comrades from Stoke, Sheffield and Bradford went out on commando-style training manoeuvres with the miners from the villages who were to become the core of the hit squads. The Fitzwilliam lads had been unimpressed with the veganism of some of the Sheffield Class Warriors and decided to see if they were 'up for it'. One night coming back from the pub, they dressed up in stolen cop helmets and riot shields

Me with Fran and Lee from
Bristol

and stormed into the house the Sheffield mob were staying in. Armed with a vegetarian diet and baseball bats the Sheffield mob battered the fuck out of the first two 'cops' through the door. 'Fair do.' they groaned, and the vegan 'weaklings' were well trusted from then on.

In reverse, Bristol Class War told us that a trip to South Wales by some Bristol anarchists had resulted in a withdrawal of support for the miners, 'because they ate meat'.

The miners' strike meant CW groups were springing up all over the country. There was no quality control. Anyone could call themselves Class War. But me and Adrienne used to visit the more lively groups – Liverpool, Sheffield, Bristol, Cambridge. CW-style local papers were springing up all over. One day a magazine called *Angry* arrived, proclaiming itself to be 'The theoretical journal of *Class War*'. What the fuck? We didn't want a fucking theoretical journal! We made a virtue of having no theory! But it was fucking good. Acerbic, slicing through the usual leftie platitudes, rigorous and spot-on. It came from Edinburgh. Was there a gang of Class War intellectuals we'd missed out on, churning out theory from the buffet bar at Waverley Station? No. It was produced by a 14-year-old schoolboy from Bridge of Allan. Our newly acquired theoretical journal was edited by a 14-year-old called Chris Low who quickly became another trusted confidante of Ian Slaughter and the side-of-the-mouth brigade. Chris was a fucking excellent comrade to boot! It was like that.

Things were happening we knew nothing about, events tumbling into each other. We had a weird trip to Bristol with Chris Low. In Bristol, we learnt that Paul Lashmar and David Leigh of *The Observer* were trying to set up some sort of sting on us by infiltrating someone into the London group. But the infiltratee had blurted it out to Bristol CW. We went looking for him. Bristol Class War seemed to be made up of plumbers and builders so a motley crue of punks and scaffolders boarded an open-topped lorry, armed to the teeth with spanners and planks and toured the city looking for

Ron and me in the George Canning

him. It must have made for a comical sight. Eventually we tracked him down and Chris Low was first through the door with his cosh in one hand and sherbert dab in the other!

Our intelligence units had foiled the plot but we hardly had time to stop and bother as Thatcher's face flickered on the TV screens against the backdrop of Orgreave and nightly picket line violence. We were becoming full-time revolutionaries – in permanent session. Nightly phone calls between me and Martin updating on the latest events from around the country. Everything else was on the back burner. Those were the days my friend. Oh yes, those were the days.

Fast forward to 1992... 'Rioting on the streets won't get rid of the Poll Tax, only the return of a Labour Government will do that,' said Neil Kinnock. Well, not quite right there, eh Kinnockio. You didn't get elected but civil disobedience and street rioting did for the Poll Tax and Thatcher. Seven years earlier.

At the start of 1985, it truly seemed to us in Class War that a combination of striking miners and inner city rioters could bring down the Thatcher government. If the inner cities were to go up on the same scale as they had in 1981, then there is no way the police would have had the numbers to police the strike picket lines and the inner cities. In the event, the miners' strike ended in April 1985 and Brixton went up in October 1985 – five months apart – and closely followed by Handsworth

Bash The Rich

and Broadwater Farm. If Brixton and Tottenham had erupted six months earlier who knows what might have happened. The probability was that Moss Side, St Paul's, Chapeltown and Toxteth would have followed suit. The Met would have had to divert their overtime-saturated boys back to London to prevent the Hackneys and Notting Hills erupting. If Sheffield, Bradford and Leeds went up, what price the policing of the pit villages like Grimethorpe, Rossington and Maltby, leave lone the picket lines outside power stations and the needs to protect the Notts scabs? It couldn't have been done. The Army would have had to have been called out and who knows, given Thatcher's unpopularity, whether public opinion would have stomached rubber bullets cutting down striking miners.

Only ten years earlier, Heath had been in conflict with the miners and when he asked the question 'who runs Britain?' he got the surprise answer 'not you, mate.'

Fanciful? Wish fulfilment? I didn't think so then and I don't think so now. Class War's perspective was a lot more on the ball than the parasitic Trots rattling collecting buckets and selling their papers. At Orgreave, the SWP had actually been trying to shift their crock of shit paper to miners fleeing mounted police. The oligarchic leadership and corduroy-trousered poly lecturer megaphone robots of the SWP didn't want the inner cities to go up. In 1981, they tried to foist their ludicrous demands – 'jobs jobs jobs' – on the rioters. The rioters had no need for anyone to mediate their anger but they weren't going to stick around to give interviews afterwards, leaving a vacuum for the leaders of the left to fill in with their outdated demands for jobs, youth clubs, leisure centres and ping-pong with the fucking vicar.

Similarly, while the SWPers were eager to support the dignity of labour, the right to work, the miners as noble aristocrats of labour, the miners we met were just like us: totally pissed off with work, Thatcher, and the poverty of everyday life. Yorkshire miners talked to us about flooding the fucking pits, about how they never wanted to go back to work. They were having a much more fun time during the strike –

alcoholically, sexually and joyfully – than when they were working. I was at a miners' rally in Islington Town Hall addressed by Arthur Scargill. He was preceded by a passionate speech by a miner's wife: 'My father died of silicosis, his brother of pneumoconiosis, my husband was disabled in a pit accident, my brother has white finger – but I'll fight for that future for my children and children's children'. Tumultuous applause from the Islington class tourists of the left. We looked across at our comrades from the Fitzwilliam pits sitting across the hall. They grinned at us, pulling their fingers across their throats in cut throat manner – rather die than

Thatcher was always visiting victims in hospital, after
various public transport disasters like
Kings Cross. I devised the THATCH CARD to counter
this vile possibility.

suffer that shit again. Imagine how cheated and disgusted the Islington lefties would have been if one of the Fitzwilliam boys had stood up and replied 'fuck that for a lark'.

Unlike the left, we devotedly did not want a return to the bad old days. We didn't want a return to fucking 'normality'. The Trots wanted normality, so they could teach the defeated heroes of labour the reason for their defeat – that is 'follow our leadership'. Even if the strike ended, we wanted the hostilities to go on. Who needed an excuse to fight with the cops and attack Thatcher and her Tory scumbags? Not us. Were the kids suffering the stultifying boredom of the pit villages really only wanting a return to the status quo. We wanted the RIOT to work not the fucking RIGHT to work. It was summed up in a picture in *Class War* No. 1 of a black kid's face pressed to a coppers during the 1981 Brixton riot; the caption read 'Look at this geezer, is he asking the way to the job centre?' During the Stop The City, I got knocked over in a push and shove outside the Royal Exchange with lots of people falling on top of me. Someone hauled me out by the leg – it was Attila the Stockbroker. Someone by the arm – it was one of the Fitzwilliam miners. Someone by the other arm – it was one of the Jethros. And a couple of punks helped me finally struggle free. It was our rainbow coalition. I had no doubt that we could bring Thatcher down that year. We fucking could have, you know.

HERE'S MUD IN YOUR EYE

For two years we had dogged CND: Hyde Park, Islington, Coventry, Cardiff, because we wanted to detach the more radical elements away from pointless hot-air rallies and into direct action. CND, like the later Stop the War Coalition against the Iraq war, must rank as one of the most ineffective protest movements ever. They marched their troops up and down to Hyde Park again and again and did nothing with them till they grew bored and faded away.

The projected Ring the Base action at Molesworth in 1985 offered us the opportunity to take some direct action however. A peace camp had been set up there for months and a peace chapel erected. On the contrary, we proposed a war camp and had designs to kick over the ludicrous peace chapel. We took a van load down to Molesworth and linked up with Class Warriors from all over the country, including Chris Lowe our theoretical organ editor from Edinburgh and Fran and Lee from Bristol, who were no longer shocked by the sight of a short-sleeved shirt and were, as usual, up for a rumble. In the event, the action didn't amount to much more than rattling the fence for a bit and lobbing mud over at the security guards in the pissing rain. However, Bone had already saved the day! On our arrival in a Glastonbury-style mud bath, it became apparent there was a VIP-only tent where the CND leadership was entertaining the media. This was in pristine condition with matting on the floor and cars were able to pull up to the entrance.

In the meantime, the sodden protestors were left to their own devices with no Champagne reception from the CND leaders inside in the warm. I inveigled myself into the press tent just as the insufferably smug Joan Ruddock (complete with fetching and mud free hat and scarf) was welcoming the VIP press visitors and apologising for the mud. Apologising for the bloody mud! 'Fuck that' I thought, picked up a handful of mud and smeared it over Ruddock's smug features. 'Infantile!' she screamed at me, as the press snapped away, the TV pictures appearing on the national news bulletins that night. Once again, a piece of 'infantile' action had got CW in the headlines and kept our momentum going. It was the last time we bothered with CND. We had our own mobs now. Time to try them out elsewhere.

Chapter 26

THE WEEKLY MEETING

Like the first conference in Portobello Road, Class War meetings were always in pubs and were often chaotic drunken affairs. In other words, they were always a good night out. For a supposedly secretive group, the meetings were open to anyone who turned up and quite a few nutters did. By now we needed a bigger room so we moved up to Kings Cross to The Copenhagen in York Way. We told the landlord we were CND but he was a canny operator and quickly sussed we where something a bit livelier. It turned out he was the man in the Licensed Victuallers Association (LVA) who had had the TGWU thrown out of the TUC for a day for ignoring an official strike. One day he said to us when we came in: 'There's someone for you lot in the other bar.'

'How do you know?' we inquired.

He pointed us to a bloke in a ski mask, like the gimp in *Pulp Fiction*, drinking his beer through a straw. 'Yes, looks like one of ours,' I acknowledged.

Then there was Mad Mark who proposed we blew up the whole of the South East of England.

'But millions of people would die,' we rationally counter argued.

'Yes, but it would get in the papers,' replied Mark with inexorable logic. He turned out to be a girlfriend beater so the Stamford Hill mob kidnapped him tied him naked to a stone at Stonehenge and said he'd be killed if he ever came back to London. As you do. Then there where Vicky and Nick and a whole succession of sociopath casualties who would normally have been tolerated in the anarchist movement but quickly got the heave-ho from ours. One night, I came straight from my mum and dad's to the meeting carrying a six-foot fluffy penguin they'd got for my kids. The penguin was elected chair of the meeting and maintained good order throughout.

We'd invited Colin Jerwood and Paco from *Conflict* over to the meeting one night for the first time. There had been an Irish wake going on downstairs all day and things were pretty heavy from the start. We went upstairs to the meeting room and after five minutes, a guy raced through the room and jumped head first through the glass window pursued by five or six others with chairs and broken bottles. Colin looked on approvingly – we obviously weren't bullshitters!

Oliver came along one night. Afterwards, he came up to me. He'd enjoyed the meeting but lived out in Ealing so thought he'd go to his local branch in future as Kings Cross was a long way to come. 'Local branch... er... no this isn't the Kings Cross branch... this is Class War... all of it'. He looked at me disbelievingly. Yes, the 20 or so people upstairs was Class War, all of it, the fuckin' lot, everyone! Sometimes the paper's triumphalism led to slight disappointment for newcomers when confronted with reality.

Usually meetings were 20 to 30 strong and attended by sane rational human beings unlike the aforementioned nutters.There were regular visitors from out-of-town groups. There was a lively mob in Brighton including Viking Tony and Mark the Destroyer, a one-man avenger squad on the property of the rich, and Glyn who would go on to be one of the major players in Class War and a rock-solid comrade.

The Sheffield crew were made up of Jesus, Mary and Barn! Barn being Mark Barnsley who would later go on to get ten years after being framed by the Sheffield coppers. The Bradford mob were coming out of the One in Twelve Club and its excellent paper *Knee Deep in Shit*. Howard and Simon from Keighley were also regular visitors to the London meetings.

Manchester Class War were mainly from the huge Hulme estate while the Liverpool anarchist group was one of the biggest and most working class-based groups in the country with Paul Newton a leading light, along with Brian and Psychic TV Dave. The informal organisation of Class War meant that you hardly ever knew anyone's second name, often only a name like Sean from Southampton. This wasn't because of some brilliant security conscious cell structure, it was just the haphazard nature of Class War!

The meetings made all the decisions about what we were doing, where we were going, and the next issue of the paper as well as consuming prodigious quantities of booze. Eventually, we moved on to The Rosemary Branch in Islington. There had been a violent riot in Trafalgar Square that day at the end of an anti-Apartheid march in which the Class War mob had played a central role. Everyone arrived at the meeting on a high of adrenaline. Fabian Tompsett addressed the meeting:

> 'Things had moved on to a different stage – a different level in the Class War. We had moved out of the ghetto and our ideas where resonating within the working class. But now we must expect repression. There would be arrests, the paper might be suppressed. Oh yes, but much worse, we could expect long prison sentences for conspiracy, maybe even life sentences or death as the police move to smash us. This was inevitable. The door was open (it was), it was make your mind up time we weren't play fighting anymore. Those who weren't up for it, to face the future, should leave now before the going got tough.'

He gestured towards the door. An uneasy silence followed. The comrades thought about the seriousness of what Fabian had outlined. A minute went by. Then everyone got up and walked through the door! We had rejected Fabian's future of death and life imprisonment for one of immediate gratification of booze, sex and rioting street violence. The same thought bubble had appeared about everyone else's cranium. We weren't martyrs. We giggled hysterically as Fabian sat on his own in the room. But, in reality, he wasn't so far off the mark. Pete Mastin was already earmarked for a jail sentence for his role in the Trafalgar Square riot that afternoon. Tim Paine was in prison for smashing up Barclays Bank in Islington. The landlord of The Rosemary Branch told us he'd been visited by Special Branch. Things had moved on to a new level. Big brother was watching us in 1984. 1985 could be revolution or bust.

NUREMBURG

It sometimes felt Class War was in permanent session. In just over a year we'd had three conferences in London, one in Stoke, one in Bristol and one in Sheffield, all open to anyone.

It would be fair to say that (although I'm no Beau Brummell) the Stoke group were sartorially challenged. When we met them for the first time Steve Sutton gasped 'Fucking hell! It's like a scene from Macbeth!' A vast tub of glutinous vegan stodge was served up as home-cooked conference fayre. There were no takers and Martin quickly added a deathshead logo and the warning 'poison' on the side of the trough.

The London group held weekly meetings in contrast to the torporific sloth of the other anarchist groups who could hardly get it together to meet once a year. Most of them seemed to be populated by vitamin-deficient charisma-by-pass types with an abject poverty of expectation that they could ever change anything. They were just going through the motions. Meeting weekly gave us the opportunity to actively intervene rather than just tailend events with some lame analysis.

One night, someone said there was a press conference of TUC windbags outside Congress House so we dived down there and I stuck a *Class War* over Jack Dromey's head on live news 'Childish' scolded our anarchist intellectuals who always had far better things to do – but which were sadly never visible.

In May 1985, we decided to organise not another conference but a

Bash The Rich

rally. This was a sure sign of our growing confidence. English anarchists weren't used to rallies. They'd never had enough fucking numbers for one for a start! There were to be no chairs arranged in circles, handwritten agendas, or talking sticks (oh how we laughed!). There would be a designated chair for each session and speakers to kick each topic off. Speakers' tables and microphones – fucking microphones whoopee! – and the audience arranged out front in traditional rows. The whole affair was to be videoed by John and Jake for possible distribution worldwide!

There were bound to be objections but we had the confidence in our own abilities to win the day. In fact, we were looking forward to being challenged because it would give us a chance to show a clear break with the past. We were something new and exciting and weren't going to be hamstrung any more by the inertia and woolly thinking that passed for English anarchism. It was our Clause 4 moment. No doubt Blair has seen the video and copied our style.

All our best speakers were lined up – Martin, Me, Angie, Tim, Jake, Pete, Dick, Tina and comrades from outside London. Once they'd kicked off the topic anyone could speak from the floor. The agenda was:

(1) *Class War*, the paper
(2) Henley Regatta
(3) Football hooliganism
(4) Schools
(5) Bash The Rich
(6) Miners' Strike
(7) Riots
Oh, I almost forgot…
(8) Stonehenge!

The 1985 rally really marked Class War at the height of its powers. We'd just come out of the miners' strike and we were expecting the inner cities to go up. We'd had the Stop the City rampage, our own Bash The

Rich march and the movement-jolting publicity of Andrew Tyler's *Time Out* article. We had in place a hardcore of 50 to 60 people who were wildly disparate but also seriously ooomphy! We were no longer a 'current' in a wider movement, we were the fucking movement! We were Class War. If you don't like it, tough shit, get used to it. There's a lot more coming your fucking way. That was our mindset at the start of the day.

On a bright sunshiny day in Caxton Hall, more than 200 people had turned up, a far cry from the 40 who'd turned up to our last conference. There was a real buzz about the place and, more to the point, I didn't know at least half of the people there. I'd confessed to Phil Gard I'd never before belonged to a political group where I didn't know everyone. Now I did. Even better. There were fucking paper sellers outside our rally – I swear it. After a lifetime selling papers outside other people's meetings, what a delight, they were selling papers outside our rally! We must have fucking made it at last!

The meeting kicked off with objections to videoing, the lay out, who'd drawn up the agenda, and then, my fingers twitched with excitement as the mouse stuck its head in the trap, who the hell sold out by doing an interview with *Time Out*!

I strode to the front. I noticed Martin eager with anticipation. This was our fucking moment. I apologised for the *Time Out* article. How wrong it was to get our views across to so many new people. Let's not tell anyone about our ideas. Let's keep it to an exclusive club. Let's be anonymous, have no confidence in our politics, hide behind anonymity.

Fuck that for a lark – those bad old days were over, crawl back to that safe warm anarchist ghetto if you must, roll on interviews with the News of the Screws, the train was leaving the fucking station, if you didn't like it, fuck off!

Wild applause, cheering, cacophony. Now it was Martin Wright's turn. How could he follow that, he said self-deprecatingly. He could. For those who'd never seen Martin speak before, it must have been a right fucking eye-opener. Coruscatingly-biting, erudite, vein-popping, head-nodding Mussolini-style, ferocious, side-achingly funny, as virtuoso piece of rabble rousing as anyone there had seen. And the rabble was roused.

After Dick had introduced the footie hooligan section, with graphic tales of his Pompey crew fighting the cops, an unknown young casual strode confidently to the front. He was like a mini-Martin, a Sean Mason gone right. Politics was all bollocks, lefties were bollocks, anarchists were bollocks, Class War was the dogs bollocks!

Angie Wardle delivered a storming speech in her knees-up Mother Brown cockney rhyming slang putting to the sword the notion Class War was a macho boys club. 'We ain't playing any more,' she finished. It hung in the air over lunch. The buzz was palpable. 'We ain't playing any more' should've been on a huge screen behind her like some spin-doctored Labour party slogan behind Blair.

There were nostalgic reminders of the old anarcho scene that we were leaving behind, however, when Mad Mark announced to the conference in triumphalist tone that he had liberated the worms from the wormery in the pre-school crèche. The collective groan was groaned!

We all got pissed at lunchtime in the pub opposite. I got pissed. The afternoon was building for the Henley Regatta. 'Let's 'ave 500 people with sledgehammers steaming across the bridge to the royal enclosure' That was the lucid bit. I was struggling to make a point about the class divide in health terms but the brain cells were too addled with warm beer: 'Old people are dying of hypothermia'... pause... long pause... 'Young people are dying of fucking hypothermia'... Pause. Desperate look for an offstage prompt... bewildered eyes... 'Everyone's dying of fucking hypothermia' A large shepherd's crook drags me off stage.

Job well done my son. Still available on fuzzy video.

WILDE IN THE (WEST) COUNTRY

At the end of 1983, we went down to Bristol for a quiet weekend with Lee and Fran — our now full-on Class Warriors. As we walked down from the bus station, we saw an Army recruiting van was stuck in the traffic. Fran jumped in front of it screaming abuse, windmilling her arms, banging on the doors and windscreen. The soldiers looked bemused at this crazed punk dervish spitting fire at them. We walked towards Broadmead passing a bridal wear shop. Well Adrienne, Lee and me passed it — Fran didn't! She was inside screaming about fucking marriage enslaving women, shoving over the bridal gown mannequins.

We moved on through Castle Park. Kim Wilde had the misfortune to be doing a photo shoot to promote some new make-up range for *Smash Hits* or the like, surrounded by happy snappers. Not now she ain't. Fran is berating her about make-up and dressing up to please men and being a plastic corporate whore. Fuck me! We've only been in Bristol ten minutes and it's permanent war! But being in Class War was like that — exhilarating and without any concept of deferred gratification. If you didn't like something, you'd go for it in the here and now — give 'em grief. You wouldn't develop a ten-year plan to abolish it, or a transitional demand, or organise a meeting to discuss how bad it was. You'd fucking shout and rage at it whenever you saw it! That summer, kids all over the country were leaping in front of Mercedes

Bash the Rich

denting the panels and shouting 'Rich scum!' at the occupants. People didn't get it. We didn't want to 'Kick the Tories Out' as the Left did. We wanted to 'Kick the Tories In'

OI AZNAVOUR — FUCK OFF!

A few of us were walking up Park Lane one evening when we saw Charles Aznavour going into The Dorchester. We shouted and jeered. He waved back thinking we were fans. The change on his face when a can whistled over past his head was a joy to behold.

CRANE SPOTTING

We were at Glastonbury paper-selling. A geezer with 'Security' written large on his back walked past us. 'Fucking hell, that's Nicky Crane!' exclaimed Sean Kenny (Southampton Class War). Could it really be Nicky 'Strength Thro Oi' Crane heading up security at Glastonbury? Carole, Sean's partner, had no doubts and led Sean in haring after him. I, famously, stopped to do up me shoelace! Carole caught up with Crane, and his minder, and started battering him about the head. Crane and his pal legged it up the path towards the security compound with Carole and Sean in hot pursuit shouting 'fucking Nazi' at Crane. Two Rastas leapt out of a darkened tent and one of them floored Crane with a right rural haymaker!

FRIAR TUCK!

We met up with Brother Silas in the White Hart in Whitechapel — not far from Peter the Painter's old watering hole. Brother Silas was not a trade union kind of brother, he was a full-on Class War monk from a monastery in the East End. We didn't have any trouble spotting him, he was in brown hooded Friar Tuck outfit. He didn't carry money (rules of the order) but downed a swift six pints, propping up the bar in his sandals and ranting against the rich. He was impressed with my 'camel through the eye of a needle' quote but provided plenty more of a class vengeance nature. He said he'd always wanted to be in a riot. Fucking cor blimey! What kudos a rioting monk would bring! Friar Tuck and his merry men and us as Robin Hoods. The imagination ran riot if nothing else! The Wapping strike, on Silas' doorstep, was only weeks away. Unfortunately, he never made it. We got a postcard. Brother Silas had been given a free transfer to Lindisfarne by his evil Abbot where he could contemplate 'certain issues'.

WE ARE ALL MESRINES
Two very cool revolutionary criminals from the French gang and publication *Os Cangeceiros* turned up — both Jacques Mesrine to a tee. We never normally had foreign anarchist contacts because no one 'could place us in their tradition'. Ho! Fucking Ho! But *Os Cangeceiros* located us right in the middle of their tradition alright. 'We are insurrectionists,' they'd grin approvingly. They had a fearsome array of slingshots and martial arts weapons. One day, they were watching the news at Adrienne's flat. A Moroccan prisoner had taken a judge hostage at gunpoint in a courtroom in Lyon. They leaped up. 'It is our comrade,' they said. 'We must go'. They went.

Chapter 27

HOORAY HENLEY

Summer 1985, Henley

5am: 'Brring, brring'. It's Keith Allen with a film crew already up and about in Henley. 'Where are the boys?' Somewhere in the *Comic Strip* vaults, there are still four hours of unseen Henley Regatta film.

10am: Paddington Station. Clock lots of Class Warriors trying to look inconspicuous. People in the ill-fitting suits you wear to magistrates' courts. Promising. Looks like a full turnout. No bottle jobs. Board the train to Henley, full of Hooray Henries and Henriettas. Not time to start kicking off now and get nicked before getting to Henley.

10.15am: Ealing Broadway. A load of black kids get on heading for some fun at Henley. They rip the piss out of the toffs and shove them around.

10.20am: Southall. About ten casuals get on, well-armed with Special Brew which they shake up and accidentally soak a few frocks. Fucking good! For sure, we wanted to attract many independent groups to Henley so it wasn't just the CW hardcore and the early signs were promising. Martin and Adrienne had, for once, done a recce the week before. Our avowed aim was to storm across the bridge to get in amongst the hospitality tents and royal enclosure. The publicity in *Class War* meant that there were sure to be tons of cops so all would depend on numbers on the day. But, for once, we had a plan B – which quickly became Plan A. We would take the cops by surprise by launching an audacious pre-emptive attack on Henley Police Station at 11.30am. These plans made at the weekly meetings were always distinguished by a typical gung-ho lack of detailed planning. But this time, at least we knew where the fucking police station was!

Hooray Henley

As the train neared Henley, there were tons of cop vans and coaches parked up in fields and two helicopters overhead. Fucking good I thought – let the fuckers be under siege with wall to wall cops to protect them. We could make good propaganda out of that later.

The cops were turning back people at the station. The black kids don't make it off the platform. My cunning disguise, short-sleeved summer shirt, gets me through. Still half an hour until we attack the cop shop. Will any of the pubs let us in? There are bouncers on all the doors but our disguises see us through. Three pints of Brakespears in 20 minutes does the brain blitz and sets the adrenalin flowing.

11.25am: Hit the cop shop. Or maybe not. The place is wall-to-wall copper, maybe 200 of them right outside in riot vans.

11.35am: Back for more Brakespears.

1pm: It's time to wander off for the serious business of the day. Fuck me, there's tons of punks wandering around. Everyone had been told to come in disguise, but there's groups of mohicanned punks all over. We spot Trevor's gang of Swansea punks. It's not hard, Trevor and some kilted punkette are shagging in a shop doorway! So much for the low fucking profile. 'All right Ian, look at this,' says Trevor. 'We stayed on a boat last night'. They've nicked the steering wheel and are bowling it down Henley High Street. Winks and nods of acknowledgement as we clock lots of other groups. John Preston's mob from Llandeilo, the Jethros from Exeter, lots of the old Mutants from West Wales, the Portobello mob including Ray Jones, Jake Arnott and Keith Allen, and most of our own networks are here. There are, surprisingly, a lot of the more serious libertarian socialist and autonomist types such as Ed Emery of Red Notes come to clock the fun. Excitement and booze is geeing me up. Must start doing something. We walk along the bank by the river where gingham tablecloths and hampers are out. About

Bash The Rich

30 of us walk along kicking chairs and hampers into the Thames and nicking Champagne bottles. Some protesting toff is sent sprawling on his arse by the Jethros. Elsewhere the Henries and Henriettas are being jostled and spat at. Boaters knocked off, and the sound of the first shop window caving in electrified everyone to make it towards the bridge. Its low-level guerrilla warfare out of the sight of the cops – tripping the toffs up, accidentally barging into them, opening shook up beer cans next to their faces, spitting, threatening, standing in their way, smashing their sunglasses. There are over 1,000 cops on duty, but they can't protect the fucking toffs. By now, there's over 200 of us by the bridge jeering the hoorays as they pass by, and the first can of Special Brew is caressed in a looping arc through the air.

We are now surrounded by the cops outside the Red Lion pub but the toffs are still too scared to cross the bridge. We launch into a few choruses of *The Rich, The rich, We Gotta Get Rid of the Rich* and assorted battle cries of 'rich scum'. The bridge is blocked by cops and their tow-away vehicles. The cops pick me out and threaten to arrest anyone who doesn't move on. We've got to break out of here before we get corralled in. We filter away in twos and threes to resume our guerrilla marauding around Henley. A BMW is turned over to cheers, the Tory Club window goes in, fists start to fly, and some hoorays decide to sunbathe fully clothed in the streets. First celebrity victim – a straw boatered Rick Wakeman is knocked out cold and hospitalised! Bricks and bottles fly over back lanes into the gardens of rich mansions as startled sunbathers flee inside. Now a Mercedes has gone over, all its windows caved in. Posh cars are booted as their drivers try to speed pass us, cops vans sirens blazing are racing around trying to keep up with the action. A few vicious little rucks break out with the steroid-rich rowing crews.

There are 43 arrests including Martin Wright whose boot imprint somehow matches the dent on a passing roller, but still the toffs are soaked in their own Pimms and strawberries, and a flotilla of crushed straw boaters drifts forlornly under the bridge.

Hooray Henley

After my rant at the bridge, I have a farcical personal police escort everywhere I go. Time to drift away again and the cops shepherd us back to the railway station where, amazingly, we are left alone with a lot of fleeing hoorays who decide to give our train a miss.

On main TV news that night, there's pictures of me ranting like a preacher at the bridge. Next day at a GLC rally in Battersea Park Ken, Livingstone is doing a live TV interview when a passing scaffolder intervenes: 'Why weren't you with the boys at Henley Ken?' On the *Wogan* show, a stripey-blazerred George Melly is asked if he went to Henley: 'No' replies George, 'but if I did, it would have been with the anarchists.'

We'd broken out of the anarchist ghetto and impinged on the national consciousness – and had a fucking top day out to boot. I write in the next *Class War*:

> *Of course, our sophisticated intellectual revolutionary friends on the left will continue to deride us for actions such as Henley. From their well-paid sinecures as lecturers, social workers, probation officers and teachers propping up the system they allegedly despise, they will laugh patronisingly when we talk of jostling the rich in the streets. In Hampstead and Islington, these wankers will prattle on about Nicaragua, Marxism Today, yesterday and every fucking way. Cosily insulated from the rising class anger on the streets, for them, politics is a trendy hobby. For us, class hatred is a daily reality and one these wankers will find out about soon enough.'*

The left might not realise it yet but, as far as Henley was concerned, we were truly on our way brothers and sisters!

MOONRAKER

Kate Davies finally got her way — the Class Warriors went to Stonehenge. Well, Pete Mastin and Steve Sutton did. The 'peace convoy' had been built up by the press into folk devils and we wanted to see what was going to happen as they pushed for the banned festival at Stonehenge. We also wanted to spread the word about our projected attack on the Henley Regatta the following month. If we could persuade the convoy to come to Henley, it would create a major panic. We were into building alliances with groups fighting back against Thatcher whether it was travellers, miners, animal liberationists, or riotous youths from Toxteth to St Paul's.

What happened at the Beanfield was a total fucking shocker to us all. I truly mean shocked! We'd seen the cops laying into the miners, their wives, their kids. We'd seen it at Stop The City and the inner city riots. That's what the cops did for fuck's sake — no point bleating about it — it was a war. They hit us, we hit them. I said 'we hit them' — not 'hit them back', because we didn't pretend our violence was retaliatory in response to some police excess as the lefties whined. We got our retaliation in first. That's why we ran our ever popular Page 3 'Hospitalised Copper' pin up in every issue.

But Stonehenge was different. It seemed like an unprotected massacre. What film there was that was allowed to be shown on TV was gut-churning. People we knew being hammered by the cops with unrelenting ferocity and unable to protect themselves in view of the tooled-up overwhelming odds against them. I actually watched in stunned silence — you couldn't joke it away. This was the way it was going to be in Thatcher's Britain. There were strong rumours for months that the cops had killed someone at the Beanfield. Pete and Steve were banged up for days around the South Coast nicks before arriving back with their war stories.

Coming at the end of the miners' strike, it seemed that Thatcher was rewarding her police force by letting them batter the fuck out of anyone they didn't like, with impunity. The demonisation of the travellers had run for months in the press, softening the public up for the attack. It has to be said that if it wasn't for the very honourable toff Lord Cardigan and the equally honourable Kim Sabido of Independent Radio News, I've no doubt there would have been deaths at the Beanfield. Against this background, we were not lying low but preparing to march into Henley-on-Thames mob handed. Who knew what the police response would be to that?

Later the police attacked the convoy again at Nostell Priory in Yorkshire — where miners and their families came to their aid in a fine example of anti-Thatcher solidarity.

Personally, the attack on the convoy in Wiltshire angered me more than I could imagine. I am still fucking irked by it today. Don't know why. Maybe it is because I'm a proud Moonraker myself — born just west of Salisbury in the same room in the same house in Hindon that my mum was born in. So we were proper Moonraker people. Now the Wiltshire cops had shamed us Moonrakers. We might be slow to rile but there's still some avenging to be done in my book.

WEATHERMAN

Many people in Class War were heavily influenced by the events in Italy in the 1970s and autonomist politics around groups like Lotta Continua and Potere Operaiea, but Autonomia had passed me by in Swansea. American radicalism hadn't. In 1966, I'd visited the Wooden Shoe bookshop in Old Compton Street where serving at the counter were Albert Meltzer and Stuart Christie. I was, of course, too shy to talk to them but I did pick up copies of *Heatwave*, *King Mob Echo*, *Black Mask* and *Resurgence*. They were all mind-blowing radical reads for a tyro-anarchist like me but they certainly moved my politics on a bit.

I was particularly entranced by *Resurgence*. This *Resurgence* (not to be confused with the English title, not that you could once you opened the front page) was the paper of the Resurgence Youth Movement in Chicago which seemed to be an anarchist street gang allied with The Blackstone Rangers (a famous Chicago gang) and later with The Young Lords (the Puerto Rican version of the Black Panthers). It was full of apocalyptic violence and threats which suited my impressionable brain. Other journals were written by one or two situationists, *Resurgence* claimed to be a gang of toughs. It might have been bollocks but the politicised street gang concept stayed with me. The Watts uprising in LA and the black revolts in the American cities made many of us believe insurrection was possible in the affluent west and that it wasn't going to come from any ideology-bound leftist, or anarchist, organisations. Sure, the Black Panther leaders were inspirational, but we weren't so deluded to think of ourselves on a similar level of struggle to the murderous repression they faced. Anyway, Mick Farren's English version (the White Panthers) had already cleaned up that franchise years before *Class War*.

The Weathermen (and Weatherwomen) who came out of the SDS during the Vietnam War were influential on me but only in one way. I didn't share their Marxist-Leninism, their contempt for the white working class, or their little rich kid commitment to bombing our class into revolution. 'The Days of Rage' in Chicago might have inspired our desire for all-out confrontation by marching into rich areas looking for confrontation but they also prefigured the problems with that tactic — you could only do it once before the cops knew how to deal with it. Still they did look good marching in their combats, helmets and baseball bats! And doubtless fed into my psyche somewhere what a gang of Class Warriors might look like in the UK.

Blocking the bridge at Henley. Inset:
The pub name seems appropriate

CLASS WAR

...OU RICH BE JOKI//
FUCKING SCUMBAG...

WE 'RE GONNA GET YOU.

IN THE CLASS WAR SPRING OFFENSIVE AGAINST THE RICH

CLASS WAR

WE HAVE FOUND NEW
HOMES FOR THE RICH

Outside the Warwick Castle in Portobello Road with Cynthia Payne

243

BOMBS NOT

Xtra!'s neat subversion of CND logo

244

JOBS

245

SECTION FOUR

THE FUNCTION OF THE ORGAN

Chapter 28

THE BEANO

Very few journalists ever wrote perceptively about *Class War*. One exception was Ian Jack – now editor of *Granta* – in *The Observer* who picked up on Class War's use of language. He was intrigued by our use of archaic terms for the rich, such as 'Toffs' and verbs like 'Bash'. He thought these both echoed back to Victorian street urchins argot with overlays of Lord Snooty and his pals from *The Beano*. 'Was it deliberate?' he mused. 'And what did it portend?'

'Something crude and curious is happening to the English language here,' wrote Jack. 'As though it was being howled by a cockney mob which had been plied with gin and then let loose among the landaus at Derby Day, around the time Frith painted it.' He went on: 'Ian Bone takes a great delight in this linguistic revivalism – the invectacive of Victorian outcast London.'

Invectacive journalism,' I called it, hoping to have coined another winner. Iain Sinclair asked the same in the August pages of *The London Review of Books*. Was *Class War* the first sign that the dispossessed and guttersnipes from the runnels and rookeries of Victorian England were coming back to get what was their own? On reflection, he thought not! But Sinclair and Peter Ackroyd's sense of the past infecting the present hung over us on still days.

Ackroyd identified Clerkenwell as the radical heart of London where both Marx and Lenin had toiled at writing desks and the Peasants' Revolt had culminated. *Class War* was printed just round the corner. Our first gatherings were in, by chance or not, The Crown and Woolpack in Islington where the Bolsheviks in exile had met.

Well the Bash Street Kids were obviously a major influence on *Class War* but we were consciously trying to resurrect images of the rich from Lord Snooty and his pals. 'Rich snobs' and 'Snooty rich bastards' resurrected the old certainties of 'Them' and 'Us' which the left had been attempting to blur for years with their 'Marxism Today' hogwash. Leftist politicians were always announcing 'the end of class struggle' or claiming 'we are all middle class now' or some other bollocks. We were saying nothing had changed. The Lord Snootys of this world are still running the show. When the lefties used to secretly buy *Class War* off us on demonstrations by way of ameliorating their

Hasek

crime they'd say 'I only buy it cos it's a laugh' or 'It's just like a comic' or even make direct comparisons to *The Beano* itself. We liked *The Beano* comparison. I'd always been keen on the chapter in Robert Tressell's *The Ragged-Trousered Philanthropist* called *The Beano* which describes the Charabanc outing and the beer bottles with their rubber stoppers and crates. We did consciously echo back to earlier English images of class struggle and Robert Blatchford's 'Merrie England'.

It was working-class English writers, such as Robert Tressell, the early Robert Blatchford and particularly Jack Common who I desired to imitate in their determination to describe socialist ideals in everyday language and articulate a political philosophy which was rooted in the day-to-day experience of working-class people. Common, mixed his laconic but class-conscious rejection of work in the 1930s with an almost Reichian analysis of politics. It was a joy to discover him writing 'the world has been their lido long enough. Now we're going to have some fun.'

Bash The Rich

The Party for Peaceful and
Moderate Progress within
the Bounds of the Law

Our real political influence was the English mob and we intended to be the proud inheritors of that mob tradition stretching back to the Peasants' Revolt but finding its first real form in the London mob of the civil war period. The books that influenced me were *The World Turned Upside Down* by Christopher Hill, *Albion's Fatal Tree* by Peter Linebaugh and others and EP Thompson's heroic *The Making of the English Working Class*. The new school of history of ordinary people pioneered by Hill and Thompson enabled us to discover our own antecedents. I was thrilled reading all of them and far more influenced by these history books than any anarchist theory.

Hill's account of the New Model Army, the Levellers and the Agitators, the *Putney Debates* and the recorded vox pops of ordinary people of the time ('I just as well worship a lump of dung as any god or king') were both funny and revelatory. The execution of the Leveller rebel Robert Lockier gets under my skin and saddens me still to this day. The real goose-pimple moment comes in an episode from the *Putney Debates*. Cromwell and Fairfax are increasingly exasperated by the Leveller's demands for equality – not apparently made with any reference to religion, Christ, or god, as was the custom.

'By what right or power do you make these demands?' inquires Fairfax. After a pause the reply came.

'By the power of the sword, master Fairfax, by the power of the sword.' Whoops! Jesus Christ! What did he fucking say! Stick that up your warty old nose Master Cromwell! They don't like it up 'em do them. Them masters! Historically, this shouldn't have happened. There was no class-consciousness according to Marx till the establishment of the proletariat 200 years later. But imagine the frisson of fear that must of flittered across Fairfax and Cromwell's cerebellums as they exited to consider their positions. What the Leveller agitator meant was that the force Cromwell had created – the New Model Army – was, or more to the point, could be, the power in the land who could have their way by physical force, not by divine right or permission of their betters! What a fucking moment! Fairfax and Cromwell scuttled off to send the mutinous regiments to Ireland and murder those who refused to go at Burford.

EP Thompson's *The Making of the English Working Class* was the most influential book of the lot on me with its proud and previously unwritten history of the ordinary man and woman and more particularly the mobs they coalesced and ran with.

Thompson describes the failed Luddite raid on Rawfold's Mill in Yorkshire. The authorities were convinced Luddite attacks were masterminded by one General Ned Ludd himself. They carried off a young wounded Luddite to a nearby inn where a priest was fetched to encourage the mortally wounded youth to reveal all about General Ludd's identity.

'Who is General Ludd?' inquired the priest.

'Father, can you keep a secret?' whispered the Luddite

'Yes, yes my son,' ingratiates the priest.

'So can I,' says the Luddite with his last breath.

That's some fucking bottle you wankers, I thought to myself.

We were Class War. We were with the Levellers and the Agitators, the smugglers, poachers and mobs battling the surgeons at Tyburn Tree. We were with the Gordon Rioters, Dic Penderyn's Merthyr Uprising, the Scotch Cattle, the Hosts of Rebecca, the Luddites, Captain Swing, John Frost's March on Newport, the looters and rioters in Queen Square, Bristol in 1831, the physical force chartists, the men of no property, the defeated but unbowed from James Naylor to Bronterre O'Brien. In the 20th century, we might have been Red Clydesiders with John Maclean, James Connolly's Citizen Army and Sylvia Pankhurst's suffragettes but our closer identities were with the unnamed, the forgotten, the anonymous class strugglers, the rioters, the dispossessed.

Another English influence was George Orwell. The obvious read was *Homage to Catalonia* with its early eulogy to Anarchist Barcelona: 'I had never been in a city before where the working class were in the saddle', but Orwell's kind of pipe-smoking English radicalism was a greater influence than Bakunin or Kropotkin. Orwell's attempts with Tom Wintringham to turn the Home Guard into a revolutionary fighting force in 1941 showed that it was not just 1919 or 1968 that were the radical years of the century.

The people who formed the core of Class War early on were politically well-sussed and well-read. Invited guests to Martin's 'inner sanctum' could see an unrivalled library of revolutionary literature. There were council communists, workers' councilists, autonomists, situationists, libertarian Marxists as well as anarchists. People like Martin and Phil Gard knew their Anton Pannekoek from their Herman Gorter, their Paul Mattick from their Raya Dunayevskaya. They were well- read but didn't have to wear their learning on their sleeves or talk in that strange language that comes over people when they start to babble about 'theory'. To have such knowledge and still be able to write simply was the true marvel of early *Class War*. Jake's much quoted article 'What do we do when the cops fuck off' could have been written ' The creation of pre-figurative forms of struggle, blah, blah.' But Jake was cleverer than that.

I had obviously been heavily influenced by Solidarity and in particular by their analysis of the Kronstadt uprising of 1921. Kronstadt was for years the benchmark to divide Trot from anarchist. By 1985, I was happy to accept the label 'anarchist' or 'workers' councillist' but at heart I was a Victor Sergeist. Serge had his faults but, to me, he was a revolutionary humanist besides being a great novelist. *Memoirs of a Revolutionary* – a painstakingly honest read – was never far from my bedside table. Nor was *The Good Soldier Schweik* by Jarsolav Hasek. If Serge was a Bolshevik then Hasek was just bolshy. Hasek's true-life adventures, in particular the establishment of The Party of Peaceful and Moderate Progress Within the Bounds of the Law, and his sly subversion masked as doltishness were an early influence. He demonstrated to me that humour as well as commitment was a necessary component of revolutionary propaganda. Hasek and Serge bizarrely inhabited the same

Lucy Parsons

country in same year – 1919 in revolutionary Russia. You wondered if, by accident, they might have unknowingly bumped into each other. But there were others at the same time: Rosa Luxemburg, Ret Marut, Gustav Landauer, Eric Mühsam, Maria Spiridonova, Simon Radowitzky, Lucy Parsons, Buenaventura Durruti, Francisco Ascaso, Nestor Makhno, whose actions and lives (and deaths) were inspirational.

The thought of the wrangling during the brief flaring of the Munich Soviet about who should be Minister of Agriculture brought to an end by Landauer's exasperate (but realistic) 'Does it matter? We'll all be shot within 48 hours' was heroic in my book. Maria Spiridonova of the Left Socialist Revolutionaries (now one of history's forgotten movements because the peasants of the SRs have no modern heirs) was the one person who just might have overthrown the Bolsheviks and certainly had the bottle to have a go at it. She was murdered by Stalin in 1941. Simon Radowitzky escaped from prison at Ushaia on Tierra Del Fuego – the prison at the end of the world – and stepped blinking into the daylight in Uruguay a fighter in two continents like Durutti and Ascaso.

As any reader of the first two *Class Wars* will notice from their front page quotations that Lucy Parsons was a particular heroine of mine. The ferocity of her writing in her *Letter to Tramps* heavily influenced my

Bash The Rich

Class War house style. It was published in *The Alarm* in 1884, hence the name of our Swansea paper.

In fact, the whole of Parsons' vitriolic writing was the rationale behind *Class War*'s very existence and the inspiration for our Bash The Rich campaigns. It's not hard to see how:

> *'Stroll you down the avenues of the rich and look through the magnificent plate windows into their voluptuous houses and here you will discover the robbers who have despoiled you and yours. Then let your tragedy be enacted here. Awaken them from their wanton sports at your expense! Send forth your petition and let them read it by the red glare of destruction.'*

Fucking magnificent exposition of class hatred. How could anyone not come to Henley with a steely resolve after dosing on Lucy's incandescent rhetoric. I couldn't do better myself – though I tried, believe me!

Chapter 29

THE FUNCTION OF THE ORGAN

Any thinking revolutionary with the merest hint of a self-critical faculty would have to ask 'Why are there so few of us?' But they don't. Recently, the leader of the Anarchist Federation revealed they had 75 members – this after 20 years existence. Far from being downcast, however, he considered this figure to be something of an upturn. 'The flow is towards us comrades. Our politics are increasingly finding resonance,' etc etc. It was reminiscent of my own joy at the 'seven' Solidarities Ian Garvie had sold at Milford Haven in 1972. A couple of letters in a week asking to join your organisation can send you giddying into heights of optimism. Maybe a third person has asked a friend in Manchester about joining? What next? Is the flood about to become a torrent?

Delusional triumphalism has been refined to perfection by the SWP which keeps its members in a permanent state of retarded ejaculation by news of a cleaners' strike in Barnoldswick, five papers sold in Rugby, or a tide of global events interpreted by the leadership as proof that their cogent analysis of capitalism has, yet again, been demonstrated correct by events. Those who believe they hold the truth are always delusional. Take the 75 members of the Anarchist Federation. They believe that, if they can explain rationally to the other 54 million of us that capitalism is an unjust system, they will have their Damascene conversion.

God Bless You Young Sirs.

It had never occurred to me before that 2% of the population owning 96% of the wealth was anything other than a fair and just system. But now you have lifted the veil from my eyes I can see it clearly. My whole life has

Bash The Rich

been wasted in the erroneous belief that we lived in a fair and democratic
system. Please enlist me in the next talk on the platformist programme of
Nestor Makhno.

   Yours in solidarity,
   Horny-handed Son of Toil

The truth of course is that people do not respond in a rational way, so painstakingly explaining injustice in rational terms gets you nowhere. If Horny-handed Son of Toil was to turn round and accept this new analysis, he'd have to be saying he was wrong for the last 60 years, an idiot, a wasted life. So he's hardly likely to do so. This particular veil was lifted from my eyes by Chris Pallis in his Solidarity pamphlet *The Irrational in Politics* which, in turn, was largely based on the pioneering sex-pol work of Wilhelm Reich in Austria and Germany in the 1930s.

In *What is Class Consciousness,* Reich had written: 'One of the reasons for the failure of the revolutionary movement is that the real life of individuals is played out on a different level than the instigators of social revolution believe'. He'd continued that if revolutionaries are to bring about international socialism, then they 'must find the connection with the petty, banal, primitive, simple everyday life of the broadest mass of the people'. Finally, he argued 'they should politicise private life, fairs, dance halls, cinemas, markets, bedrooms, hostels and betting shops'.

Foretelling the Situationists 'those who make a revolution without explicit reference to everyday life speak with a corpse in their mouths'. But the anarchists did speak with corpses in their mouths – usually Spanish or Ukranian – and their papers seemed to have no connection with the ordinary lives of anyone, let alone the street insurrectionists of 1981. We'd noticed at our first conference at The Colville in front of an uninvited crowd of regulars, it was the discussions on sex that animated them to get involved

There are three remarkable early issues of *Class War* which show attempts to grapple with the issues Reich raised. There was Aleks and Leah's *What is class consciousness* issue, Kate's *One from the girls* issue and the *Thatcher Best Cut of All* issue, which was the most adventurous of the lot.

In the Thatcher issue, there were three page-long articles simply headed 'Sex' 'Porn' 'Crime' – not a snappy title in sight – and dealing with

Matt, Jo and Becky flogging Class War

issues you'd never normally see discussed in a 'political' paper. Martin introduced his 'sex' article:

> *'We think that sexual politics are relevant but only if realised and talked about in our own terms. This means kicking out the specialised language along with the middle-class trendies who drone on boring us with it. We've got to make revolutionary and sexual politics the property of the working class, ourselves. Why, in our anarchist circles, is there so much animated discussion about the subject of sexual politics? It's a reflection of the society we live in. Working-class people aren't usually motivated in a revolutionary direction because of a handy ready-made ideology available like a packet of Daz, or the sufferings of the Third World peasantry. No, the primary motivating factor for many of us is our own individual experiences of oppression and that includes the intimate, personal desires and feelings which effect us in every conceivable manner. This is part of sexual politics.'*
> *Wright on Reich!*

To kickstart the discussion, he went on: 'We ultimately regard a diversity of sexual expression as desirable, preferably with as much experimentation and pleasure as possible.'

Bash The Rich

On the 'Porn' page opposite Martin's article, Lynn and Tina let rip with two passionate attacks on pornography turning the 'take your desires for reality' argument on its head. Tina wrote:

'If I'm not supposed to suppress my fantasies, right-off or right-on, then why should I suppress my anger? I'll fucking trash sex shops if I want. I'm doing it for myself and every woman who's being fucked over by men. Eat shit. It's not freedom of expression that men pay for but the chance to see their fucked-up fantasies enacted – see I'm not wrong for having my fantasies, I can't be they're on film. And we all know the camera doesn't lie. If it is one thing that validates societies standards, it's seeing them on a film or photograph.'

Further on, under 'Crime', I'd written the much-quoted piece:

'We're totally in favour of mugging the rich, burgling posh neighbourhoods, looting, assaulting the police and putting the boot in whenever we can.'

The article was in reality an attempt to get away from irrelevant anarchist platitudes on crime in the here and now and went on:

'When I'm walking down the street, I don't want to be beaten up or my house broken into by thugs in or out of uniform. Unless we can develop realistic strategies for dealing with uniformed and non-uniformed thugs then, to most people, anarchists will remain living in cloud-cuckoo land.'

I didn't have the answer to stopping working class on working class crime any more than Tina had the answer to why certain images aroused people or Martin knew how to end mass monogamous misery! We had never sat down and talked about applying Reich's ideas into a paper any more than, when doing *Alarm*, we discussed Antonio Gramsci's ideas. But we did know that we wanted to create a different kind of paper and social movement which took as its starting point experiences of everyday life not 'politics'. For this to happen, there had to be open debate both in the paper and in our organisation. And there certainly fucking was. We spent far more time in Class War's first two years discussing sexual politics than we ever did violence.

For me, I wanted in a vague way to marry Reich's ideas with Gramsci's. To deal with everyday issues in a way that our ideas were seen as common-sense ideas rather than the usual 'anarchists as loonies'. We'd won that battle in Swansea with *Alarm* and now it seemed we could do the same with *Class War*. In the Thatcher issue, there was another article on young women's access to contraception without their parents knowing. Of course, we supported this. But the *Daily Mail* and moralists like Victoria Gillick were demanding an end to it. It was classic Reichian terrain of an end to sexual misery but also where we could win the battle of ideas – where our idea of sexual autonomy and independence for young people found ready resonance among young people themselves. Let the battle for hegemony commence.

One day, on a miners' rally down at Jubilee Gardens, a load of miners had laughingly snapped up copies of this Thatcher meat-cleaver-in-head *Best Cut of All* issue of *Class War*. Three hours later, we saw them in the pub – reading the porn, sex, and contraception articles – then arguing the toss about them. We were bloody politicising the bedroom and the pub, even if we hadn't got to the fairs and circuses yet!

Outside the windows, the *Socialist Worker* sellers were demanding the recall of the TUC. I knew we were on a fucking winner!

THE GRAVY TRAIN'S A COMING...

The Greater London Council (GLC) was just a big fucking gravy train for radicals who wanted to get on the payroll, to get their snouts in the trough after years of having their noses pressed to the windows from the outside. Every leftie in the capital hotfooted it to County Hall to get on Ken's payroll or some risible GLC-sponsored quango.

It wasn't just odious elocution-lessoned wannabe toffs like Paul Boateng — 'jolly Boateng weather' we used to sing at him — out to further their own careers but practically every leftie in town was abandoning their principles for the chance of a mickey mouse job with a fat paycheck. I blame the GLC for the whole whinging radical ethos that you can't do anything without funding. Fuck fucking funding! Just as Bill Hicks slammed comedians who advertised anything saying taking funding totally and irrevocably neuters your ability to be radical and independent. Take a look at the 'Newham Seven Defence Campaign' which was funded to radical death into the 'Newham Monitoring Project'. It was the professionalisation of protest by those who read *The Guardian*'s Wednesday job pages. Radical hari-kari by equal opportunities bollocks The only people left outside looking in were the working class who, when they complained you could only get a GLC job if you were a black, one-legged lesbian, were sent to gulag seminars for retraining to have their incorrect thinking altered. Lobotomy by smug radical fat cats — the Galloways of the 1980s.

It spread out to the mini-empires of Ted Knight in Brixton, Margaret Hodge in Islington and Linda Bellos in Hackney where similar floods of cronying lefties thought they were pigs in clover. The left collectively abandoned their critical faculties — which weren't many anyway — in the collective rush to grasp at power and the wealth it brought through funding, sinecures, nepotism, or perks.

Class War to its credit didn't wait for a leftie sell out to be critical. We knew this funding patronage was bollocks and said so unequivocally from the start. 'Fuck the GLC' ran the *Class War* headline as we spilt out our anger at the countless Ken-organised rallies while the rest of the left fawned in self interested brown—nosing.

The GLC's powerful economics committee was like a haven for retired International Socialists such as John Palmer as it decided to fork out millions to support *The News on Sunday*. *The News on Sunday* was a total crock of leftist whinging and bleating shit, full of victimhood, boredom, torpor, self-righteousness and political correctness gone bonkers. As far as we were concerned, there was already a populist paper out there filling that gap in the market. It was funny and unfunded, vitriolic and venomous and the punters loved it. It was called *Class War*.

Chapter 30

THE SMOULDERING RUIN

The Hampstead Bash the Rich march in September 1985 was to prove a disastrous farce for Class War. A typically apocalyptic article in the paper, written by Chris Low the schoolboy editor of our newly-discovered 'theoretical organ', warned that Hampstead would be left 'A smouldering ruin after our visit'. We had successfully managed to hype up our great victory at Henley all summer but, even if we didn't totally believe it, the cops certainly did. I played my usual tricks with the local press, in this instance with the *Ham and High*, making wild threats of damage and violence with a view for maximising our turn out. In the event all it did, was to maximise the turn out of the cops.

We gathered as usual for the pre-match pints in The Flask in Hampstead and I'd thrown about six down me with even greater rapidity than usual. As we walked down Chalk Farm road in our supposedly inconspicuous twos and threes the whole long street was lined with cops in riot vans with green coaches parked up every side street. I wasn't too alarmed because if we could still get to Hampstead surrounded by hundreds of riot police, we could still claim the usual 'They cowered behind their curtains but a thousand riot cops could not stop us' line and pass it off as what a threat the cops took us for and eventually mythologize it as 'another great victory'. But just in case, I popped into an offie for another four cans on the way down to fortify my revolutionary confidence that we could still somehow win this one.

At Chalk Farm Station, we had assembled about 300 comrades with many more skulking along the side streets waiting to see the way things worked out. The top cop was keen to get us to move off right away, ordering us to begin the march or be arrested. We'd learnt from our mistake at Ladbroke Grove, however, and refused. I said, 'It's our march and we'd move off when we want to'. He snarled into my ear that he'd have me in the station later 'no doubt about that, son' but backed off. This minor triumph emboldened the more timid comrades hanging around in the adjacent pavements to come a join us, so at 3pm, we set off up Chalk Farm Road surrounded by riot vans and troop carriers.

As always, we had no clearly thought out strategy beyond marching through Hampstead High Street to Bishops Avenue (Millionaires' Row) geeing the troops up with some spurring words of self congratulation and heading back to the boozers in the evening. However, Nemesis! The cops had taken us seriously and had learned their lessons. They were determined we wouldn't piss them about again. Halfway up the road, they

'It's our march, and we'll start when we fucking want to.'

put a line across the street and pointed us down a side road. Our rag-tag and bob-tail army was completely outnumbered and out manoeuvred, we stood our ground refusing to follow their directions in a complete impasse. 'Two minutes to move off or you're all nicked,' sneered the top copper into my ear. I thought, 'Fuck it. At least 300 arrests will make the news and anything's better than following the cops' orders.' Even then, I was mulling over how we could snatch a propaganda victory from the jaws of defeat!

Someone shouted that they'd started nicking people at the back and being pretty pissed anyway, I ran from the front with some vague idea that we should at least go down fighting for the benefit of the press. My fearless act of leadership for once failed to inspire the comrades to follow me. However, a cop tried to halt my onward charge so I punched him in the face while other cops homed in on me. Several desultory scuffles and collective arrest resisting broke out with Adrienne gamely attempting to free me from the clutches of the law. In all, there were about 40 arrests but the bulk of the marchers remained inactive, probably quite sensibly.

Eventually, while the rest of us where being processed at the cop shops, which were all on alert for a mass arrest, the rest of the marchers where forced to go on a three-mile detour of humiliation, being bossed about, taunted, derided and abused by the cops. Total demoralisation, defeat and a fiasco. Even I couldn't dress this up successfully. Not even small smouldering ruins!

For me the fiasco got even fiascoer. My prison paranoia was rapidly gaining hold and I imagined the usual charge of conspiracy to riot plus assaulting the police, bail refused and a possible kicking organised by sneering top cop and a three year sentence. I felt sure they'd know my name but tried on my usual 'Ian Lewis' false name more out of habit than hope. We where banged up in three or four big communal cells and gradually names where called out. People didn't return so they were obviously being bailed. There was some hope now. I might even be on for a few pints at the Warwick Castle later on after all. Eventually, I was the last one left and darker thoughts returned. At any time, about four cops and chief sneerer were going to come in and give me a good kicking. I hid my glasses under the seat. It was obvious why I had been left to last. Liddle Towers and Steve Biko came to mind. I'd probably die in agony of a ruptured spleen. The door rattled. The falsely jovial desk sergeant came in. 'Well you're the unlucky one old son,' he quipped. Oh fuck! This is it. Here comes the goon squad, goodbye teeth. 'You're wanted on a warrant from Hackney so you'll be cautioned and taken over there.'

Whaat! Hackney? What? Caution? No kicking? No charges? Maybe it was a trick and they'd kick me in Hackney? I was cautioned for hitting the copper (as all the other 40 arrested were. Nobody was charged with anything) and shipped off to Hackney Central cop shop for failing to answer bail on a criminal damage charge.

Then I twigged it. Oh Bone you fucking dick head! You arsehole! I'd been so concerned with the heavy riot conspiracy charge that I'd only gone and given the same false name as I'd done for painting Class War on the Marks & Spencer's shop in Graham Road and then never turned up to answer bail. You fucking pillock. If I'd only used my own real name I'd have been drinking down the Warwick by now. *Citizen Smith* or what! From Che Guevara to laughing stock in one afternoon.

On arrival at Hackney, I saw the stomach-sinking 'no bail' on the charge sheet and was banged up to Old Street magistrates' court on Monday morning. This wasn't quite the end of the shocks though. I pleaded guilty to get it over quickly because of the false name. Then the prosecutor said Marks & Spencer's were claiming I'd committed criminal damage to the tune of £10,000 for the cost of painting the entire outside of the fucking shop. The bastards where making me pay for their annual refurbishment programme. Ten grand of criminal damage would mean a remand for reports job with no bail since I'd failed to appear once already. Bollocks, Pentonville here I come.

But wait! Hold hard my boy! The magistrate is cracking a joke! 'Ten thousand is a bit steep for a bit of painting and decorating,' the magistrate quipped. 'If that's the going rate, I'm in the wrong job.' There's laughter in court I'm splitting my fuckin' sides. Oh, what a rib tickler, your honour. I'm a bit of light relief for the bench after dealing with several murder charges. 'Fined £100, if Marks & Spencer's want £10,000, they can pursue you through the civil courts.' I'm out! I'm congratulated by my former cohabitates of the ice box and head straight down the boozer. A good result my son.

But in truth, we'd been well and truly rumbled. We'd either had to engage in some serious street fighting with the cops with inevitable arrests and prison sentences or continued hyping was out of the question. As at Stop the City, the cops had been confused at first but got their act together later by saturating policing. It was put up or shut up time. The fact of the matter was that we were still a small group with a hardcore of about 30 activists. When it had come to the showdown, we weren't prepared to risk going to jail to match our rhetoric with violence which was the only possible step forward with this tactic. With five or six of us jailed, the movement would collapse. We'd have to rethink our entire strategy.

In November, there was one last damp squid Bash The Rich march in Bristol. After the march, the Avon cops followed the van load of us from London around all night despite the manic driving attempts of Pete Mastin to shake them off. In a cafe two obvious police plain clothes man came over to talk to us in the most astonishing police anarchist negotiation I ever experienced. They told us they were on overtime till 10pm to make sure we didn't go on a night-time wrecking spree. But they where knackered and wanted to go home so they'd stop following us if we gave them guarantees that we wouldn't 'fuck about' as they put it. Later on we got lost looking for a punk party we'd been invited to. Martin wound down the van window and asked the obvious plain clothes cop car following us: 'Where's the party we're going to?'

'No. 79, first left,' came the reply.

It was a suitably farcical end to the Bash The Rich campaign.

I get nicked on the way
to Hampstead

Chapter 31

PHEW! WHAT A SCORCHER...

We were laying out the next issue of the paper at Calverts North Star Press. We were in high good humour because the 9 September 1985 had been the scene of the biggest uprising since 1981.Who could forget the newsflash headline 'Home Secretary Stoned in Handsworth'.

'Well everyone is stoned in Handsworth' was the grinning response. Our strategy was vindicated. The1981 riots weren't isolated incidents, footnotes in history, as some learned comrades opined but were going to be the new form of class warfare. Our front page was a photo of a petrol bomber from Handsworth under the caption 'The working class strikes back'.

Thatcher had been using the police force as a political hammer to crush our class. The miners had been battered at Orgreave – on television – yet it was the miners who were facing conspiracy to riot charges. Three miners had been killed on picket lines. At the Beanfield, the travellers had been smashed to fuck but it was the travellers who faced riot charges. In the next two months, two black women – Cherry Groce and Cynthia Jarrett – would be shot by the police with impunity. In the face of this onslaught, getting out on the streets with a brick in your hand seems a less than proportionate response.

Where next, we were wondering when news came over the radio that a riot had broken out in Brixton. The police were under siege in Brixton cop shop cowering from angry mobs outside. Fuck the paper! We hot footed it to Brixton, arriving at Angel Tube station to see the chalked sign: Brixton Tube closed due to riot! Fucking whoopee! Phone every fucker we know. This is a three-line whip. We jump off the tube at Stockwell. There's a pall of smoke rising over Brixton. It's about 4pm. A Roller comes round the corner. Without hesitation XXXXX throws a brick through the windscreen. The atmosphere is Electric Avenue.

The rioters control central Brixton with the cops adopting only defensive positions. They're proper Aunt Sallies with the bricks raining down on them. Earlier in the day they'd been besieged in their own cop shop by petrol bomb-throwing mobs outside. You can feel the anger and vengefulness. All the shops are being looted, cop cars are burning and there's the usual riot atmosphere of unity, working together and looking out for each other. As usual, we try to work out where the cops will attack from and start building barricades outside the Ritzy. It's a Class War wet dream with hundreds out on the streets all up for it as the smoking haze descends into early evening. All the usual faces appear. These aren't the 'official' anarchists who are far too snooty to dirty their hands with a common riot, but all the Brixton and London-wide faces we've got to know over the last 12 months.

We build barricades on Acre Lane. The offie is looted. A magic moment. We're behind the barricades drinking looted booze, but there's crates and crates of the stuff so we have the joyous luxury of hurling full beer cans at the cops rather than the usual flimsy empty ones which do no damage. Bigger fires are burning. It smells like the excitement on bonfire nights except multiplied by a times 10 adrenalin buzz. The Brixton Class Warriors are giving a good account of themselves setting fire to a group of abandoned cop cars. We race down another road past Aleks and Leah's house – the Situationists who'd produced the detested *Class War* No. 4. Phil Gard knocks on their door.

'There's a fucking riot going on outside your fucking front door! Phil shrieks to a bewildered Aleks who retreats inside to compose more tomes on the autonomy of the working class!

We're all pissed and high as fuck.

Far from the usual press descriptions of 'race riots' black and white are united as in 1981 against the common enemy – the police. But people have learned the tactical lessons of 1981 and are using new methods to counter police advances. Burning cars hold back the police who, when they finally break through, face an empty street and another burning barricade. People are masked up to avoid identification. The fighters hold the estates making hit and run attacks and retreating to where the cops are to scared to follow. There's a carnival atmosphere, people are grinning, laughing, joking about the sheer outrageousness and joy of what they're doing. People are ecstatically looking at each other in a 'fuck me, are we really doing this' kind of way.

Amidst the smoke, and with the assist of looted booze, the scene takes on a dreamlike quality of silhouetted figures flicking through the flames and burning buildings I somehow end up near Stockwell Tube station and walk all the way back to Hackney. As the birdsong starts up, I'm gleeful with tales to tell. Was that it or will Sunday bring more? If only, if fucking only Brixton and Handsworth had gone up six months earlier during the miners' strike. Still, who knows what tonight might bring? There was more rioting on the Sunday but it was mostly legging it from the cops who'd got their act together and were looking for heads to crack.

On Monday the papers implicate Class War in the riot. In particular, a self-serving article by David Rose in *The Guardian* echoes Brixton Chief Inspector Marnoch's crap about outsiders causing the trouble and Rose fingers Class War for his paymasters.

In a blisteringly ferocious article in *Class War* – another piece of top quality heat-of-the-moment 'invectacive' journalism – Pete described the riot and demolished the press and police lies:

> *'Marnoch drivels on with mindfucking stupidity about 'visiting agitators from Handsworth' What a load of fucking bullshit! No, as EVERYONE knows, the riots were started, organised and led by Communist Alien Stormtroopers from the red planet Bolleaux who landed on the roof of the fucking Ritzy.' As for the conspiracy*

theories emanating from the wooden head of moron police commander Marnoch that we in Class War were behind the riots, all we can say is bollocks! The people of Brixton don't need us to spark them off. We fully admit many of us were there and took an active part in the proceedings. And fuck it – why shouldn't we pour into the riot area to fight alongside our comrades and our class.'

Another notch in the strategy of tension is racheted up. Maybe Fabian is Nostradamus after all. I re-read Pete's article:

'We fight the bastards with all their force and all our strength with bricks and petrol bombs, we confront them and maim and kill them. Because we hate them.'

If a copper was killed, how far away could incitement to riot or conspiracy or incitement to murder be with articles like this? We knew Special Branch was watching us, the papers were already fingering us for Brixton. Where next? When? If it was soon then the press would be demanding the cops lifted us.

Three years earlier, I'd left Swansea because it missed out on the 1981 riots. Now a new wave of riots were rocking Thatcher in 1985 and *Class War*, the paper I'd created in riotless Swansea, was right in the fucking middle of it. Exhilarating, exciting. 'It's your head that'll be in the fucking noose Ian,' comedian Tony Allen offered by way of words of warning. I was already the 'most dangerous man in Britain' according to *The People*. Surely the cops would move against us soon.

'There comes a tide in the affairs of man which if he does not take he is forever in the shallows.' This was my tide. Forward ever – backward never. Worried as fuck though. Where next indeed?

SCOTS ANDY

We met Scots Andy in the Railway pub in Brixton. He was a garrulous ex-Communist in his 60s who was ferociously furious now he'd had the veil of Stalinism lifted from his eyes. Mind you, he was ferociously furious about everything. He came to Henley with us and spat out his class hatred and vitriol at the astonished frocks and their beaus through cans of Special Brew and broken teeth. He got nicked in Greenwich Park after an afternoon of anarchist football, picnicking and drinking to commemorate Martial Bourdin who had blown himself to smithereens attempting to blow up the Greenwich Observatory 100 years earlier. He got arrested for venting his spleen on a copper. He died from pneumonia in a police cell 12 hours later.

His daughter showed up for the funeral plus Vera his partner, me, Martin, Pete, Steve, Mike Gilliland and a couple of others. Andy wanted to be buried and he had a suitably shambolic internment — a few desultory words on the wind and a Special Brew can thrown onto the coffin. A full Special Brew can. Someone climbed onto the coffin to retrieve it 'Andy wouldn't appreciate waste' he said as he drank the can and left it crumpled on Andy's coffin. 'Oh yes he would' someone said. We drifted off through the yew trees in the late afternoon sunlight. Mike Gilliland — editor of the excellent Brixton squatters' paper *Crowbar* — drove me back to central London.

We didn't say a dickie bird.

Chapter 32

IT WAS THE BEST OF TIMES

Up to the autumn of 1985, everything had been going in our favour. Then came PC Blakelock's death. The Broadwater Farm uprising was a defining moment. A policeman had been hacked to death. The police dragnet was cast wide and people were being sweet-talked and plea-bargained into the main frame. No one from Class War had been anywhere near the riot. Unlike Brixton, Broadwater Farm felt 'personal.' It was an estate riot only. It was for those who had endured harassment for years. It was a score to be settled between the estate and the coppers. Any intervention from us would have been an intrusion into private grief. Broadwater Farm really was personal. But the lessons were not. People were going to get life sentences – maybe never coming out again. The charge of 'common cause' was likely to be made. If you were involved in a riot and a copper was killed then, even if you were only present, you could be charged with murder. And what about if you'd incited the riot or encouraged it or conspired to incite it? More life sentences? The exhilaration of the Brixton riot suddenly gave way to goose-bump nervousness, hesitation and doubt about continuing to advocate rioting when merely writing could get you a life stretch for incitement.

It was put up or shut up time in more ways than one. The cops had rumbled our Bash The Rich tactics at Hampstead and when push came to shove, we hadn't shoved. If we were to repeat the tactic, we'd have to do it Weatherman style – with clubs and helmets and fight our way through with the certainty of arrest and long sentences. Maybe Fabian hadn't been too far off the mark after all. The other problem with our violent rhetoric was that violence was becoming the sum total of what we were known for. But violence wasn't the answer to every question, every action didn't have to be violent to be a success because it was tactically inept apart from other considerations. We had to find some way into Class War for people who wanted more than a rumble. 'Hospitalised Copper' was funny. 'Dead copper' wasn't funny. 'Dead copper' may have appeal to a few sniggerers but we would be marginalising ourselves as psychotics if we went down that route. We needed to embrace our class not marginalise ourselves by walking into the 'loonie category' noose being dangled before us.

Other factors were beginning to loom on the horizon. There were the beginnings of a discussion about whether Class War should become a federation with democratic decision-making at national conferences, rather than the loose collection of autonomous groups. It hadn't crystalised as yet but it was far from certain that me and Martin would be on the same side of the argument. A 'split' could be fatal and nasty! Me and Martin had always got on well and shared ideas as well as side of the mouth conspiratorial phone calls about the way forward. We joked about being the Bakuninist invisible leadership but any visible disagreement over the federation aspect could be catastrophic for Class War.

Post-Broadwater Farm, these questions were still to be resolved but it was all far from doom and gloom. Any sober assessment (not often done) of Class War's rapid progress from 1983 to 1985 would be well on the credit side. From nowhere (well Swansea), Class War had established itself as the major force in the anarchist movement with its brand of street insurrectionism. Class War had broken out of the much talked about 'anarchist ghetto' to a wide audience of the Left and beyond.

To produce an anarchist paper with a circulation of 15,000 was a major achievement. We were only 5,000 behind such august journals as the *New Statesman*. Its house style – to out-tabloid the tabloids – had come as a culture shock to many anarchists but had found its target audience with unerring aim. We had the product the punters wanted – there was no reason that we couldn't hit 25,000 to 30,000 in the coming year. The defeat of the miners' strike was a major blow to those of us hoping for immediate insurrection but the strike had put raw, unremitting class war on the agenda. We had built contact with the most combative elements from the miners. The paper was still widely circulating in South Yorkshire coalfields and beyond. The inner-city riots would continue even if the ante was upped on both sides.

Thatcher was still in power but there was a sizeable and combative minority in the country determined to bring her down. Eventually they did in 1992 with the Poll Tax riots. But this was 1985. Where could our strategy go from here? Phil Gard brought us exciting news. A printers' strike was looming as Murdoch moved his printing press to Wapping with non-union labour. This could offer us the mix of industrial struggle and community and estate-based uprising we'd been looking to aggravate. The miners' strike picket line clashes had taken place miles from London with ourselves only in occasional attendance, but Wapping Highway was right on our doorsteps. The estates around Wapping offered a myriad of back lanes to wage guerrilla war on Murdoch's distribution lorries. The local youths and football crews would be well into the fun and games in their back alleys. Once they'd cleared Wapping they'd still have the rest of London to negotiate and their distribution depots around the country would come under similar attack.

Printer Phil knew a lot of the print casuals, in particular Pete Gold and his renegade crew of fighting printers who were well into *Class War*. The print union might well be able to close Wapping's gates as other trade unionists had done at Saltly Gates a decade earlier. Arnie, a mate of ours, was planning to bring out a Saturday night special called *Picket* with up-to-date news on the picketing and the Saturday afternoon football results. We seemed to have all the angles covered. We even had a rioting monk gagging to chance his arm on Murdoch's TNT lorries. As always we needed to keep the core CW groups together and avoid any splits over the federation issue or personal squabbles. Nightly action on the streets was sure to be a great unifier. Roll on Wapping.

Chapter 33

WHAT THE BUTLER SAW

My mum and dad weren't 'Labour voters'. They were just 'Labour'. 'We're Labour,' my dad would say cheerily by way of introduction. 'Labour' wasn't just something you voted for every five years, it was what you were. If you were Labour people, it was what you were every day, it was part of your being. You were Labour for life. My dad could never understand it when some Labour MP lost his seat and was 'wondering what to do next'. The question didn't arise – you just went on being Labour.

They remained hopeful about politics during the 13 years of Tory misrule and under Heath and Thatcher. Labour might be out of government but so what. You were still Labour weren't you? They were sustained by their social networks – my dad in his union branch at Vessa and mum with her customers in Celia's clothes shop on the High Street. Then there was the British Legion, the community centre, the pubs, market day. Walking through Alton with my mum and dad felt like walking through Liverpool with John Lennon. Every five yards, they'd be stopping to listen to someone else's woes or happy stories. It took hours to do the shopping. My experience of Labour was totally different. In the Shire counties where we lived in Kent, Sussex, Wiltshire, Hampshire, it was still radical to be Labour into the 1960s. In Swansea, Labour had been the party of power for ever and was totally corrupt. So when I went home, I just saw Labour voters sustaining a corrupt and reactionary party. I didn't see Labour people.

Like a lot of the 60s radical students, I had the feeling and arrogance to believe we were the first radicals there'd ever been in England. At least since the general strike in 1926 when the students had been on the other side. But since then, there seemed to have been nothing – a radical black hole. Their incomprehension at my new world of long hair, drugs, underground magazines and rejection of work sustained my belief of the grey, boring 1950s. Mum and dad's dream – what they'd worked so hard for – was that I would be a teacher. They still had that respect for teachers that leaving school at 14 gave that generation. I didn't want to be a teacher 'mass producing quiescent wage slaves.' I didn't want to be defined by work at all. I didn't want to work at all. After early arguments we hardly talked about politics on my home visits. It would only lead to more arguments, as mum the peacemaker would say.

Like a lot of my generation of radicals I didn't like my country much. I didn't like our empire, our queen, our Tory and Labour parties, our narrow morality, our racism... the crimes of Britain were endless. I'd support anyone against us. This was incomprehensible to my mum and dad who'd fought and lived through the war and were proud to be British, patriotic and Labour. They seemed almost as bad as the Tories.

I'd never take copies of *Class War* home. They'd be worried about me getting into trouble. It wasn't aimed at them. Our readers were mostly young. They were people who'd get out on the streets and make it happen. It was aimed at people in struggle. My mum would have been horrified by our 'Hospitalised Copper' just as she was horrified by Himmler in the *Sunday People*. Best just talk about the kids. Then came the miners' strike. We were supporting the miners on the picket lines and fighting with the coppers. But behind that, there was the whole infrastructure of miners' support groups, miners' wives groups, bucket collections outside supermarkets every day and evening. These spread well beyond mining areas and the cities to market towns and the Shires. My mum and dad's generation of Labour people were the backbone of these miners' support groups. There were miners on fundraising speaking tours in Alton and being put up and fed by mum and dad. In Alton! The infrastructure of support for the miners was just as important as the picket line fighting but one that got not quite as much coverage

Bash The Rich

in the paper. I went home in early November during the strike. Mum was out collecting for the miners one day and selling poppies for the Legion in the supermarket the next. When I was a kid I used to hate Remembrance Sunday. It meant being dragged round windy village war memorials in Binsted, Froyle and Bentley as old people with medals marched down deserted lanes. It was the one time every year my mum and dad went to church. That Remembrance Sunday in Alton, my dad stood ready to go to the war memorial with his Coal Not Dole badge next to his poppy. I'd never dreamed you could wear the two together. How could I not go with them. I saw them standing there together in the wind, a tear in my dad's eye. Dignified, respectable working class people with noble aspirations. Labour people. Proud among the Alton Tories. Labour people and British people. All their hopes for the future after the war reflected in the Labour landslide, the years of austerity and ration books giving way to racy kipper ties and huge Echo televisions with minute screens. They were betrayed by the politicians they trusted, but rewarded now as their social networks (like sleeper cells) sustained the miners with their support.

I read Orwell on the war years and studied the radical journalism of the *Daily Mirror* and *Picture Post*. There was a feeling of betrayal and disgust with the aristocracy and Tory government that had appeased Hitler. There was a sudden sense that the ordinary people would have to get us out of the mess they had made. Tom Wintringham and 9,000 local defence volunteers training at Olney Park for guerrilla war against the German invaders – and just maybe against our own ruling class!

There was a sense that Britain hovered on the brink of radical social change for months during 1940. The refusal of deference and rejection of going back to the status quo after the war. The Commonwealth Party victories in the wartime by-elections and the Labour landslide of 1945. The mass squatting movement after the war. We weren't the only radicals since the general strike after all. The next year, I wore a poppy. I didn't hate England any more.

Thatcher still hated the English working class though. But her 'no such thing as society' gave the game away. She didn't just want to smash the miners and displace the inner-city inhabitants. She wanted to destroy the idea there was any communality of interest among ordinary people. My mum and dad's caring Alton social networks counted for nothing compared to the Thatcher-eulogised, hideous, braying yuppies in the city making themselves overnight fortunes in selling off our social assets. I might have stopped hating my country but I loathed its ruling class more than ever. But this time, commonsense was on our side. Thatchers 'no such thing as society' was seen as bollocks by most people including mum and dad. We had some common ground again we were no longer the loonies, the crazed Thatcher was 'the mad cow'. There were millions of people like my mum and dad all over the country. *Class War* needed to reach them. We needed to emphasis the positive self-organisation that had come out of the miners' strike which was in direct contradiction of Thatcher's 'we're all selfish bastards' analysis. I remembered *Solidarity's* 'As we see it' statement which I'd reprinted in the first *Class War*:

> '*Meaningful action for revolutionaries is whatever increases the confidence, the autonomy, the initiative, the participation, the solidarity, the equalitarian tendencies and the self-activity of the masses and whatever assists in their demystification.*'

The organisation of support groups during the miners' strike had certainly done that. These people were still there. We needed to get *Class War* to them in 1986 then who knows what might happen. We still had to politicise the markets, the CIU clubs, the British Legions as Reich had said, but Thatcher was doing her best for us.

Some might already be more radical than I thought. My mum showed me a press cutting from the Alton Gazette of 1974 reporting dad's retiring speech as chair of the Petersfield Constituency Labour Party after the

Bash The Rich

return of the Heath government:

> 'The result of the general election had been disastrous. Now the general public were paying the price in cuts in social services, the slowing down of the comprehensive schools programme, and the Industrial Relations Bill set against a backcloth of hiving off the profitable parts of publicly-owned industries into private pockets. It seems the crass determination to go ahead with the sale of arms to South Africa will be pursued to the bitter end.

> 'There was a rising feeling of anger and a sense of outrage. In recent times, there had arisen a very frightening aspect, something new to Britain, the intrusion into personal freedoms.

> 'The Rudi Dutschke Affair illustrates this clearly. Freedom and civil rights are being threatened... not just of one individual but of us all.'

I marvelled how the Glenbuck miner's son and the Hindon munitions girl had mutated to butler and housemaid and come out the other end fighting for black South Africans and wounded Berlin radicals. How the 1940s optimistic post-war egalitarianism of Flanagan and Allen and the demob happy hopes for a better world had never dimmed with mum and dad. How had the Glenbuck Cherrypicker and the Chilmark Dynamo sustained each other through the times of no hope?

I also wondered how the next year would turn out for their son. Wapping Highway beckoned. The cops were watching.

I'd need to be tough. Like Uncle Tough – mum's brother.

'Why was he called Uncle Tough,' I asked mum.

'Because he pulled a turnip out of the ground when he was only a year old,' she replied.

Forward Ever – Backward Never!